The
DISCIPLE'S
MANUAL

The DISCIPLE'S MANUAL

WILLIAM MacDONALD

🖘 GOSPEL FOLIO PRESS
304 Killaly St. West, Port Colborne, ON L3K 6A6
www.gospelfolio.com

Abbreviations:

KJV	King James Version
JND	New Translation, J. N. Darby
NASB	New American Standard Bible
NIV	New International Version
ME	Modern English, J. B. Phillips
TEV	Today's English Version

Published by Gospel Folio Press
304 Killaly Street West
Port Colborne, ON L3K 6A6
Web store: www.gospelfolio.com
Order phone line in North America: 1-800-952-2382

ISBN 1-882701-86-0

Printed in the United States of America

FOREWORD
WE EACH HAVE A PART TO PLAY
by Jabe Nicholson

It will be obvious to the astute reader that this book was not merely an academic exercise of the author. For more than half a century Christian discipleship has been his life and ministry. The book is intended to pass on practical aids for both the disciple and the disciple maker. It is not a small book designed for a casual read. Although written in a brisk and direct way, it requires time, careful thought, and action.

But because of its comprehensive nature, some may be discouraged from becoming involved in the discipling of young believers. "There are things I can't teach others," you might respond, "because I don't practice them myself."

Well, because you can't do *everything,* don't let that keep you from doing *something*. No school teacher is expected to take a student from kindergarten to grad school. No construction project as complex as the church is expected to be handled by one tradesman. The Lord intends everyone to share in the project.

Having described the various gifts given to the church, Paul writes: *"But one and the same Spirit works all these things, distributing to each one individually as He wills"* (1 Cor. 12:11). Each of us has been given a strategic part to play in God's overall plan.

The enemy may whisper discouragement in your ear, telling you where you have failed, and what you are not equipped to do. But don't listen to him. The Lord will give you the strength and ability for anything He wants you to do, *"For it is God which worketh in you both to will and to do of His good pleasure"* (Phil. 2:13).

So what can you contribute to the cause of making disciples? What are the areas where you believe the Lord has helped you to accomplish something for eternity? What has He taught you that you could pass on to an eager understudy?

Do you visit the sick? Do you encourage the widows? Take a young man with you and give him a taste of what James calls *"true religion."* Show him how to make the visit short, sweet, and spiritually beneficial.

Can you teach a few young people how to use a concordance or Bible software, or discover a word meaning from Vine's Dictionary? Then have them over for a Sunday lunch and spread out the books on the kitchen table afterward. It will be a life-changer for them.

Some young fellows with an aptitude for music need help in song leading. All new believers could use a course in the appreciation and appropriate use of hymns at the Lord's Supper.

Many of our youth feel outside the local church. Asking them along on a work project for some of the needy or elderly will give them a vested interest in the Lord's work and a taste of honest toil for the Savior.

My 10 year old son was taken by a young disciple maker to help move a senior's furniture. Later, on the phone he told me, "Dad, I'm learning it's a good thing to sweat for the Lord." It is indeed.

No young believers in your assembly to disciple? I daresay if you are willing to help and ask the Great Disciple Maker for some young charges, He will be more than happy to comply.

TABLE OF CONTENTS

TABLE OF CONTENTS

Section V: Conclusion

Appendixes

A WORD OF EXPLANATION
ON-THE-JOB TRAINING

It would be easy for a teacher to conclude that if his disciple simply reads a book like this, he would be properly trained. Wrong! The material in the manual is important but it is not enough. It covers some of the major subjects involved in Christian discipleship, but it leaves untouched the practical knowledge of how to do the work.

A disciple must be given on-the-job training as well as book learning. He must be introduced to various branches of Christian service. It does not mean that he will be doing all these things the rest of his life. But it will help him find out where his gifts lie.

This was the Lord's *modus operandi*. He lived with the Twelve, taught them by word and example, then sent them forth on the glorious mission. His method must be the best one. If there were a better way, He would have employed it.

To be a mentor is threatening to a person. You make yourself vulnerable. Your disciple will get to know you as you really are—warts, wrinkles, and all. Not to worry. Young people don't expect perfection. They just want sincerity and transparency. They will accept you as you are.

A U.S. Marine officer leads his men into battle. He doesn't sit back while they charge. He goes before them into the fray. They have already learned the basics and have had practical training; now they put it into practice by following his example.

Failure to follow this model is the reason why so many discipleship-training programs have faltered or failed. The leaders had no trouble finding Bible teachers to handle the book learning. But they did not find men who would be living role models. Some teachers might object that they could not possibly do all the things that are desired in an on-fire disciple. In that case, they should import men who are experts in various fields. It takes a little forethought and planning, but it can be done.

For too long mentors have satisfied themselves with imparting tons of information to their disciples, but have left them without being able to do the work smoothly and efficiently. This ability is gained step by step through practical experience.

A graduate of one of the successful assembly discipleship programs wrote from the mission field, "If it were not for the practical training I received in the program, I would have landed here and asked myself, 'Now what do I do?'" Fortunately when he arrived, he knew exactly what to do. He was able to plunge into the work and see it prosper under God.

A good place to start is with a Daily Quiet Time. The mentor should show how he reads the Word, gets a message from the Lord, and prays effectively.

Then it is desirable to go on to ministries that are relatively non-threatening. A disciple should see the teacher passing out tracts at checkout counters, tollbooths, and wherever there is contact with another person. Then he should carry some tracts and do likewise.

Every trainee should be encouraged to be a serious student of the Word. Otherwise he will want to run, but he doesn't have a message. If he is going to have sound doctrine and answer the critics, he must know his Bible. Please, Mr. Teacher, show him how to study the Word or get someone else to do it.

When the mentor speaks at a meeting, he can encourage the trainee to give his testimony. We all have to start somewhere.

If the disciple is timid, he could be assigned every Sunday to introduce himself to someone in the local church to whom he has never spoken and start a conversation. This will make it easier for him to share the gospel with strangers outside the local church.

Next he should be coached in how to prepare and deliver a gospel message. Hopefully at the end, his mentor will encourage him and give him helpful advice on how to improve.

As he progresses, the young believer should covet the privilege of teaching a Sunday School class or a home Bible class.

Preaching in the open air is invaluable training. At first it is extremely intimidating, but usually it leads to a real love for this outreach. One great benefit is that it teaches a fellow to project his voice. If the audience can't hear him, they drift away. You have to maintain their interest. They are not a captive audience.

We learn much about prayer by praying with others. It should be a primary subject in the disciple's curriculum. The trainer should share his prayer life.

Visitation is important. The mentor arranges the time for going to retirement homes, hospitals, and convalescent institutions. And home visitation can be for gospel contacts or the edification and comfort of Christians. The mentor does the talk; the intern sits back and listens. He learns how to make a transition from introductory conversation to pertinent spiritual matters.

It is ideal if the trainee can sit in on sessions where his mentor or a church elder is counseling. The number and variety of problems for which people need help will amaze him. And he will be impressed to see the counselor go to the Word for answers. Those with profound knowledge of the Bible have a great advantage here.

Whenever there is a wedding or funeral, the trainee should take notes in case he is ever asked to officiate at one.

Maybe some day the disciple will be an elder in an assembly. In view of that, it is excellent if he is allowed sometimes to sit in on non-confidential parts of an elders' meeting.

I hope the mentor will provide coaching to his young charge on how to lead singing and how to chair a meeting. This will spare audiences from fumbling exhibitions that are completely devoid of class.

A disciple should be taught to see things to be done in the meeting place and to do them. There are often chairs to be arranged, hymn books to be placed, messages to be recorded on tape. A trainee can show his greatness by serving.

Even young people can be trained to be hospitable. They can be encouraged to greet visitors and to arrange for them to be taken for a meal.

I like to see young people showing random acts of kindness in the name of Jesus. It's a habit that can be developed.

SECTION I
CHRISTIAN DISCIPLESHIP

ONE
TO BE A DISCIPLE [1]

The words *disciple* and *discipleship* are not only overworked, they have come to mean whatever the user wants them to mean. They remind us of Humpty Dumpty's use of the word *glory*. When Alice asked him what he meant by it, he said, "When I use a word, it means just what I choose it to mean—nothing more nor less."

But if we want to understand the teaching of Jesus on discipleship, we must understand what *He* meant by the term—not what we mean by it. We must examine the descriptions of discipleship in Jesus' teachings and in His apostles' writings to learn what concept of discipleship Jesus was presenting.

By doing that, we find that a disciple is a student, a learner. Discipleship is the process by which a master or teacher trains a student in his doctrine and practice. It is seen in the way the Lord

---

1 In this book we have used male pronouns almost exclusively. We hope that women will not feel slighted. Nothing like that is intended. Much of the teaching applies as well to them as to men. It's just that the constant repetition of *"he or she,"* *"his or hers,"* and *"him or her"* becomes monotonous. It is also unnecessary because it is generally recognized that the male pronoun can be used as generic for male and female. Older women are distinctly taught that they should be disciplers also (Titus 2:4).

Jesus appointed twelve disciples *"that they might be with Him and that He might send them out to preach"* (Mk. 3:14). These men lived with the Savior, heard His doctrine, observed His lifestyle, and then moved out to spread His message. It was on-the-job training.

Discipleship is also seen in Paul's instruction to Timothy: *"And the things that you have heard from me among many witnesses, commit these to faithful men who will be able to teach others also"* (2 Tim. 2:2).

We can easily see that there are four generations of believers in this verse—Paul, Timothy, faithful men, others. The expansion of the Christian faith depends on the active involvement of every believer in this multiplication process.

This method of training must be the best way. If there were a better form of indoctrination, the Lord Jesus would have used it.

The goal of discipleship is that the learner becomes like his teacher. *"It is enough for a disciple that he be like his teacher, and a servant like his master"* (Mt. 10:25).

A teacher cannot lead his student beyond his own level of achievement. *"A disciple is not above his teacher, but everyone who is perfectly trained will be like his teacher"* (Lk. 6:40). "You can't teach what you don't know. You can't lead where you don't go."

Every true believer is a disciple of the Lord Jesus Christ. In addition to the Twelve, there were many others who followed Jesus and whom He acknowledged as disciples. Among these there are degrees of discipleship. Their faith and obedience determined this. *"According to your faith let it be to you"* (Mt. 9:29). *"If you abide in My word, you are My disciples indeed"* (Jn. 8:31).

Even unbelievers are sometimes referred to as disciples. In John 2:23-24 we read of some who believed in His name, but Jesus did not believe in them because He knew that they had never been born again. Again in John 6:66, *"Many of His disciples went back and walked with Him no more."* They showed by their desertion of the

Son of God that they did not belong to Him. Their discipleship was only on the surface (see Jn. 8:31-33).

The Lord Jesus is the true Disciple. In Isaiah 50:4-5 He says, *"The Lord God has given Me the tongue of the learned* [the word learned is a synonym for disciple], *that I should know how to speak a word in season to him who is weary. He awakens Me morning by morning, He awakens My ear to hear as the learned* [disciple]." Every morning He got before His Father to receive instructions for that day.

The curriculum for the Christian disciple is found in the pages of the Bible. To be a mature disciple, one must know his Bible and obey it. One of the key emphases in the New Testament is the development of Christian character.

- Matthew 5:1-12 describes the character of citizens of the kingdom.
- In John 15:1-17 it is called the *"abiding"* life.
- In Galatians 5:22-23 it is *"the fruit of the Spirit."*
- Ephesians 6:10-20 speaks of it as *"the whole armor of God."*
- 2 Peter 1:5-11 deals with some essentials of good character.

It seems that character is more important than service.

Discipleship is more than merely reading the chapters of a book like this one. It is on-the-job training. It means spending time with the teacher and engaging with him or her on various forms of Christian service. In the case of men, it might mean becoming actively involved in such ministries as preaching, teaching, personal evangelism, open-air evangelism, counseling, and visitation, In the case of women, it might mean teaching as in Titus 2:3-5, counseling, and visitation. As a disciple exposes himself or herself to these activities, he will soon be able to recognize his gift(s) and to serve independently of his mentor. He should then find one or more young believers whom he could disciple.

The discipler should be his student's friend, even though the learner's progress might be slow. The mentor should not be too rigorous or demanding. He should take time to listen. It is good if he can meet with his protégé on social or athletic occasions and be ready to meet at unscheduled times to help in times of crisis.

Rather than following the same stereotyped program for each person, the discipler should look to the Holy Spirit for individual guidance. The Spirit is sovereign; He does not always act in the same manner.

In the pages to follow, you will find many of the subjects that you would want to teach a young believer for whom you are serving as a mentor. There are many more that you can add to the list. But these will at least serve as a beginning.

TWO
THE REVOLUTIONARY
TEACHINGS OF JESUS

The Lord Jesus Christ was a revolutionary. However, when we say that, we do not mean that He was an armed terrorist bent on destroying the government. His was a revolution of love, not hatred; of service, not tyranny; of salvation, not destruction. When we say that Jesus was a revolutionary, we mean that His teachings were the most radical teachings that have ever swept across this planet.

There is nothing in all literature like the Sermon on the Mount. No other great leader ever laid down such stern demands of discipleship as the Lord Jesus. No other teachings have ever produced the spiritual, moral, and ethical changes that the Christian faith has.

The trouble is that we have become so used to the words of Jesus that we have lost sight of their revolutionary meaning. It's a tragedy that we can read them and still be comfortable. They were never designed to make us comfortable. They were intended to transform our lives and send us forth as burning lights, as heralds of a flaming passion.

We often think that it must have been a wonderful experience to travel with Jesus when He was here on earth. We can see Him and His disciples sauntering along, enjoying a continual Bible conference. But it wasn't like that. It was more of a scalding experience in which the disciples learned their own sinfulness and failure, and in which they were called to a pathway of persecution, suffering, and death.

If we can read the statements of Jesus and still be comfortable, then we do not understand them properly. If we can read them and think that they are easy, then we have missed the point. The demands of Jesus are humanly impossible. The life of Christian discipleship can only be lived by the supernatural power of the indwelling Holy Spirit.

Modern man has developed the dangerous art of taking the radical teachings of the Lord Jesus and so robbing them of their true meaning that there isn't enough left to make soup for a sick grasshopper. Instead of taking His words literally, we devise sixty theological ways of explaining them away. The result is that there is a vast difference between the Christianity we see about us today and the Christianity of the New Testament. Today it means attending church whenever convenient, putting money in the collection, and giving Jesus one's spare evenings. Is that true Christianity? No! True Christianity is a life of radical discipleship, of sacrificial service, of total commitment to the Son of God. It means seeking first the kingdom of God and His righteousness.

In his book *Born After Midnight*, A.W. Tozer wrote:

Christ calls men to carry a cross; we call them to have fun in His name. He calls them to forsake the world; we assure them that if they but accept Jesus, the world is their oyster. He calls them to suffer; we call them to enjoy all the bourgeois comforts modern civilization affords. He calls them to self-abnegation and death. We call them to spread themselves like green bay trees or perchance even to become stars in a pitiful fifth-rate religious zodiac. He calls them to holiness; we call them to a cheap and tawdry happiness that would have been rejected with scorn by the least of the stoic philosophers.[2]

In another place, Tozer said:

Our Lord called men to follow Him, but He never made the way look easy.

---

2   Tozer, A. W., *Born After Midnight*, Camp Hill, PA: Christian Publications, 1989, p. 141

Indeed one gets the distinct impression that he made it appear extremely hard.

Sometimes He said things to disciples or prospective disciples that we today discreetly avoid repeating when we are trying to win men to Him. What present day evangelist would have the courage to tell an inquirer, *"If any man will come after Me let him deny himself and take up his cross and follow Me. For whosoever will save his life shall lose it and whosoever will lose his life for My sake shall find it."* And do we not do some tall explaining when someone asks us what Jesus meant when He said, *"Think not that I am come to send peace on earth. I come not to send peace but a sword...."*

That kind of rugged, sinewy Christianity is left for an occasional missionary or for some believer behind one of the various curtains of the world. The masses of professed Christians simply do not have the moral muscle to enable them to take a path so downright and final as this. The contemporary moral climate does not favor a faith as tough and fibrous as that taught by our Lord and His apostles. The delicate, brittle saints being produced in our religious hothouse today are hardly to be compared with the committed, expendable believers who once gave their witness among men. And the fault lies with our leaders; they are too timid to tell the people all the truth. They are now asking men to give to God that which costs them nothing. Our churches these days are filled, or one-quarter filled, with a soft breed of Christians that must be fed on a diet of harmless fun to keep them interested. About theology they know little. Scarcely any of them have read even one of the great Christian classics. But most of them are familiar with religious fiction and spine-tingling films. No wonder their moral and spiritual constitution is so frail. Such can only be called weak adherents of a faith they really never understood.[3]

E. Stanley Jones said something similar:

Men do not reject Christianity; they would simply render it innocuous. They would inoculate men with a mild form of Christianity so that they would become immune against the real thing (in *Christ's Alternative to Communism*).

---

3   Tozer, A. W., *That Incredible Christian*, Camp Hill, PA: Christian Publications, 1964, p. 87

The Lord Jesus is looking today for people who are willing to accept His teachings literally and obey them even if they don't see anyone else obeying them. He is looking for men and women, young men and young women who are tired of living self-centered lives; who are aware that material things don't bring happiness, who realize that Christians are here for bigger business than to make money. He is looking for disciples who hate the tyranny of the fashion parade, the food fair, the social whirl and the cult of the body beautiful. It's sadly true that we often find more reality in the average communist or the average cultist than we do in the average Christian. People are willing to do for political and social causes more than we are willing to do for the Savior of the world. They show more dedication to false religions than we do to the Christ of God. They are more motivated by the dollar than we are by love to the Savior.

Thank God there is hunger, especially among young people, for something better. Recently, I spoke at a meeting about some committed young people who are finding fulfillment in lives of sacrificial service overseas. After returning home, I received the following letter from a young lady who had been in the meeting. She entitled it: *Reality—How Is It Found?*

During the past few days, we have been hearing of the courage, persecution, and sacrificial living of some young people in countries of Europe and Asia. They have found REALITY in the Christian life, something for which I and dozens of other young people have searched for a long time. I want that reality more than anything in the world. Yet I am trapped. Because we American young people have every luxury, every convenience, every opportunity to witness, there has ceased to be any challenge, if you know what I mean—nothing to fight for. I desire desperately to throw off all the things and selfish ambitions for the cause of Christ, but it seems a losing battle. Do you know how this feels? It's a trap, a live devil-put trap that I can't seem to break through. I'm sick, sick, sick of living for self. I want and need a challenge. A chance to forget me and live for the Lord. I'd give anything for the chance to be hungry for the sake of God, be imprisoned, persecuted, etc., anything, but here in the enlightened USA, there is no challenge, no opposition and because of this we young people can't help but be complacent and carnal. Please help, there has to be all for God or nothing as far as I am concerned. Is there an answer?

We started off by saying that the teachings of the Lord Jesus are revolutionary. Let us now turn to the New Testament to see just how revolutionary and radical they are. I think if we could just read the New Testament for the first time, we would realize what a revolutionary book it is.

First of all, the Lord Jesus taught His disciples that they should adopt a revolutionary standard of living. In Luke 14:33 He said, *"So likewise, whoever of you does not forsake all that he has cannot be My disciple."* And Paul echoes this in 1 Timothy 6:8 where he says, *"Having food and clothing, with these we shall be content."* The Savior says we should forsake all that we have. Paul says that we should be satisfied with food and covering. Now this is a revolutionary standard of living. It points to a life of simplicity. It points to a life of sacrificial living.

Not only so but the Lord Jesus taught what we might call a revolutionary social life. He said in Luke 14:12-14,

> *When you give a dinner or a supper, do not ask your friends, your brothers, your relatives, nor your rich neighbors, lest they also invite you back, and you will be repaid. But when you give a feast, invite the poor, the maimed, the lame, the blind. And you will be blessed, because they cannot repay you; for you shall be repaid at the resurrection of the just.*

These words of the Lord Jesus strike a blow at the common policy among men and women today to invite people who will invite them in return, a sort of reciprocity. And this is what underlies most modern society. But the Lord Jesus said to not do that when you invite guests. Invite those who can't repay you, and you will be repaid at the resurrection of the just.

Then the Lord Jesus taught that we should take a revolutionary attitude toward earthly relationships and toward our own lives. He said in Luke 14:26, *"If anyone comes to Me and does not hate his father and mother, wife and children, brothers and sisters, yes, and his own life also, he cannot be My disciple."*

Now when it says, *"does not hate his father and mother, wife and children, brothers and sisters,"* the Lord did not mean that we should show animosity, a bitter, acrimonious spirit towards our loved ones, but He did mean that He must come first in life and that all other loves must be hatred by comparison.

But I think that the most revolutionary part of this verse is that expression *"...yes, and his own life also." "If anyone comes to Me... and does not hate his own life also, he cannot be My disciple."* This means, of course, that we must put the cause of Christ ahead of our own lives; we should be willing to fling our body and soul down for God to plow them under. In another place the Lord Jesus says that if any man loves his life he will lose it, but if he hates his life for Christ's sake and the gospel's he'll find it.

Then in Matthew 6:33, the Savior taught that the central reason for our existence is to seek first the kingdom of God and His righteousness. He said, *"But seek first the kingdom of God and His righteousness, and all these things shall be added to you."* This is revolutionary. Most people think that they are born into the world to be plumbers or electricians or doctors or teachers or nurses or something of this sort, but there is a difference between our calling and our occupation. The calling of the child of God is to serve the Lord Jesus Christ. His occupation is merely a means of putting bread and butter on the table but not to get rich or find fulfillment in it. Paul was a tentmaker but in starting his epistles he never said, "Paul called to be a tentmaker." He always said, *"Paul called to be an apostle."* His calling in life was to be an apostle and he made tents to supply his temporal needs.

Then in Matthew 19:19, the Lord Jesus said something that some people consider to be His most revolutionary statement. He said, *"You shall love your neighbor as yourself."* Now we have become so used to those words, they really don't grip us and we don't seem to realize just how potent they are. Just think about it for a moment, *"You shall love your neighbor as yourself."* Think of how we love ourselves, how we cater to ourselves, how we make sure we are fed and that we brush our teeth and take care of our body and we have all the Bibles and the good things of life. Jesus said, *"You shall love your neighbor as yourself."* Who is my neighbor? Anyone who is in need. If I really love my neighbor as myself, I won't be satisfied until men and women all over the world are introduced to the Lord Jesus Christ and until they have copies of the Word of God as well.

Our Lord taught a revolutionary view of greatness. In His kingdom greatness means keeping and teaching His commandments (Mt. 5:19b), serving, even slaving, for others (Mt. 20:1-16; Lk. 17:7-10; 22:26) and taking the lowest place (Lk. 9:48). How different this is from the world's view. There the greatest man is the one who throws his weight around, barks out orders and lords it over others.

Finally, the Lord Jesus taught a revolutionary view of security for the future. Matthew 6:19 says,

> *Do not lay up for yourselves treasures on earth, where moth and rust destroy and where thieves break in and steal; but lay up for yourselves treasures in heaven, where neither moth nor rust destroys and where thieves do not break in and steal.*

And then in verse 25 of that same chapter, He said, *"...Do not worry about your life, what you will eat or what you will drink, nor about your body, what you will put on. Is not life more than food and the body than clothing?"* Here the Lord Jesus absolutely forbade His disciples to spend their lives saving for a rainy day. He says to them in effect, "Look, put My interests first. Work hard for the supply of your current needs and the needs of your family. Put everything above that in the work of the Lord and I'll take care of your future. I call you to a life of faith, a life of trusting in Me to provide your needs. And if you seek first the kingdom of God and His righteousness, then all these things shall be provided for you."

One final verse is John 3:3. Jesus said, *"Most assuredly, I say to you, unless one is born again, he cannot see the kingdom of God."* Nicodemus, a religious leader, came to the Lord Jesus by night and the Lord Jesus faced him with this revolutionary truth. He said, "Nicodemus, you need to be born again if you're ever going to see the kingdom of God: The new birth is an absolute necessity." And incidentally, this is where the life of discipleship begins. You don't become a Christian by living the life of discipleship, but you live the life of discipleship after you become a Christian, and you become a Christian by being born again.

Of course that raises the question, *"How can a man be born again?"* and the answer is, first of all, by repenting of his sins. In order to be saved, a person must acknowledge that he is a sinner and that he deserves to go to hell. When he comes to that place, he should then realize that the Lord Jesus died as his Substitute on the cross of Calvary, that He paid the penalty for the sinner's sin. Then by a definite act of faith, he must put his trust in the Lord Jesus Christ. In this very same chapter, the Lord Jesus said, *"For God so loved the world that He gave His only begotten Son that whoever believes in Him should not perish but have everlasting life"* (Jn. 3:16). The moment you receive the sinners' Savior by that definite act of faith, you can know on the authority of the Word of God that you are saved, that you have been born again. Would you like to start on the road as a disciple of the Lord Jesus? Then put your faith and trust in Him and go forth to tell His excellencies to the entire world.

In the chapters that follow, we will examine some of the radical teachings of the Lord in greater detail.

THREE
IT'S RADICAL TRAINING: Part 1
LUKE 6:12-26

Soon the Lord Jesus was going to the cross to die as a substitute for sinners. He would provide a way of salvation that would be available to all mankind. But that means that there must be a worldwide proclamation of the good news. The world must be evangelized. How could this be done?

The Savior's strategy was to choose twelve men, indoctrinate them with the principles of His kingdom, then send them forth as flaming heralds. If He could just find twelve men who loved Him with all their hearts, feared nothing but sin, and obeyed Him implicitly, He could turn the world upside down.

His first step was to spend a night in prayer on a mountain. Picture the holy Son of God, prostrate on the ground, seeking the will of His Father. There is little doubt that the main subject of His prayers was the choice of disciples. Ever dependent on God for guidance, He made the choice a matter of earnest and prolonged prayer. This shows us the priority He gave to prayer. And it rebukes our prayerlessness, we who seldom if ever spend a night in prayer.

The next day He met with His followers and singled out the twelve whom we know as the apostles. His choice was remarkable in several respects: the number selected; their age; their general qualifications; and the inclusion of a traitor. First, as to the number chosen—not 12,000, 1,200, or even 120. Only 12. Why such a small team? For one thing, discipleship can only be carried on effectively with a small group. In addition, the number must be so small that any success will be attributed only to the Lord.

The disciples were probably in their twenties at this time. The Lord Himself was about thirty, and normally a teacher is older than his students. Also, the Lord knew that youth was His best opportunity to mold, change, and ignite the human soul.

The disciples' qualifications were unimpressive. They were ordinary men, homespun and unlettered in the higher institutions. None had theological credentials. None was wealthy. Robert Coleman describes them as "a rather ragged aggregation of souls, by any standard of culture…representing an average cross-section of the society in their day." We can say of them, as of anyone else, the only wonderful thing about them was their connection with Jesus.

There is mystery connected with the selection of Judas Iscariot. Certainly the omniscient Lord knew that Judas would betray Him, and yet He chose him anyway. It is best just to let the mystery stand.

Immediately the disciples are given on-the-job training. They watch the Lord and listen to Him as He teaches the crowd, heals the sick, and casts out unclean spirits. They cannot help but be impressed as they see the people surge forward to touch the Master. They learn that people can tell when God's power is flowing through a man.

The Savior's message sounds like a partial repeat of the Sermon on the Mount in Matthew 5–7. But it is not the same. This message was given on a plain or level place (v. 17), not on a mountain. The beatitudes are different. In Matthew the blessed are the poor in spirit and those who hunger and thirst for righteousness. In Luke they are those who are physically poor and hungry. This sermon, addressed primarily to the disciples (Lk. 6:20), includes four woes: there are none in Matthew.

First, our Lord tells His apostles that they are to go forth as poor men. We know He means literally poor rather than poor in spirit by the contrasting woe in verse 24; *"Woe unto you that are rich."* He does not say rich in spirit; that would be meaningless. He is referring to a lack of affluence or wealth. But is it a blessing to be poor? People all over the world are locked in grinding poverty, and to them it is a curse rather than a blessing. In what sense, then, were the disciples to be blessed by being poor? The key is found at the end of verse 22: *"for the Son of Man's sake."* Rather than amassing personal fortunes for themselves, the Twelve were to impoverish themselves that others might be enriched spiritually.

When we stop to think of it, it was only proper that they should be poor. They were representatives of One who was born into a poor Jewish family, who is never reported to have carried money, who had nowhere to lay His head. They were agents of One who had been rich but who voluntarily became poor that we might be rich. They were envoys of "the one perfect life that has been lived in this world...the life of Him who owned nothing and who left nothing but the clothes He wore" (Denney).

It would have been a contradiction if they had worn expensive clothing, had displayed high-priced coiffures, had flashed big rolls of bills, and had paraded costly jewels. It would have given a completely wrong impression of the One who cared for none of these things. E. S. Jones tells of going into an ornate cathedral and seeing a statue of the baby Jesus which the church had draped with priceless jewelry. Then he went out to the street and saw the faces of children pinched with hunger. The thought crossed his mind, "I wonder if the Bambino is enjoying His jewels." Then he said, "I decided that if He was, I could no longer enjoy the thought of the Bambino." And yet in many ways the professing church has draped Jesus with expensive livery, presenting Him to the world as a Man of wealth, living in luxury instead of a Man of God, living in simplicity.

If the disciples had gone forth as rich men, they could have attracted countless followers whose only motive would have been to better themselves financially. People will profess religion to get a bowl of rice, but their great need is repentance toward God and genuine faith in Jesus Christ as Lord and Savior.

If the Twelve had gone forth wealthy, any success would have been attributed to the power of money rather than the power of God. In addition, they might have been tempted to embark on expensive projects that might not have been the will of God. Poverty in Christian service keeps men dependent on the Lord and confident that He will pay for everything He orders.

It is doubtful that the disciples could have accomplished what they did if they had not gone forth poor. Wealth would have been a liability whereas their poverty worked for them. These men could have been rich, but they chose not to be rich in a world where thousands died of starvation and where the name of Jesus was still unknown to multitudes.

Not only were the disciples to go forth without wealth; they were to know the blessing of being hungry. Is hunger a blessing? Yes, but only if chosen for the Son of Man's sake. The disciples were not called to be gourmets, sampling choice foods and lingering over vintage wines. Rather they were to live economically, using their resources to the maximum for the spread of the gospel.

Next their ministry was to be one of weeping. But this does not refer to the weeping that is pandemic in a suffering world such as ours. This is a special sorrow, a kind that is endured for the Son of Man's sake. They were to shed bitter tears for the dying souls of men. They were to mourn over the divided condition of the church. They were to grieve over their own sins and shortcomings. If they went forth weeping, bearing precious seed, they would come again with rejoicing, bringing their sheaves with them (see Ps. 126:6). "Winners of souls must first be weepers for souls."

Not only were they to be poor, hungry and weeping; they were to be unpopular for the Son of Man's sake. Their faithful association with Jesus would bring them hatred, excommunication, reproach and slander. But not to worry! This would be cause for great rejoicing. They would be sharing the experiences of the godly prophets of the Old Testament and would be guaranteed a great reward in heaven.

Some might be tempted to ask, "What could Jesus ever do with such a four-ranked army of fools—poor, hungry, weeping and despised? The answer is: He could turn the world upside down with them. And He did!

As if anticipating how future generations of disciples would turn away from a sacrificial lifestyle of self-denial and grasp after "the soft and effeminate luxuries that kill the soul," the Lord pronounced four woes.

Woe unto you that are rich! These are professed disciples whose motto is "Nothing's too good for the people of God." They quote 1 Timothy 6:17b, *"(He) gives us richly all things to enjoy,"* forgetting that enjoyment is not by self-indulgence, but, as the next verse says, by doing good, being rich in good works, and distributing to the needy. They refuse to see how sinful it is to hoard wealth when that wealth could be used in the evangelization of the lost. They forget that the holy Son of God said, *"How hard it is for those who have riches to enter the kingdom of God! For it is easier for a camel to go through a needle's eye than for a rich man to enter into the kingdom of God"* (Lk. 18:24b-25).

Woe unto you that are full! These are professed disciples who live to gratify their appetites. Self is the center and circumference of their lives. They eat in elegant restaurants, gorge themselves on pleasure cruises that lead nowhere, and luxuriate at the finer clubs and hotels. Their life is all kitchen and dining room. The fact that Lazarus is hungry outside their door concerns them not at all.

Woe unto you that laugh now! Their sin is not that they enjoy a good joke, but that everything in life is a joke to them. They don't seem to be serious about the great issues of time and eternity, about dying souls, about sobbing humanity, or about eternal hell. Spiritually they are featherweights. Life is just a bowl of cherries. Their minds are empty; their speech is empty; their lives are empty.

Woe unto you, when all men shall speak well of you. They say they are disciples of Jesus but they are actually slaves of status. They love man's praise more than God's. They avoid speaking the truth clearly and fearlessly lest it would offend. These men are chameleons, adapting the message to the audience. They can speak out of both corners of the mouth simultaneously. They are in the ignoble line of the false prophets of the Old Testament.

So disciples must make a deliberate choice. On the one hand there is poverty, hunger, tears and unpopularity for the Son of Man's sake. On the other there is riches, abundant food, gaiety, and man's approval. Those who choose the latter receive their reward now and remorse later. Those who choose the former inherit the kingdom with all the joys that go with it.

FOUR
IT'S RADICAL TRAINING: Part 2
LUKE 6:27-38

As the disciples go forth into the battle, it is imperative that they have a suitable weapon, so the Savior now unveils a secret weapon in the arsenal of God. It is love. His is a revolution, not of hatred, but of love; not of violence, but of kindness.

This love is different from anything that the world knows. It is a supernatural, otherworldly love. It is not mere human affection, of which unbelievers are capable. It is something that only those with divine life can display. And even believers cannot show it by their own strength. It can only be shown by the power of the indwelling Holy Spirit.

This love is more a matter of the will than of the emotions, although the emotions are, of course, involved. It is not something that is contracted, like a common cold, but something that is cultivated by sitting at the feet of Jesus. It does not come from Hollywood but from heaven. Whereas lust cannot wait to get, love cannot wait to give.

Unconverted people are completely taken off guard when they encounter this kind of love. They are nonplussed. They know how to respond to human affection and they can certainly fight back when they meet hostility. But when their discourtesies are repaid with kindness, they don't know what to think, say, or do.

That is the whole idea. Disciples will never make an impact on the world if they don't rise above flesh and blood. They have to shock men and women with a great explosion of love.

In verses 27 through 31 the Savior tells how love treats others. For instance, it goes out to enemies, not just to friends. Now that isn't natural. To love one's enemies cuts across the grain of human nature. Or to repay hatred with deeds of kindness. Or to ask God's blessing on those who curse us. Or to pray for those who mistreat us. And yet, "It is the way the Master went. Shall not His servants tread it still?"

Does it really make an impact on men when Christians love their enemies and pray for their persecutors? Let me tell you a story.

Mitsuo Fuchida was the Japanese pilot who led the attack on Pearl Harbor in December 1941. It was he who radioed back to Tokyo, "Tora, Tora, Tora," announcing the complete success of the mission. He was intoxicated with victory until the tides of war eventually turned. Finally his country had to surrender.

Now crushed by defeat, Fuchida determined that the victors should be tried for war crimes before an international tribunal. To gather evidence, he interviewed Japanese servicemen who had been held as prisoners of war in the United States. Instead of hearing of atrocities, he repeatedly heard of a Christian woman who visited the POW camp, showed kindness to them, and gave them a Christian Book called the New Testament. When they asked why she was so good to enemy prisoners, she told them that her parents had been missionaries in the Philippines, that they had been executed by the Japanese, but that before their death, they had prayed a certain prayer. It was because of that prayer that she decided to love and care for needy Japanese prisoners.

Mitsuo Fuchida couldn't get the story of that mysterious prayer out of his mind. It nagged him continually. He located a copy of the New Testament and began reading. When he reached Luke 23:34, he knew right away that he had discovered the prayer: *"Father, forgive them for they know not what they do."* "He no longer thought of the American woman or the Japanese prisoners of war, but of himself a fierce enemy of Christ, whom God was prepared to forgive in answer to the prayer of the crucified Savior. At that very moment he sought and found forgiveness and eternal life by faith in Christ." Mitsuo Fuchida spent the rest of his life preaching the unsearchable riches of Christ all over the world.[4]

Love does not retaliate or give tit for tat. Rather it turns the other cheek. "By turning the other cheek you disarm your enemy. He hits you on the cheek and you, by your moral audacity, hit him on the heart by turning the other cheek. His enmity is dissolved. Your enemy is gone. You got rid of your enemy by getting rid of your enmity...The world is at the feet of the Man who had power to strike back but who had power not to strike back. That is power—the ultimate power" (E. Stanley Jones).

Love holds such a light touch on material possessions that it gladly parts with more than is asked. The reason it is so difficult for us to follow this example is because we own so much and it has a grip on us.

Love manifests itself in giving.

> *Love ever gives, forgives, outlives,*
> *And ever stands with open hands.*
> *And while it lives it gives,*
> > *For this is love's prerogative—*
> > *To give and give and give.*

The disciples must know at the outset that their ministry is to be a ministry of giving. The question is not, "What will I get out of it?"

---

4   Adapted from an oral message by Harry Foster, English Bible teacher

but "How may I give more and more?" They must not expect to be on the receiving end, but on the giving end. They will constantly see genuine cases of need, and, though poor themselves, they will be enabled to contribute. The only time they would not be expected to give is when it would harm a person, either by subsidizing laziness or by financing an evil habit. If ever in doubt, the disciple should err on the side of grace.

The basic rule is that Christ's followers should treat others as they like to be treated. This means that they should be courteous, generous, patient, unselfish, impartial, forgiving, helpful—the list is endless.

Now Jesus goes on to emphasize that our behavior must be superior to that of unregenerate men (vv. 32-35). It is not enough to love our relations and friends. Even gangsters do that. It is not enough to show kindness to those who treat us kindly. Murderers and adulterers are capable of that. It is not enough to lend with the hope of repayment. The local loan company will do that. We must go beyond what is merely human to that which manifests divine life if we are going to make an impact on the world. We can do this by loving the unlovely, the wicked, and the unthankful, by doing good to those who don't deserve it, and by lending without hope of getting it back. God will reward that brand of discipleship handsomely, and we will be the children of the Highest. This is not how we become children of the Highest. The only way to do that is by repentance toward God and faith in the Lord Jesus Christ. But this is how we show the world that we are God's children. We demonstrate the family likeness by being kind to the unthankful and the evil.

In serving the Lord, the Twelve would meet with all kinds of human need—the sick, blind, deaf, elderly, wayward, insane, demon-possessed, lonely, poor and homeless. There would be times when they would be tempted to be impatient, when they would be physically tired and emotionally exhausted, and when they would feel like scolding the unfortunate people. Jesus reminded them that they must be merciful, just like their heavenly Father.

"Judge not, and you shall not be judged." Many people who are ignorant of the rest of the Bible know this verse and use it as a club to silence any criticism or correction. If they would study the rest of the Bible, they would learn that there are times when we must judge as well as times when we must not.

For example, we must judge teachers and their doctrine by the Word (1 Cor. 14:29). We must judge whether others are true believers; otherwise we could not obey the prohibition against entering into an unequal yoke (2 Cor. 6:14). We must judge disputes between believers (1 Cor. 6:1-6). We must judge sin in our own lives (1 Cor. 11:31). The local church must judge extreme forms of sin (1 Cor. 5:12). The local church must judge whether men are qualified to be elders and deacons (1 Tim. 3:1-13).

But there are other areas where we must not judge. We must not judge the motives of other people because only God knows what is going on in their minds. We must not judge the service of the Lord's servants (1 Cor. 4:5). There is only One who knows whether they are building with gold, silver, precious stones, or with wood, hay, and straw (1 Cor. 3:12). We must not judge those who differ with us in matters that are morally indifferent or non-essential (Rom. 14:3-4, 13). Finally, we must not judge by outward appearances (Jn. 7:24), or show partiality of persons (Jas. 2:1-4).

"Condemn not, and ye shall not be condemned." It would give a false view of the Savior for His disciples to be forever condemning others. Jesus did not come to condemn but to save. His followers should not be critical, censorious, fault finders. True, they must earnestly contend for the faith, but that does not necessitate a ceaselessly negative ministry. Those who are forever condemning others attract people just like themselves, and such a congregation is inevitably doomed to division!

"Forgive, and ye shall be forgiven." This is parental forgiveness

and is to be distinguished from judicial forgiveness. When a sinner trusts the Savior, he receives judicial forgiveness, that is, God the Judge frees him from ever having to pay the penalty of his sins. But when a Christian sins, he needs parental forgiveness. He receives this when he confesses his sin (1 Jn. 1:9). This forgiveness is conditional. God will not grant the forgiveness that restores family fellowship if the believer refuses to forgive a repentant brother. Every child of God has been forgiven millions; he must be willing to forgive a few cents (Mt. 18:23-35).

One early lesson that disciples should learn is that they cannot outgive the Lord. If they really want to be generous, God will see to it that they will never lack the means to be generous. If they shovel it out, God will shovel it in, and God has a bigger shovel. Note how different this is from the not uncommon practice of using the ministry as a means of financial security. The scriptural way is not "Get all you can out of it" but "Put all you can into it."

When all else fails, love conquers. In one of Aesop's fables, the sun had a contest with the wind to see which one could make a man take off his overcoat. The more the wind blew, the more snugly the man pulled the coat around himself. When the sun shone on him, he quit shivering and removed his coat. The warmth had won.

A little boy was playing in a hollow where there was a distinct echo. He shouted "I hate you" and the words rebounded "I hate you." Each time he yelled more loudly and the words came back with increasing volume. He ran sobbing to his mother, explaining, "There's a little boy in the neighborhood who hates me." The mother wisely suggested that he tell the boy that he loved him. Sure enough. Every time he shouted, "I love you," he heard the welcome echo, "I love you."

The world is dying for a little bit of love. Christ calls His disciples to go forth with the love of God shed abroad in their hearts.

FIVE
IT'S RADICAL TRAINING: Part 3
LUKE 6:39-49

The ministry of Christian disciples is a ministry of character. Their spiritual and moral integrity is their whole stock-in-trade. What they are is far more important than anything they ever do or say. The cultivation of strong Christian character is what counts.

Actually, there are only a few exhortations in the New Testament to aggressive soul winning, but there are hundreds of exhortations to holy living. When Jesus said, *"Follow Me and I will make you fishers of men,"* He made the development of a Christlike life the precondition to successful soul winning.

Let me give you some examples of how this works. An unsaved sailor was impressed by the behavior of a Christian buddy. The Christian was even-tempered, self-effacing, and honest. He could actually carry on a conversation without using profanity. One night Dick said to his friend, "Bert, you're different. You have something I don't have. I don't know what it is, but I want it." It was easy for Bert to lead Dick to the Lord that night.

When a university student became repulsive through excessive drinking, his own friends turned against him. In fact, his roommate ordered him to leave. No one wanted him. Finally an on-fire believer heard of his plight and invited him to share his room. The alcoholic was disgusting, but the good Samaritan prepared meals for him and took care of his laundry. Often he had to clean up his vomit, bathe him, and get him into bed. Eventually it began to get to the drinker.

One day he shouted angrily, "Look here! What are you doing this for? What are you after?"

The Christian answered quietly, "I'm after your soul." He got it.

Then there is the story of Sir Henry M. Stanley who went to Africa in search of David Livingstone, the missionary-explorer. Stanley later wrote:

> I went to Africa as prejudiced against religion as the worst infidel in London. To a reporter like myself, who had only to deal with wars, mass meetings, and political gatherings, sentimental matters were quite out of my province. But there came to me a long time for reflection. I was out there away from a worldly world. I saw this solitary old man (Livingstone) there, and I asked myself, "Why does he stop here in such a place? What is it that inspires him?"
>
> For months after we met, I found myself listening to him, wondering at the old man carrying out the words, *"Leave all and follow Me."* But little by little, seeing his piety, his gentleness, his zeal, his earnestness, and how he went quietly about his business, I was converted by him, although he had not tried in any *way* to do it.

The outside world reads us more than it reads the Bible. Men say, with Edgar Guest, "I'd rather see a sermon than hear one any day." And too often they are forced to say, "What you are speaks so loud I can't hear what you say." When a certain preacher was in the pulpit, his congregation wished he would never leave it. When he was out of it, they wished he would never enter it. A great preacher but his life didn't match his preaching. Every one of us is either a Bible or a libel.

A poet reminds us:

You are writing a gospel, a chapter each day,
By the things that you do and the things that you say,
Men read what you write, whether faithless or true,
Say! What is the gospel according to you?

When asked what his favorite Gospel was, a man answered, "The gospel according to my mother." In similar vein, John Wesley said he learned more about Christianity from his mother than from all the theologians of Europe.

A famous minister had a brother who was a medical doctor. One day a lady came to the minister's door but became confused as to which brother lived there. When he came to the door, she asked, "Pardon me, but are you the doctor that preaches or the one that practices?" The question startled him and he determined to practice better the truths he taught.

Years ago I wrote this searching jingle in the front of my Bible:

If of Jesus Christ their only view
May be what they see of Him in you,
MacDonald, what do they see?

It is a healthy reminder that we are the only view of the Savior that many people will ever have.

In Luke 6:39-49, our Lord is talking about the character of His disciples and how important it is. First of all, He points out that there are certain limits on the extent to which we can help others. The blind can't lead the blind. If we have some blind spot in our life—some unconquered sinful habit, some command we have not obeyed, some glaring character weakness—we cannot teach anyone else how to overcome. If we try, he will probably say, "Physician, heal yourself."

A teacher can lead a disciple up to the point that he himself has attained, but he can't expect the disciple to advance beyond that. The goal of discipleship is for the learner to become like his trainer.

Jesus used the illustration of the speck and the beam to press

43

home the point. Using a little sanctified imagination, we picture a man walking past a threshing floor. Suddenly a gust of wind lifts a speck of dust and plants it securely in his left eye. He rubs and rubs, and the more he rubs, the worse it gets. Friends crowd around with assorted remedies. One says, "Pull your top eyelid down over the bottom one." But nothing helps. Then I come along with a telephone pole protruding from my eye and offer some sympathetic help. What happens? He looks up at me with bloodshot eye and says, "Don't you think you should get that post out of your own eye?"

Of course, I cannot assist someone who is suffering from some moral or spiritual problem if I have that same problem, and especially if I have that problem to an exaggerated degree. I'd better straighten out my own life before I try to help others.

To emphasize that the man is the message, Jesus used the illustrations of good and bad trees, good and evil men, and wise and foolish builders. Good trees bring forth good fruit. Trees that are not in healthy condition bring forth diseased, wormy fruit. A tree is known by its fruit. Thorn bushes can't produce figs, nor can prickly shrubs grow grapes.

It is that way with men. A good man ministers words of edification, comfort, and encouragement to others. His life is a benediction to those he contacts. A wicked man on the other hand speaks in a way that is defiling, destructive, and empty. The quality of a person's ministry is determined by what he is inside. Conversation is a barometer of character.

As the Lord Jesus comes to the end of His sermon on the plain, realizing how radical and revolutionary it is, He foresees the temptation on the part of the disciples to hear it but not obey it. They will call Him *"Lord, Lord,"* but will not do what He says. So He defines a wise disciple and a foolish one. The wise man hears His words and obeys them. That man's life is built on a solid foundation. When storms come into his life, as come they will, he stands fast. His life has been built on the sound principles of Christian discipleship that the Lord has just taught.

The foolish man is the man who hears but doesn't obey. He depends on his own wisdom and common sense. He rationalizes that the Savior's program would never work in a world like ours. So he builds his life on the shifting sands of worldly wisdom. When the storms come, the life he has built is swept away. His soul may be saved but his life is lost. He has nothing to show for the wasted years. A life is a terrible thing to waste.

SIX
HAVE A SECURE FUTURE
MATTHEW 6:19-34

The Lord Jesus has a security program for those who are His disciples. At first glance this program seems to violate everything we have been taught about security, about prudence, and about common sense. But the hard fact is that the Lord's plan is 100% safe whereas all man's plans are loaded with risk and insecurity.

First the Lord forbids laying up treasures on earth. He is speaking against the accepted wisdom of saving for a rainy day. We have always been taught that "wise bees save honey and wise men save money." We have been brainwashed that we must provide for financial independence during the later years of life. We think that if we just have enough money, we can face the future unafraid. Material wealth provides security, we feel.

Someone might object that if he lived by faith, he would have a nervous breakdown. Not so, says Jesus. It's treasures on earth that have the possibility of providing not one but three nervous breakdowns: *"Moth...rust...thieves."* In Bible times, wealth was in the form of clothing and coinage. The clothes were subject to attack by moths. The money was subject to corrosion. And both were in constant danger of theft.

The way to have real security is to lay up treasures in heaven. Instead of spending our lives accumulating perishable wealth for an uncertain future, we should devote our finest talents to investing for eternity. We do this, of course, by putting our money to work for the Lord, by serving Him faithfully and tirelessly, and by living for people instead of for things.

Before going further, we should emphasize that this passage is not dealing with the provision of current necessities. We should work hard for our current needs and the needs of our family. But when these needs are met, we should invest everything else in heavenly treasures and trust God for the future. If we do that, our treasures will never suffer loss from moth, rust, or thieves.

The fact is undeniable that the location of our treasure determines the location of our heart. In other words, our interests, affections, and ambitions are either in a bank or in heaven. Our heart here stands for that for which we live. It refers to what is central in our life. If we are intent on stockpiling wealth on earth, then that will consume us inwardly.

And make no mistake about it! We can't live for earthly riches and heavenly treasure at the same time. Jesus taught this by the illustration of the human eye. The eye is the lamp of the body. It is through the eye that light enters the body and guides the person. If the eye is single, that is, healthy, the person sees clearly where to go. If the eye is evil, that is, diseased, the way ahead is dim and indistinct.

The spiritual meaning is this: The single eye represents the determination to live for heavenly treasure alone. The person who lays up his riches in heaven will never lack the guidance of God. The evil eye stands for the desire to live for both worlds, to have treasures in both places. The person who has divided motives will experience spiritual darkness. He will lack clear direction from the Lord. Actually his darkness will be greater than that of a person who never had light on this subject. It is better not to have known the Savior's teaching about laying up treasure than to have known it and rejected it. "Light rejected is light denied." *"From him who does not have, even what he has will be taken away"* (Mt. 25:29b).

It is impossible to serve two masters without preferring one above the other, without dividing one's loyalties. Situations will inevitably arise where the interests of the two masters conflict. A choice must be made. If we live for money we can't live for God. We must choose between treasures on earth and treasures in heaven.

Our Lord gives six reasons why we should not worry about future needs, as far as the necessities of life are concerned.

First, it puts a wrong emphasis on what is important. We shouldn't live for food, drink, or clothing, as if they were the things that really matter in life. God put us here for bigger business than to eat, drink, and model clothes.

Second, anxious care about possible future crises implies doubt about our Father's care for us. Jesus suggested that we learn a lesson from the birds in this respect. He said that they do not sow nor reap. That doesn't mean that we shouldn't. They can't plant or harvest; we can. They scratch around for their daily food and don't worry about the future. Sparrows don't develop ulcers from worry, nor do they rush off to psychiatrists with tension problems. They live a day at a time and their future is in the hands of their Creator. No bird's nests have barns or silos attached. For centuries the bird population has managed to survive without hoarding for the dim, unknown future. If God cares for His feathered creatures, how much more does He care for us!

A third reason why worry is forbidden is because it is futile. Jesus asked, *"Which of you by worrying can add one cubit unto his stature?"* In other words, "Who can grow eighteen inches by worrying?" Or the Savior's question may read, *"Which of you by being anxious can add a single cubit to his life's span?"* (NASB). Here life is viewed as a journey of so many miles, and the question is, "Who can add eighteen inches to it by worrying about the future?" It is futile to try. Actually worry shortens life instead of lengthening it.

If we would only stop to think, we would realize that it is virtually impossible to provide security for our future. For one thing, we don't know how long we will live. We don't know what the dollar will be worth in the future. We don't know what expenses we will face. There are too many unknowns for us to plan for the rainy day.

Then Jesus pointed to the flowers to show that worry about clothing betrays a lack of faith in God. He was not thinking as much of potted Easter lilies, but rather of the wild anemones that grow in profusion on the hillsides of Israel. The Lord designed these flowers with exquisite care. He lavished breathtaking beauty upon them. Even Solomon did not clothe himself with such elegance. And yet those flowers carpeting the landscape with color today will be mowed down tomorrow and thrown in an open-hearth fire to provide heat for baking the flat bread of the Middle East. Now if God goes to such length to clothe wildflowers with beauty, how much more will He provide suitable clothes for His people?

John Stott said,

> To become preoccupied with material things in such a way that they engross our attention, absorb our energy, and burden us with anxiety is incompatible with both Christian faith and common sense. It is distrustful of our heavenly Father, and it is frankly stupid.

A fifth reason why we should not take anxious thought for food, drink, and clothing is that that is what pagans live for, and God doesn't want us to be like the pagans. The heathen give first place to the body. They live to cater to it. They are essentially worldly, earthy, and fleshly. Without divine life, they cannot be expected to rise above flesh and blood. But believers should be different. They should give the best of their life to that which is eternal.

The final reason is that worry is unnecessary. *"For your heavenly*

Father knows that you need all these things." The simple fact that He knows is the guarantee that He is willing and able to take care of us. Our future could not be in better hands.

Now, the Lord Jesus is ready to enter into a covenant with all of us who are His disciples. He knows that if we have to provide for our future, we will be so busy accumulating wealth that we won't have any time for our primary work, that is, for serving Him. We will give the best of our lives to hoarding money instead of to living with eternity's values in view. So He says to us, in effect, "Put my interests first. Work hard for the supply of your current needs and the needs of your family. Put everything above that in My work. And I promise to take care of your future. If you seek first the kingdom of God and His righteousness, you will never lack the necessities of life."

In summary, our Lord forbids us to spend our lives worrying about the future and trying to provide for the rainy day. Our responsibility is to live for Him today and let the future worry about itself. Attending to today's work is enough to keep us busy.

Someone has said that if a man lives for the rainy day, God will make sure that he gets it. And Cameron Thompson said, "God pours out His choicest blessings on those who are anxious that nothing shall stick to their hands. Individuals who value the rainy day above the present agony of the world will get no blessing from God."

SEVEN
HE SAID, "FORSAKE ALL"
LUKE 14:25-35

These may be the most unpopular paragraphs in the Bible:

*And great multitudes went with Him, and He turned and said to them, "If any-
one comes to Me and does not hate his father and mother, wife and children,
brothers and sisters, yes, and his own life also, he cannot be My disciple. And
whoever does not bear his cross and come after Me cannot be My disciple. For
which of you, intending to build a tower, does not sit down first and count the
cost, whether he has enough to finish it—lest, after he has laid the foundation,
and is not able to finish it, all who see it begin to mock him, saying, 'This man
began to build and was not able to finish.'*

*"Or what king, going to make war against another king, does not sit down
first and consider whether he is able with ten thousand to meet him who comes
against him with twenty thousand? Or else, while the other is still a great way off,
he sends a delegation and asks conditions of peace. So, likewise, whoever of you
does not forsake all that he has cannot be My disciple. Salt is good, but if the salt
has lost its flavor, how shall it be seasoned? It is neither fit for the land nor for
the dunghill, but men throw it out. He who has ears to hear, let him hear."*

Verse 25: *"And great multitudes went with Him, and He turned and said to them...."* The Lord was speaking to the multitude, both saved and unsaved. Jesus gave a fair presentation of His message, even to the unsaved. He did not put His best berries on the top of the box. Note Christ's sifting process. "He first woos, then winnows" (G. Campbell Morgan). "He never hid His scars to make disciples."

The previous section dealt with the gospel; this one deals with service. He wants disciples, not decisions; real G.I.'s, not chocolate soldiers; quality, not quantity. Remember how Gideon's army was reduced from 32,000 to 300.

Verse 26: *"If any comes to Me and does not hate his father and mother, wife and children, brothers and sisters, yes, and his own life also, he cannot be My disciple."* The companion passage in Matthew 10:37 says, *"He who loves father or mother more than Me is not worthy of Me. And he who loves son or daughter more than Me is not worthy of Me."* The expression *"more than Me"* shows that Jesus is using a comparative. Therefore, to put Christ first in our lives means to hate all others comparatively. It means Christ must come first. All other loves must be hatred by comparison.

God said, *"Jacob I have loved, but Esau I have hated"* (Rom. 9:13). His preferential love for Jacob means that He hated Esau by comparison. It is not that he hated Esau with a harsh, vindictive animosity, but only that He loved Esau less than Jacob, as seen by His sovereign selection of Jacob.

C. T. Studd was afraid that his fiancée might love him more than she loved Jesus, so he wrote this poem for her to repeat every day of her life:

> *Jesus, I love Thee.*
> *Thou art to me*
> *Dearer than Charlie*
> *Ever could be.*

When the poet Ruskin proposed to a Christian lady, she asked,

"Do you love me more than you love Jesus Christ?" He had to admit that he did. She said, "Well, in that case, I couldn't marry you." Ruskin tried again, even after she had contracted a serious illness. Her answer was still the same. She died not long afterward. Christ was still first in her life.

In verse 26 our Savior mentions a man's wife. There are a good many men who allow their wives to dominate them. If a man has a worldly wife, it is pretty hard to live a life of keen discipleship. But if he is a Christian, he must recognize that even his wife must take the second place. Mrs. Spurgeon tells an interesting story in Charles Spurgeon's biography:

> When Spurgeon was a young man, he had to go from place to place to find a building large enough to accommodate the crowds that came to hear him. He was only in his early twenties when he preached in Exeter Hall on the Strand. The place was always thronged.
>
> He was engaged to marry a young woman named Susan Thompson. One night he had been at her home, and they drove together to Exeter Hall for a meeting. When they got there, he hurriedly got out of the cab. There was an enormous crowd of people. The police were trying to sort things out and regulate the flow of traffic, but it was exceedingly difficult. Spurgeon had to push his way through the crowd to get to the hall. He was so impressed with the swarming multitude to whom he was to preach the gospel that he forgot everything but that sense of responsibility. And so he pushed his way through the crowd, got to the platform at last, and conducted the service.
>
> When it was over he remembered that he had come to the hall in company with somebody else, but he had completely lost her. He tried to recall whether he had seen her in the congregation. Then he remembered he had not. He feared that he would likely be in trouble, so following the service, he got a cab and hurried to Miss Thompson's home. On arriving there, he was told that she did not want to see him. She was upstairs, pouting. She imagined that she was far more important than the entire multitude. He insisted upon seeing her, and finally she came down.

He explained his position to her: "Now, I am exceedingly sorry, but we had better have an understanding. I am my Master's servant first. He must always come first. I think we shall live very happily if you are willing to take the second place, but it must always be second to Him. My obligation to Him is first."[5]

When the great ministry was ended in later years, Mrs. Spurgeon said she learned a lesson that day she never forgot. She learned that there was Someone who had the first place in her husband's life. She had the second. That is a pretty high standard, is it not? But it is the standard of the Bible. Christ demands the first place.

This seems to be the meaning of Moses' blessing on Levi:

Who says of his father, "I have not seen them;" nor did he acknowledge his brothers, or know his own children (Deut. 33:9).

When Israelites worshiped the golden calf, the sons of Levi took sides with God by destroying their own relatives (Ex. 32:26-29).

Actually the man who puts Christ first is the best kind of husband and father to live with.

Verse 26 closes with the words, *"Yes, and his own life also."* To me this is the most difficult part of the passage. We must put Christ above self. Paul did exactly that. He could say,

But none of these things move me, nor do I count my life dear to myself, so that I may finish my race with joy, and the ministry which I received from the Lord Jesus, to testify to the gospel of the grace of God (Acts 20:24).

Of the tribulation saints in Revelation 12:11 it is written, *"They did not love their lives to the death."*

In John 12:24-25, our Lord made it clear that:

...unless a grain of wheat falls into the ground and dies, it remains alone; but if it dies, it produces much grain. He who loves his life will lose it, and he who hates his life in this world will keep it for eternal life.

---

5   Shields, T. T. Dr., *The Herald of His Coming*, August 1981, p. 1.

It was T. G. Ragland, the pioneer missionary, who said:

If we refuse to be corns of wheat, falling into the ground and dying; if we will neither sacrifice prospects, nor risk character, and property and health; nor, when we are called, relinquish home, and break family ties, for Christ's sakes then we shall abide alone. But if we wish to be fruitful, we must follow our blessed Lord Himself, by becoming a corn of wheat, and dying, then we shall bring forth much fruit.

Verse 27: *"And whoever does not bear his cross and come after Me cannot be My disciple."* The cross here doesn't mean arthritis or a grouchy husband. It means deliberately choosing a pathway of rejection, shame, suffering, poverty, loneliness, betrayal, denial, hatred, insults persecution, mental agony and even death for Christ's sake. When a friend warned an outgoing missionary. "Don't go, you might die," the answer was "I have already died."

A classic in the annals of the U.S. Coast Guard is the story of Captain Pat Etheridge of the Cape Batterne Station. One night in the howling hurricane, the lookout saw a distress signal from a ship that had gone aground on the dangerous Diamond Shoals, ten miles at sea. The lifeboats were ordered out. One of the lifeguards protested, "Captain Pat, we can get out there, but we can never get back." "Boys," came the reply that has gone down in history, "we don't have to come back."

The Lord Jesus has given us our marching order. He has commanded that the gospel be preached in all the world. He has not promised His messengers an easy time. He has not given the assurance of a safe return to the home base— but He did say, "Go."[6]

The Italian patriot, Garibaldi, standing on the steps of St. Peter's in Rome, said to the men gathered around him:

---

6   A. Naismith, *1200 Notes, Quotes, and Anecdotes,* London: Pickering and Inglis Ltd., 1963, p. 83.

I offer you neither pay nor provisions; I offer you hunger, thirst, forced marches, battles and death; let him who loves his country with his heart and not with his lips only follow me.

Sir Ernest Shackleton, Antarctic explorer, placed an ad in a London newspaper. "Men wanted for hazardous journey. Small wages, bitter cold, long months of complete darkness, constant danger, and safe return doubtful. Honor and recognition in case of success." They all returned alive, and honor and recognition were heaped upon them.

> When we voluntarily embrace the adverse circumstances of life as instruments of death to the selfish and self-centered existence, we are bearing our own cross. Received aright, the sufferings, the limitations and trials of life will lead us to our true position as crucified with Christ. Whoso looketh on the white side of the Cross and taketh it up handsomely shall find it to him just such a burden as wings are to a bird.[7]

"Forgive me, Lord, for so often finding ways of avoiding the pain and sacrifice of discipleship. Strengthen me this day to walk with Thee, no matter what the cost may be. In Thy Name. Amen." (Daily Notes of the Scripture Union).

Christ was poor; He had scars; He lived for others; He died as a sacrifice.

Verses 28-32: *Which of you, intending to build a tower, does not sit down first and count the cost, whether he has enough to finish it—lest, after he has laid the foundation, and is not able to finish it, all who see it begin to mock him, saying, "This man began to build and was not able to finish." Or what king, going to make war, does not sit down first and consider whether he is able with ten thousand to meet him who comes against him with twenty thousand? Or else, while the other is still a great way off, he sends a delegation and asks conditions of peace.*

---

7   Sanders, J. O., *On to Maturity*, Chicago: Moody Press, 1962, pp. 132-133.

It is not enough to start out well. The important thing is to finish well. Many aspire but few attain. We must count the cost. The world has nothing but contempt for half-hearted Christians. When a building remains unfinished, men call it Jones's folly, or whatever the builder's name was. The life of discipleship is not only a building program. It is all-out war. It is total commitment or abject surrender.

Verse 33: *"So likewise, whoever of you does not forsake all that he has cannot be My disciple."* What does it mean to forsake all? No one can dictate to anyone else. It is different for different people. A person must get before the Lord and ask Him, "What will Luke 14:33 mean in my life?" Then He will start putting His finger on things.

Moses is an example of forsaking all. He renounced:

> The fame of Egypt (Heb. 11:24)
> The pleasures of Egypt (11:25)
> The treasures of Egypt (11:26)
> The politics of Egypt (11:27)
> The religion of Egypt (11:28)

It is not enough to be willing to forsake all. We must do it.

"If He is king, he has a right to all" (Pilkington). It would be fool-hardy to forsake all if we weren't following Him. When He says, *"Come, follow Me,"* that takes care of all our needs.

We don't think it strange when the Communists forsake all. What would happen if the Church forsook all? The world would be evan-gelized. How would it work? Through the sharing of the Christian community. In his book, *Rich Christians in an Age of Hunger,* Ronald Sider calls it "a community of sharing and love, where secu-rity would not be based on individual property holdings, but on openness to the Spirit and on the loving care of new-found brothers and sisters."

Verse 34: *"Salt is good; but if the salt has lost its flavor, how shall it be seasoned?"* Our table salt is pure and cannot lose its savor, but salt in Bible lands at that time had impurities. So it was possible for the salt shaker to have something in it but it would be tasteless.

Verse 35: *"It is neither fit for the land nor for the dunghill, but men throw it out. He who has ears to hear, let him hear."* The impure salt would be worthless. It was not good for fertilizer or for anything but to make a path to the door.

So it is with a life that does not obey the principles of Christian discipleship.

EIGHT
DON'T BARGAIN WITH GOD
MATTHEW 20:1-16

Anyone reading this parable for the first time could be forgiven for thinking that there has been a grave miscarriage of justice. Many wonder how anything so seemingly unfair could even be in the Bible. Let's review the story to understand why.

The owner of a vineyard needed some grape-pickers so he went to the town square early in the morning (let's say 6 AM) and found some men who bargained with him to work that day for a denarius. That was the going wage in that day.

At 9 AM the boss hired some more men with the understanding that he would pay them whatever was fair. Again at noon and at 3 PM he sent additional men into the vineyard, promising to do right by them. When he went out at 5 PM and found some more unemployed men, he asked why they had been idle all day. They assured him that they weren't lazy. They wanted to work but no one had hired them. So he sent them into the vineyard, again promising to pay them whatever was right.

At 6 PM he instructed his manager to pay off the men, giving each one a full day's wage. The men were to be paid in reverse order, that is, those who were hired last were paid first and those who were hired first were paid last.

This meant that the 6 AMers saw the 5 PMers getting the same pay as themselves, and their reaction was predictable. They said, "Hey, this isn't fair. We worked twelve hours in the heat of the day and these men who've worked only one hour get the same pay as we do. What kind of business is that?"

Frankly, it doesn't seem fair, does it? What, then, is the explanation?

First we must see that this parable is a continuation of what we had in the previous chapter. Notice that verse 1 begins, *"For the kingdom of heaven is like unto a man..."* The *"For"* is a connective word, bridging the two chapters. Actually the parable is an explanation of the last verse of chapter 19, *"But many who are first will be last; and the last will be first."* Notice that the parable ends with similar words, *"So the last will be first, and the first last"* (20:16).

Now let us go back to chapter 19, verse 16, where Jesus encountered a rich man who wanted to do something to inherit eternal life. Jesus tested him on two points. First, he gave the man the opportunity to acknowledge Him, not just as a good master, but as God. Second, He used the law in an effort to produce conviction of sin. The man failed both tests and went away sad. He was not willing to forsake all and to follow Jesus.

With that background in mind, Peter reminded the Lord how he and the other disciples had done what the rich man had failed to do. They had literally forsaken all to follow Him. Then Peter asked this crucial question, "What will we get out of it?"

The Lord assured him of a rich reward in this life and in the next, but then He added, in effect, "But watch out for that bargaining attitude, Peter. If you bargain with God, you'll get what you bargain for, but you might be last when the rewards are passed out. In your service, don't ask, 'What's in it for me?' Leave that to Me. I'll treat you fairly."

Then the Lord added the parable of the laborers to illustrate what He had just said. The men who were hired first had bargained with the vineyard owner. They received exactly what they had agreed on, and were the last to be paid. All the others had gone to work without any wage agreement, just depending on the owner to treat them fairly. They got more than they deserved.

When the 6 AMers complained that they had received a raw deal, the owner gave one of them a lesson on the difference between justice and grace. They had agreed to work for a denarius a day and they received exactly what they had bargained for. That's justice! The others had trusted him to do what was right and they received more than they deserved. That's grace!

Grace is better than justice, both in salvation and service. In salvation, if we received justice we would all perish eternally. As Mark Twain said, "If heaven were gained by merit, your dog would go in and you would stay out." In service for the Lord, if we received justice, we would all lose out because we are unprofitable servants. When we trust the Lord in those areas, we find that He gives exceeding abundantly above all we ask or think.

It's like the girl whose father took her into that dreamland known as a candy store. She spotted a huge jar of her favorite candy and asked Daddy if she could have some.

"Sure," he answered, "reach in and take a handful."

"No, Daddy, you reach in and take a handful."

"Why do you want me to do it?"

"Because your hand is bigger than mine."

That's it. God's hand is bigger than ours. Just trust Him to do what is right, and He will exceed our fondest expectations. Choose grace.

The generosity of the owner should be noted. He said, *"I wish to give to this last man the same as to you"* (v.14 b). Think of it this way. He knew that these men were not lazy. They wanted work but hadn't been able to find it. He also knew that they had families that needed food. So he paid them for whatever hours they had worked, but gave the last four groups enough extra money to buy groceries.

The Lord is like that. He goes by need and not by greed. The 6 AMers went by greed and not by need. They didn't care whether the others had enough to feed their families. All they cared about was themselves. They remind us of Ernest, a kid who was exceedingly good at the game of marbles. He was able to beat all the boys in the neighborhood, and had filled a sack with his prize "glassies."

Once when a preacher was visiting in the home, he noted Ernest's prowess and said:

"You are really good at playing marbles, aren't you?"

"Yes, sir, I am."

"Do you ever pray about these games, Ernest?'

"Oh, yes sir, I do."

"What do you pray?"

"I pray that I'll win."

"Do you ever pray that the other fellows will win?"

"No sir, I never pray that."

"Why not?"

"Because I want to win. I want to get all the marbles."

"Ernest, do you ever speak to the other fellows about the Lord?"

"Yes, I do, sir, but they don't seem at all interested."

"I can't say that I blame them, Ernest. The Lord you present to them wants you to have all the marbles, and He doesn't want them to have any. Try praying that they will win sometimes. That is real Christianity."

F. E. Marsh pointed out that "Too many of us are very much like that boy. As long as we win, it is well; but let us fail, and it is ill. If we are living and laboring for Christ's sake, we must remember that the very first principle is the denial of self."[8]

---

8   Marsh F. E., *Fully Furnished*, Glasgow, Scotland: Pickering & Inglis, n.d., p. 305.

Returning to the parable, we hear the owner pressing his case: *"Is it not lawful for me to do what I wish with my own things?"* The answer is, "Of course." It was his money, and he could do whatever he wanted with it. This speaks to us of the sovereignty of God. He can do whatever He pleases, and what He pleases is always just, fair, kind, and good.

The trouble was not with the owner but with the 6 AMers. In his words, their eye was evil because he was good. They had not been willing to trust themselves to his grace, and they didn't want anyone else to receive it.

Times haven't changed. Even in the matter of salvation, men don't want to be recipients of God's undeserved favor, and they don't like to see Him showing grace to others. They are turned off by His goodness, vainly preferring to earn or merit it than to receive it as a free gift.

"So the last will be first, and the first last."[9] If the disciples, who lived in the first days of the Christian era, adopted a bargaining attitude toward the Lord, they could be last in the matter of rewards. On the other hand, those living in the closing days of the dispensation might be first in rewards if they serve the Lord without trying to strike a bargain with Him.

It would be easy for us who live 2,000 years after the coming of Christ to think that all the best rewards have already been won. This parable teaches that it isn't necessarily so, especially if we serve the Lord without any thought of personal gain.

If you still feel that the 6 AMers had a legitimate gripe because they worked so much longer, think of it this way. They should have been grateful for the privilege of working for such a splendid boss. He thought more of his employees than he did of his personal profits. There aren't many like that.

---

9   The last clause of verse 16, KJV ("for many be called, but few be chosen") are omitted in many versions.

But maybe all this is hypothetical. Do we ever bargain with God today? Or was this just an isolated instance in Peter's life? Consider the following:

- Lord, I will follow You, but first let me get married.
- I will turn my life over to You if You allow me to pursue my career.
- I will do anything, Lord, as long as You don't send me to the mission field.
- Take my life, Lord—that is, when I retire from business.

All these "buts" and "ifs," all these reservations, are a form of bargaining with God. Beware of them. If you persist, you may get what you bargain for, when God has something far better for you.

F. B. Meyer was right when he said,

We must see to it that we keep nothing back. There must be no reserve put in any part of our being. Spirit, soul, and body must be freely yielded to the great Husbandman. We who are God's tillage must make no bargain with His plowshare, and withhold no acre from the operations of His Spirit.[10]

---

10   Meyer, F. B., *The Heavenlies*, Westchester, IL,: Good News Publishers, p. 50.

NINE

MAKE FRIENDS WITH YOUR MONEY
LUKE 16:1-15

At first glance this seems to be a very unlikely story to be found in the Bible. The problem is that it appears to commend dishonesty. Doubtless many believers are embarrassed by its inclusion in the sacred Scriptures. Perhaps some hope that if they don't look, it will go away.

But there is nothing to fear. When rightly understood, the story is rich in meaning. It does not commend crookedness. But it does teach that there is one positive way in which we should imitate this fore-sighted manager. Let's get to the story.

Word reaches the boss that his business manager has been stealing his funds. His reaction is predictable: he fires the embezzler, but demands a full accounting before he leaves. The employer naturally wants to know the extent of his loss.

This throws the thief into a tailspin. He now has no visible means of support and no security for the future. He is too old to do heavy physical labor and too ashamed to beg. What to do?

Suddenly a light goes on in his brain; he has a bright idea. He will take steps to ensure that he will always have friends. Doors will always swing open to him, and he will always be welcome to enter and have a meal.

He calls in his boss's customers one by one.

"How much do you owe?" he says to the first.

"I owe about 800 gallons of olive oil."

"Well, I'll tell you what to do. Pay for 400 gallons and we'll call it even."

Second customer: "And how much do you owe?"

"My bill is for about 1100 bushels of wheat."

"I'll make a deal with you. Pay for 880 bushels and I'll mark your invoice PAID IN FULL."

The manager was still up to his crooked tricks. He had no right to make such bargains. The money belonged to his employer, not to him. That is what makes verse 8 so surprising. It says, *The master commended the unjust steward.*[11] On the face of it, this seems not only to condone dishonesty, but also to commend it.

There are two keys that unlock the difficulty.

Key #1. The commendation was not for dishonesty but for wise planning. *"The master commended the unjust steward because he had dealt shrewdly."* The particular way in which he had acted wisely was in guaranteeing that he would have friends in his future.

Key #2. The Christian's future is not in this world but in heaven. *"The sons of this world are more shrewd in their generation than the sons of light."* In other words, unconverted people often use greater foresight than believers. Like the man in the parable, the unconverted take steps to ensure that they will have friends in their future, that is, their future here on earth. Christians do not have similar concern to have friends in their future in heaven.

The Lord Jesus is now ready to apply the parable to His listeners.

---

11   The King James Version reads "and the lord commended the unjust steward." It is not clear whether it refers to the Lord Jesus or to the man's employer. Actually it doesn't make any difference. The commendation would be true, no matter who made it— as we shall see.

"And I say to you, make friends for yourselves by unrighteous mammon, that when you fail, they may receive you into everlasting habitations" (v. 9). Unrighteous mammon is money. Although money itself is neither good nor bad, Jesus calls it unrighteous because it is so often gained dishonestly and so often used for unrighteous purposes. He Himself would soon be betrayed for 30 pieces of silver. Even today we speak of money as filthy lucre. Paul reminds us that *"the love of money is a root of all kinds of evil"* (1 Tim. 6:10a).

And yet we can make friends for ourselves with money. How can we do this? By using it to spread the gospel. By investing money in Bibles, Testaments, and Scripture portions. By supporting missionary work. By contributing to gospel broadcasts worldwide. In short, by investing in the work of the Lord. Those who are saved through these means are our friends for eternity.

"...that when you fail, they may receive you into everlasting habitations." Bible versions differ here. Some say, *"when you fail,"* others *"when it fails."* But the difference is unimportant, because when the disciple fails or dies, his money fails too. It has no more value for him. He must use it while he's living or not at all. When he dies, it no longer belongs to him but to his estate.

"...they may receive you into everlasting habitations." "They" here refers to the people who have been converted through the investment of our funds in the Lord's work. The everlasting habitations are the many mansions in our Father's house (Jn. 14:2). The friends we make with the unrighteous mammon serve as a welcoming committee when we reach the gates of glory. It is the fulfillment of this unknown poet's wish:

> *And when in the mansions above,*
> *The saved all around me appear,*
> *I want to hear somebody saying,*
> *"It was you who invited me here."* (Anon.)

Let me give an illustration of how this can work. When a devout Christian was approaching his 80th birthday, his sons and daughter wanted to surprise him with a party and some gift that he would really appreciate. But they couldn't decide on a gift that would be truly meaningful. After all, what does an 80-year-old man need? Finally they went to him and asked what gift he would like on his birthday. He thought for a few minutes, then said, "I'd like to see a Scripture portion printed in some language that it has never been in before."

That wasn't exactly what the family had in mind, but they decided to be good sports about it. So they went to the Bible Society and told of their father's unusual request.

"That's interesting," said the director, "we are just preparing to print the Gospel of John in an African dialect for the first time."

When the family asked concerning the cost, they were staggered at first, but there was no turning back. They enthusiastically gathered the money and presented it to the Bible Society on their father's 80th birthday. The old man was ecstatic.

Now let us project ourselves 100 years into the future. One day as this devout Christian (no longer old) is walking along the golden street, he meets a brother in Christ (there are no strangers in heaven). The conversation goes something like this:

"How did you get here to the celestial city?"

"Well, I'll tell you—I lived in Africa, steeped in pagan idolatry. But someone cared enough for me and my people to have the Gospel of John translated and printed in our language. I'll never forget the day those Gospels reached our village. When I read the wonderful story of the Savior's love, I destroyed my idols, repented of my sins, and received Jesus as my only hope for heaven."

Who can describe the joy of that man when he meets this trophy of grace who was won to the Lord through his 80th birthday gift?

Even as I write this, I see a letter from Wycliffe Bible Translators that says, in part: "Just the other day I had a check for $83,000 from an 89-year-old businessman to get the New Testament into three different dialects in Ghana. According to his nephew, this man doesn't own any stocks, any bonds, or any other major assets, but wants to give what the Lord has entrusted to him as soon as it is available. He feels the urgency of sharing God's Word around the world." Think of the welcome this man will receive when he gets home!

In verse 10, our Lord indicated that the way we handle money is a gauge of our faithfulness in other areas. He speaks of money as *"that which is least."* This, of course, is the exact opposite of what modern man thinks; he rates money as "that which is most." If we are faithful in our stewardship of something as unimportant as money, we can be counted on to be faithful in matters that are of spiritual and eternal importance. One who is unreliable with mammon would be unreliable with true riches (v. 11). By contrasting money and true riches, the Savior explodes the myth that material wealth makes a person rich. True riches are the blessings that are ours in Christ Jesus: the worldwide fellowship of God's family; the privilege of serving the Lord; the great truths of the Bible.

"And if you have not been faithful in the use of that which is another's, who will give you that which is your own?" (v. 12, NASB). The words *"that which is another's"* are intended to remind us that our money is not actually ours at all. It belongs to God, and we are stewards whose function is to administer it for Him. If He can't trust us with the wise use of His money, how can He be expected to give us what is our own? In other words, how can He give us friends in our future, won through our stewardship? How can He give us deep spiritual truths from the Word? How can He give us rewards at the Judgment Seat?

For the second time in the Gospels, Jesus said that it is an absolute impossibility to live for God and for money at the same time. There is a conflict of interests and a dividing of loyalties. In spite of the finality with which He said it, Christians still try to do it. Strange!

When the Pharisees heard Jesus' low view of money, they sneered. They felt they knew better. They probably looked on their wealth as a proof of divine favor. They loved money, and wanted as much as they could get. They were worldly-wise. Jesus exposed them as pious frauds. They sought to appear righteous before other men, but inwardly they were corrupt. The riches they valued were detestable to God. They were covetous religionists but spiritual paupers. They could take their place alongside the crooked manager—unfaithful in that which is least, undependable in that which is Another's, unworthy to receive true riches.

TEN
THE SIN NO ONE CONFESSES
1 TIMOTHY 6:6-10; 17-19

In 1 Timothy 6:3-5, Paul warns Timothy about certain religious leaders who think of the Christian ministry as a way to get rich. These men suppose that professional godliness is an easy way to line their pockets with gold. Their descendants are still with us—radio and TV celebrities who have raised fund-raising to an art form and reduced it to a science. By the use of clever psychological gimmicks, they play upon the heartstrings of impressionable Christian people. They always have some new project to add to their vast empire. They live in luxurious homes, build up fat investment portfolios, wear elegant clothes and jewelry, and display the latest attention-getting coiffures. And all this in the name of our penniless Friend from Nazareth.

The apostle warns Timothy to stay away from these religious wheeler-dealers and, by implication, from their practices. The ideal combination is to have godliness with contentment. A godly person who is content, who is rich in character and rich in the fewness of his wants, has something that money cannot buy.

Malcolm Muggeridge testified that the happiest times of his life were the times of simplicity and austerity—a small cabin, a table, a chair, some rice on a green leaf. These things, he said, bring their own ecstasy.

We brought nothing into the world, and it is equally certain that we will bring nothing out. The newborn baby's hands are clenched securely but they hold nothing. When he dies later in life, his hands are relaxed—and empty. Alexander the Great left instructions that when he died, his hands should be visible with empty palms. He had conquered the world, but he died empty-handed.

Dr. James Dobson learned this lesson by playing a game with his family. We'll let him tell the story.

> Shirley and I were married in 1960 and we had no financial problems whatsoever because we didn't have any finances. Since then the Lord has blessed us, and we have tasted a little of what the world thinks you have to have to be happy, such as a house, a car, and other things. But I'm learning more and more that happiness is not found in material possessions. The Lord has been teaching me the emptiness of materialism, even using a game to convey the message.
>
> Recently my family played Monopoly, which was the first time I've played it in more than fifteen years. Before long, a bit of the old excitement and enthusiasm came back, especially as I began to win. Everything went my way, and I became master of the board. I owned Boardwalk and Park Place, and I had houses and hotels all over the place. My family was squirming, and I was stuffing $500 bills into my pockets and under the board and seat. Suddenly the game was over. I had won. Shirley and the kids went to bed, and I began putting everything back into the box. Then I was struck by an empty feeling. All of the excitement I had experienced earlier was unfounded. I didn't own any more than those whom I had defeated. It all had to go back into the box!
>
> The Lord showed me that there was a lesson to be learned beyond the game of Monopoly. I recognized that I was also witnessing the game of life. We struggle and accumulate and buy and own and possess and refinance, and suddenly we come to the end of life and have to put it all back into the box! We can't take a cent with us! There are no trailers that accompany us through the Valley of the Shadow.

Now I understand why the Scriptures tell us, *"A man's life consisteth not in the abundance of the things which he possesseth"* (Lk. 12:15, KJV).[12]

In some countries, monkeys are trapped by putting rice inside a gourd, with a hole only big enough for the monkey's empty hand. When he reaches in and grabs a handful of rice, he can no longer pull it out. But he won't let go of the rice. He won't let go—and is trapped. Trapped by his own greed!

Earlier Paul had spoken about contentment. Now in verse 8 he defines it as satisfaction with food and covering. The word he uses for *"covering"* could mean not only the clothes that we wear but a roof over our heads. So it means the basics of life. We become so familiar with this verse that we fail to realize how radical it is. Perhaps it will help if we remember how few believers we know who are satisfied with food, clothing, and housing. As far as the majority of Christendom is concerned, the verse might just as well not be in the Bible.

In verse 9 the apostle moves on to talk about those who desire to be rich. This includes everyone, rich and poor, who is covetous. Covetousness is the greedy compulsion to get more, the determination to get it even if God doesn't want the person to have it. A covetous person can't enjoy something unless he owns it, or, at least, a part of it.

This sin may be sexual (*"Thou shalt not covet thy neighbor's wife"*) or, as in 1 Timothy 6, it may be materialistic. In either case, it is idolatry because it worships and serves that which is created rather than the Creator.

The trouble is that we have taken this sin and baptized it with Christian baptism. We have given it Christian respectability by calling it prudence, common sense, financial responsibility, thrift, and foresight. When we ask, "How much is that man worth?" we mean, "How much money has he hoarded?" "Getting on in the world"

---

12   *Decision Magazine*, December 1981, p. 12.

means accumulating material things. We call covetous people "the cream of society" and "the upper crust." Someone has pointed out that covetousness sold Jesus for 30 pieces of silver. Having sold Christ to the cross, the professing church began to sell the cross itself. And then it claimed to sell the way to heaven through indulgences, promising deliverance from purgatory.

Covetousness denies the real purpose of our existence. It forgets that we are here for bigger business than to make money or to indulge ourselves. It forgets that the best use of our money is for spiritual purposes. It is deceptive. Said J. H. Jowett,

> Riches can make a man think that he is growing bigger when all the time he is growing less. He estimates his size by the inlet of income and not by the outlet of beneficence. While the inlet is expanding, the outlet is contracting.

It is irrational. We strive to get things we don't need to impress people we don't like.

It frustrates God's plan for world evangelization by hoarding money that could be used in the propagation of the gospel.

It unfits a man for leadership in the church—an elder must be *"not greedy for money"* (1 Tim. 3:3)—but, worse than that, it excludes a man from the kingdom of God (1 Cor. 6:10).

Here in our passage Paul warns Timothy that the desire to be rich leads to temptation. A covetous man will resort to illegal means to get what he wants. And it leads to a trap. It is like holding a live wire; he can't let go. Or like drinking salt water; it creates the thirst for more.

A man said to his friend, "When I had $50,000 I was happy. Now I have a million and I'm miserable."

"That's no problem," said the friend, "give away $950,000."

The millionaire whined, "I can't."

The desire to be rich leads to *"many foolish and harmful lusts, which drown men in destruction and perdition."* This is strong language. Paul warns that covetousness leads to eternal ruin. How strange, then, that Christians should speak approvingly of that which God condemns unsparingly!

The love of money is a root of all kinds of evil. For example, it is the root of lies. J. H. Jowett told of asking help of a wealthy man in New York for an exceedingly worthy cause.

> His face immediately answered my appeal, and he spoke as one who was on the verge of poverty: "I really cannot give any more. What with one thing and another I do not know what we are coming to!" A few weeks later he died, and his will amounted to over 60 million! And I wonder, I wonder if at the end of the day he heard the messenger of the Lord saying to him, *"Thou fool, this night thy soul shall be required of thee; then whose shall these things be?"* [13]

The love of money leads to frauds, thefts, and even murders. It breaks up marriages and ruins children. It causes nervous and emotional disturbances, and has led to suicide. Wealthy people live in fear of theft, kidnap, and extortion. They worry about inflation and market collapse. They suffer from unrest, boredom, dissatisfaction, and envy. Sometimes they bring on themselves prison and disgrace.

Because the Scriptures condemn their whole lifestyle, they wander from the faith rather than change. They twist, turn, and rewrite the Bible to justify their affluence. Not only so, they pierce themselves through with many sorrows. When Howard Hughes died, he left an estate estimated as high as $2.3 billion. Yet one newsmagazine reported:

> For all his power, he lived a sunless, joyless, half-lunatic life...a virtual prisoner walled in by his own crippling fears and weaknesses. Once a dashing, vibrant figure, he neglected his appearance and health during his last fifteen years until he became a pathetic wraith. He was hooked on drugs. His physical appearance was horrifying. Although four doctors rotated in taking care of

---

13   Jowett, J. H., *God Our Contemporary*, New York: Fleming Revell Co., 1922, p. 147.

Hughes, his medical condition was appalling. His main amusement was watching movies. He lived week in and week out on a diet that a ten-cent store clerk would have spurned, yet he was finicky about its preparation. He would eat a spoonful of soup and then get interested in a movie. The same soup would be reheated twelve times.[14]

In closing this section, Paul tells Timothy to charge those who are rich in this world. They should not strut pride and arrogance, nor trust in uncertain riches. Rather their trust should be in the living God who gives us richly all things to enjoy. This latter expression, *"who gives us richly all things to enjoy"* has often been used to justify the stockpiling of wealth. But the following verse explains all. We don't enjoy money when it lies sterile in the bank but when we use it to do good, to distribute to the needy, and to share with our less fortunate neighbor. In that way, we stockpile a rich reward in the world to come and enjoy life that is life indeed.

The conclusion? Ronald Sider gives it in his book, *Rich Christians in an Age of Hunger.*

> The rich fool is the epitome of the covetous person. He has a greedy compulsion to acquire more and more possessions even though he does not need them. And his phenomenal success at piling up more and more property leads to the blasphemous conclusion that material possessions can satisfy his needs. From the divine perspective, this attitude is sheer madness. He is a raving fool.[15]

---

14   *TIME Magazine*, December 13, 1976, pp. 20-41.
15   Ronald J. Sider, *Rich Christians in an Age of Hunger*, Downers Grove, IL: Intervarsity Press, 1977, p. 123.

ELEVEN
ONLY THE BEST FOR GOD

There is a golden thread that runs through the Scriptures, a truth that constantly reappears in the weaving of the Word. The truth is this: God wants the first and God wants the best. He wants the first place in our lives and He wants the best we have to offer.

The Bible opens with a statement of historical fact, *"In the beginning God..."* But the words should be true in our lives. God should be first. He who is worthy of first place will not be satisfied with anything less.

When the Lord instituted the Passover, He instructed the Israelites to bring a lamb without blemish (Ex. 12:5). They were never to sacrifice to Him any animal that was lame, blind, defective, or flawed (Deut. 15:21; 17:1). That would be detestable.

Now it should be clear that God does not need any animals that man can offer to him. Every beast of the forest is His, and the cattle on a thousand hills (Ps. 50:10). Why then did He legislate that only perfect animals be offered to Him? He did it for man's good, not for His own. He did it as a sort of object lesson to teach His people a fundamental truth, namely, that they can only find joy, satisfaction, and fulfillment by giving Him the proper place in their lives.

In Exodus 13:2, God commanded His people to set apart their firstborn sons and firstborn animals to Him. *"Consecrate to Me every firstborn male. The first offspring of every womb among the Israelites belongs to Me, whether man or animal"* (NIV). In ancient cultures the firstborn stood for that which is superlative and most highly esteemed. Thus Jacob spoke of Reuben, his firstborn, as *"my might and the beginning of my strength, the excellency of dignity and the excellency of power"* (Gen. 49:3). The Lord Jesus is spoken of as *"the firstborn over all creation"* (Col. 1:15) in the sense that He is most excellent and that He holds a position of highest honor over all creation.

In telling His people to sanctify their firstborn sons to Him, He was touching a very sensitive nerve, because the oldest son has a special place of affection in his parent's hearts. However, it was designed to teach them to say, in effect:

> *The dearest object I have known, whate'er that object be,*
> *Help me to tear it from the throne, and worship only Thee.*
>
> (William Cowper)

Abraham had learned this lesson on Mount Moriah (Gen. 22). Now his descendants must learn the same lesson.

Next, God instructed the farmers to bring the first of the firstfruits of the land to the house of the Lord (Ex. 23:19). When the grain crop began to ripen, the farmer was to go out to the field, reap an armful of the first ripe grain, and present it as an offering to the Lord. This sheaf of firstfruits acknowledged God as the Giver of the harvest, and pledged that He would receive His portion of it. Once again, it is obvious that God didn't need the grain, but man needed the constant reminder that the Lord is worthy of the first and best.

When sacrificial animals were cut up, the priests were sometimes allowed to take certain parts, and the offerers were permitted to eat other parts, but the fat was always offered to the Lord (Lev. 3:16).[16] The fat was considered to be the richest and best part of the animal, and therefore belonged to Jehovah. Nothing but the best was good enough for Him.

This obligation of putting God first extended to every area of life, not only to the place of worship but to the kitchen as well. The Lord's people were instructed to offer a cake of the first of their dough for a heave offering: *"Of the first of your ground meal, you shall give to the Lord a heave offering throughout your generations"* (Num. 15:21). Mixing a batch of dough seems like a fairly mundane task, one that is not especially spiritual. But in offering the first of the dough to the Lord, a godly Jew was confessing that God must have first place in all of life. He was also denying any distinction between the secular and the sacred. While he knew that God didn't need the dough, he realized that the Lord must be acknowledged as the Giver of man's daily bread.

Jehovah laid it on the line when He instructed the Levites, *"You must present as the Lord's portion the best and holiest part of every-thing given to you"* (Num. 18:29, NIV). Since man becomes like what he worships, it is imperative that he entertain a proper appreciation of God. Low thoughts of God are destructive. Only when the creature gives the Creator the place He deserves will he rise above flesh and blood and attain the dignity for which he was designed.

As we follow this thread through the Old Testament, we see the lesson acted out when Elijah met a destitute widow in a place called Zarephath (see 1 Ki. 17:7-16). He asked the woman for a drink of water and a piece of bread. She apologized that all she had was a handful of flour and a little oil—just enough to make one last meal for her son and herself before they died of starvation.

---

16   Some of God's kindly laws were also designed to safeguard the health of His people. Here, for instance, the prohibition against eating the fat might protect the people from arteriosclerosis, thought to be caused by excessive cholesterol. But the primary intent of this was to teach the people to give the best to God.

"Not to worry," said the prophet, *"first make a little bread for me, then use the rest for yourself and the boy."*

Now that sounds like a shockingly selfish request, doesn't it? It seems as if the prophet was guilty of inexcusably bad manners. We have always been taught to see that others are served before ourselves. To say "Serve me first" is a callous breach of etiquette. But we must understand that Elijah was God's representative. He was standing there in the place of God. He was not guilty of selfishness or rudeness. He was saying, "Look, I am God's man here. In serving me first, you are really giving God first place, and as long as you do that, you will never lack the necessities of life. Your flour barrel will never go empty and your olive oil jug will never run dry." And that's exactly the way it turned out.

Solomon reinforced God's prior claim on our lives in the familiar words, *"Honor the Lord with your possessions, and with the first-fruits of all your increase"* (Prov. 3:9). That means that every time we get a raise in pay, we should be sure that the Lord is the first to get His portion.

Coming over to the New Testament, we hear the Lord Jesus insisting that God must have first place. *"But seek first the kingdom of God and His righteousness, and all these things shall be added to you"* (Mt. 6:33). It is the same truth that Elijah shared with the widow: those who give the Lord the place of supremacy in their lives will never have to worry about the basic necessities of life.

Perhaps we become so familiar with the Lord's Prayer (Mt. 6:9-13) that we miss the significance of the order contained in it. It teaches us to put God first (*"Our Father in heaven, hallowed be Your name"*) and His interests (*"Your kingdom come, Your will be done on earth as it is in heaven"*). Only then, and not before, are we invited to bring our personal petitions (*"Give us this day our daily bread,"* etc.).

Just as God the Father must be given the place of supremacy, so must the Lord Jesus, as a Member of the Godhead. Thus we read in

Colossians 1:18, NASB: *"...so that He Himself might come to have first place in everything."*

The Savior insisted that His people's love for Him must be so great that all other loves are hatred by comparison. *"If anyone comes to Me and does not hate his father and mother, wife and children, brothers and sisters, and his own life also, he cannot be My disciple"* (Lk. 14:26). Jesus must have first place in our love.

Now unfortunately the Lord does not always get the first and best from His people. In Malachi's day, when it came time to make an offering to the Lord, a farmer kept the best animals for breeding or for sale, and gave the Lord the cast-offs. He was saying that anything is good enough for the Lord. A profit in the marketplace came first. That is why Malachi thundered, *"And when you offer the blind as a sacrifice, is it not evil? And when you offer the lame and sick, is it not evil? Offer it then to your governor! Would he be pleased with you? Would he accept you favorably?"* (Mal. 1:8).

But that was in Malachi's day. What about today? How can we give the Lord the first and the best? How can we make it practical in our lives? We can do it in our business by obeying those who are over us; by working heartily as for the Lord, not for men; by realizing that it is the Lord Christ whom we serve (Col. 3:22-25). If the claims of work begin to gain priority over the claims of Christ, we must be prepared to say to them, *"This far you may come, but no further, and here your proud waves must stop"* (Job 38:11). We should be willing to do more for the Savior than we would ever do for a corporation.

We can do it in our homes by faithfully maintaining a family altar, during which we read the Bible and pray together. Yes, we can do it by raising children for the Lord and not for the world, for heaven and not for hell.

> *Give of thy sons to bear the message glorious;*
> *Give of thy wealth to speed them on their way;*

Pour out thy soul for them in prayer victorious;
And all thou spendest Jesus will repay.

(Mary A. Thomson)

A Christian mother thought she was putting Christ first, but when her daughter came home from Bible school and announced, "Mother, God has called me to the mission field," the mother answered, "Over my dead body, Isabel."

Another mother was working feverishly in the kitchen while a preacher was visiting with her son in the living room. The preacher was holding forth on the wonderful opportunities for this young man's skills in the work of the Lord. Then a strident voice came from the kitchen, "Don't talk like that to my son. That isn't what I've planned for him."

On a happier note, Spurgeon said to his son, "My son, if God should call you to the mission field, I should not like to see you drivel down into a king."

We can do it in the local assembly by faithful attendance and enthusiastic participation. George Mallone tells of an elder who turned down an invitation to a presidential dinner at the White House because his eldership responsibilities did not allow him to have the evening free. After Michael Faraday had given a brilliant exposition on the nature and properties of the magnet, the audience voted to have a statement of congratulation. But Faraday was not there to receive it. He had slipped away to the midweek prayer meeting at his church, a church that never had more than twenty members.

We can put God first in our stewardship of material things. We do this by adopting a simple lifestyle so that the entire surplus can go into the Lord's work. We do it by sharing with those who have spiritual and physical needs. In short, we do it by investing for God and for eternity.

But the greatest way we can give God first place is by presenting our lives to Him, by committing ourselves to Him not only for salvation but for service as well. Nothing less than this is enough, when we think of all He did for us.

The current wisdom is for Christians to spend the best of their lives making money, to live in luxury and ease, and to give their retirement years to the Lord. By then many are suffering from burn-out and have few years left. A greater wisdom is to surrender to Christ in the springtime of life when strength, love, and enthusiasm are at their height. Better to do that than to give Him what Thomas Gill called our weak desires; our poorer, baser part; our fading fires; the ashes of our heart.

God wants the first and God wants the best.

He is worthy of both.

The only question left is, "Will He get them—from me?"

TWELVE
20/20 VISION
2 CORINTHIANS 5:9-21

No one has absolutely perfect vision, but some have impaired eyesight to the extent that they have to wear glasses. If they are anything like myself, they go to the ophthalmologist fairly regularly for an examination.

I am now seated in the examination room. The doctor enters, snaps on a light and says, "Now, Mr. MacDonald, cover your left eye and read the top line on the chart."

"What chart, Doctor?"

"Ah yes, this is a serious case. We'll have to increase the power of your prescription."

Whereupon he swings a black, two-eyed gadget in front of me and asks me to look through the right opening. As I do, he turns a wheel controlling various lenses and asks, "What can you see now?"

All I can think of is the Bible verse, *"I see men as trees walking"* meaning, "It's better but still blurry."

Then as he flips the lenses, he asks, "Is this one better than this one?" Soon several lines on the chart become clear, and he is satisfied that with new lenses, I will have 20/20 vision.

Now it is also true that no one has perfect spiritual vision. When sin came into the world, it affected man's spiritual eyesight, and we all need corrective lenses. In 2 Corinthians 5:9-21, there are seven such corrective lenses which we must wear all the time if we are going to see things the way God sees them.

THE FACTS OF HELL (5:11a)

The first is the fact of hell. Paul says, *"Knowing, therefore, the terror of the Lord, we persuade men."* Now I realize that terror here means reverential awe and that it was this holy respect for God, this fear of displeasing Him that led the apostle to persuade men as to his integrity in the ministry. But I would like to apply the verse differently. I would like to apply it as meaning that the knowledge of the horrors and terrors of hell led Paul to persuade men to trust Christ to save them from that place of torment. So in our spiritual frames we should have a corrective lens in which we see the flaming fires of hell. This will constantly remind us that our unsaved relatives, friends, neighbors, yes, all unbelievers are in imminent danger of this awful fate. It will inspire us with a sense of urgency in sharing the good news of salvation with those with whom we come in contact. It will move us to marshal our resources for the spread of the gospel.

Hell is a fact. The Lord Jesus spoke more about hell than He did about heaven. Just as sure as there's a heaven, there's a hell. It is the eternal destiny of all unbelievers. It is a place of conscious torment. There is neither light nor love in hell. It is everlasting hopelessness. The more keenly we are aware of its awfulness, the more we will persuade men to escape from it through faith in Christ.

THE LOVE OF CHRIST (5:14-15)

The second lens is the love of Christ—not our love for Him but His love for us. If we have this lens in our glasses, we will see a blood-stained cross, and on that cross the Son of God dying for our sins, paying the price that we should have paid. If He were only a man, we ought to be forever grateful to Him, but how much more so when we realize that He is the Lord of life and glory, the Creator and Sustainer of the universe.

Such love constrains us. His work on the cross has a certain logic connected with it. If He died for us, that means that we were all dead in trespasses and in sins. He wouldn't have done it if we had been spiritually alive and well. But there is more. He didn't die for us so that we would continue living sinful, selfish, senseless lives. Rather He died for us so that from now on we might live for Him. "Love so amazing, so divine demands my soul, my life, my all" (Isaac Watts). That conclusion is inescapable.

THE VALUE AND ETERNITY OF A SOUL (5:16)

"Therefore, from now on, we regard no one according to the flesh. Even though we have known Christ according to the flesh, yet now we know Him thus no more" (v. 16). When we are saved, we look on people in a different way. Previously we were concerned with people's physical appearance, with their personalities, or even the amount of their wealth.

But things are different now. Grace teaches us to see them as precious souls for whom Christ died. We see them as potential worshipers of the Lamb of God for all eternity. We realize that the most unimpressive, nondescript person is worth more than all the gold, silver, platinum and diamonds in the world. At Calvary, the Lord Jesus put a value on each one—the value of His own life's blood.

An unknown poet wrote:

> *Only like souls I see the folks thereunder,*
> *Bound who should conquer, slaves who should be kings;*
> *Hearing their one hope with an empty wonder,*

Sadly contented with a show of things.
Then with a rush the intolerable craving,
Shivers throughout me like a trumpet call.
O, to save these, to perish for their saving,
Die for their life, be offered for them all.

When we have this corrective lens in our glasses, we realize that it is people who are important. We can no longer spend our lives accumulating things. We must live for people—for their eternal welfare.

THE PURPOSE OF OUR CREATION (5:17)

In verse 17, Paul says, *"Therefore if anyone is in Christ, he is a new creation."* If we are new creatures, part of a new creation, that raises the inevitable question, What is the purpose of our creation? Are we here to make money? To make a name for ourselves in the world? To accumulate material possessions? To luxuriate in better homes and gardens? To drink the cup of pleasure? To pursue trivia? Must all our plans end at the grave? Have we no higher destiny than to build a nest in a tree that is marked for destruction?

The answer, of course, is that we are here to glorify God and to represent the Lord Jesus on earth. We are here as the salt of the earth and the light of the world. We are called to tell forth the excellencies of Him who called us out of darkness into His marvelous light. As His ambassadors, we must urge men and women to be reconciled to God. Everything else is a distraction. Everything else is irrelevant.

THE PLAIN COMMAND OF CHRIST (5:18)

The Lord has committed to us the ministry of reconciliation. This means that He has sent us forth to tell men and women how they can be reconciled to God. Christ's work on the cross has provided the only way by which they can come into right relations with God. But they must hear the message and receive it. The only way they can hear it is by our telling it. We are responsible to go.

In the military, when a commanding officer expresses a desire or extends an invitation, his subordinates are expected to interpret these as commands. When King David wished for a drink from the well at Bethlehem, his men looked upon that as an order, even though the well was behind enemy lines (2 Sam. 23:15-17). Our Captain has given us the Great Commission: *"Go ye into all the world, and preach the gospel to every creature."* This is more than a request or a suggestion. It is a direct command. It is not given for discussion or consideration but for obedience. Each of us must face the possibility that when we meet the Savior, He will ask us, "What did you do with the Great Commission?"

THE RESPONSIBILITY OF POSSESSING THE ANSWER (5:20)

It is no exaggeration to say that Christians have the answer to the world's problems. Sin is the basic cause of humanity's troubles. No one but Christ has dealt with sin effectively. Nothing but His work at Calvary has given man deliverance from the penalty and power of sin. Christ is the answer!

It is a solemn thing to have the answer and not to share Him. It would be like having the cure for cancer and keeping it off the market. Or seeing a house on fire and failing to sound an alarm or try to rescue the occupants.

In the days of Elisha there were four starving lepers who unexpectedly came upon a huge stockpile of food. At first they gorged themselves without thinking of anyone else. Then their consciences smote them. They were withholding the good news from the people in the city nearby. So they sent word to the city that there was plenty of food to break the famine. The people flocked out and were saved from starvation.

In a sense we are all lepers, commissioned to tell others where to find food. We cannot afford the possibility of having unsaved people ask us in eternity, "Why didn't you tell us?" As ambassadors for Christ, we cannot afford to be guilty of the blood of our neighbors.

THE JUDGMENT SEAT OF CHRIST (5:10)

In the final corrective lens, we see a judgment seat. The Lord Jesus is the Judge. Each of us is standing before the bench. We are not being tried for our sins; they were judged at the cross of Calvary and the penalty was paid in full. This is a trial when our service for the Lord will be evaluated and rewarded. It is like a state fair rather than a criminal court.

Everything done for God's glory, for the blessing of His people, and the salvation of sinners will be rewarded. Everything done for selfish or impure motives will go up in smoke. There will be special awards for endurance, for holy living, for faithful leadership, for winning souls, for resisting temptation, and for loving Christ's appearing.

We should live every day with the truth of the soon coming judgment seat of Christ before us. It will not have the effect of terrorizing us, but it will inspire us to make the moments count for eternity.

PUT THEM TOGETHER

Here then are seven lenses to correct our spiritual astigmatism and to give us 20/20 vision: the fact of hell; the love of Christ; the value and eternity of a soul; the purpose of our creation; the plain command of Christ; the responsibility of possessing the answer; and the Judgment Seat of Christ. Wear these and you will see life in its true perspective. Without them life will be a blur.

SECTION II
CHRISTIAN CHARACTER

THIRTEEN
AIM TO BE LIKE JESUS

The answer to most of the problems that we face is holiness or Christlikeness. For instance, one of our problems is how to know the will of God. Most of the verses that answer the question have to do with our character (Prov. 3:5-6; Ps. 25:9). We want to know how to be effective in evangelism. The answer is in holiness (Mt. 4:19).

If we want to have an effective prayer life, the Lord says, *"If you abide in Me and My words abide in you, you will ask what you desire, and it shall be done for you"* (Jn. 15:7). As soldiers fighting for the Lord we need protection and effectiveness. How? The believer's armor is found in Ephesians 6:11-18. It is Christian character.

And so it is in all aspects of the Christian life. God does not give us a neat set of ten How To's. Rather He emphasizes our personal life. The rest will fall into line.

We should always pray, "Lord, make us more like Christ and less like ourselves." No Christian would quarrel over the fact that we should be more like the Lord Jesus. That is a given. There is no higher goal, no loftier ambition than to be Christlike. One of God's great purposes in His people is to conform them to the image of His Son. There is no need for us to press the matter further. God's purpose is to make us like Jesus. It is taught throughout the New Testament, and we often hear it in sermons.

But there is still the question, "How?" In a practical way and on a day to day basis, how can we work with God to achieve increasing likeness to our Lord Jesus? It is one thing to know what to do and another to know how to go about it.

"The image of God is not seen in the shape of our bodies, but in the beauty of the renewed mind and heart. Holiness, love, humility, meekness, kindness, and forgiveness—these make up the divine character" (Daily Notes of the Scripture Union).

Paul tells us that we are changed into His likeness by beholding Him (2 Cor. 3:18). This means that we study His life as a Man here on earth and also His present life for us at God's right hand, then with the discipline of determination, we seek to follow Him, to walk as He walked, to be guided by His example.

There are two clear verses in the New Testament where the Lord Jesus is set forth as an example for us to follow. They are John 13:15, *"For I have given you an example that you should do as I have done to you"* (He had just washed their feet). Also 1 Peter 2:21, *"For to this you were called, because Christ also suffered for us, leaving us an example, that you should follow His steps."*

It goes without saying that we can never achieve His perfection down here or share those attributes that belong to God alone. But that should not be used as an excuse for satisfaction with the *status quo*. We should still strive toward the goal.

Although Christ Himself is our supreme example, we can often learn valuable lessons on how to imitate Him when we see Him reflected in the lives of His people. Isn't it true that sometimes we can read about His excellencies but they seem somewhat removed from us? But when we meet a believer who exhibits some Christlike quality in an unusual way, we see the truth made flesh. It is no longer far off or theoretical or impractical. The whole subject of discipleship, for instance, may never come alive until we see it lived out by a blood-earnest disciple with a passion for obeying the clear commands of Scripture.

So that brings us to the central questions. What is Jesus like and how can I be more like Him? How can I so live that others will see Christ in me? How can I imitate His character, His behavior, and His speech?

He was a Man of the Book. Christ's mind was filled with Scripture. He quoted the Word as His final authority. The verses He quoted were always on target—just the right words for that particular occasion.

He was a Man of meditation. He was the blessed Man of Psalm 1 whose delight was in the law of the Lord. In that law He meditated day and night.

He was a worshiper. Our Lord's supreme act of worship was His sacrificial death at Calvary in obedience to His Father's will.

He was not conformed to the world. Did He not say concerning His disciples, *"They are not of the world, just as I am not of the world"* (Jn. 17:16)? He was not of the world at all.

He did not fight with carnal weapons. When our Lord was on trial before Pilate, He said, *"My kingdom is not of this world. If My kingdom were of this world, My servants would fight, so that I should not be delivered to the Jews; but now My kingdom is not from here"* (Jn. 18:36).

Moral perfection. Not only did the Lord Jesus live without sinning, He lived without even knowing sin, and there was no sin in Him. He was tempted from without but never from within. There was nothing in Him to respond to sin.

Thou would'st like wretched man become

In everything but sin,

That we as like Thee might become

As we unlike had been. (Joseph Stennett)

He could not do anything in self-will or act independently of God the Father. Twice in John 5 He said that He could do nothing of Himself (vv. 19, 30). In saying this, He was not denying His omnipotence but affirming His absolute equality with the Father and the perfect unity of His will with the Father.

In his book, *The Sinless Savior,* J. B. Watson paid this glowing tribute to the Lord Jesus:

> No pang of repentance was ever felt by Him. He was never conscious of fault, no word did He ever need to recall…. He never expresses regret for any word or act, never admits mistake, never utters any syllable of confession, or suffers anyone to dictate His path or actions. He moves unhurried through each day, every hour finding it appointed work fulfilled, so that in His life there were never any arrears, rather did each evening find Him holding unspotted and unsoiled that peace with which He began the day.

Another admirer has said, "He was as spotless as Man as He was as God; as unsullied in the midst of the world's pollutions as when daily He was the Father's delight before the world began."

Joy. The joy of the Son of God was to do His Father's will and to bring many sons to glory. With that joy in view, He endured the cross, despising the shame. His joy was unaffected by the trials and sorrows that men heaped upon Him.

Peace. Peace and poise characterized the life of the Redeemer. No matter what adversities crashed down upon Him, He was calm and unruffled. The threats and insults of His creatures left Him unmoved.

Longsuffering. Jesus was longsuffering with His disciples, a *"faithless and perverse generation"* (Lk. 9:41). He is longsuffering with the world of lost mankind, *"not willing that any should perish but that all should come to repentance"* (2 Pet. 3:9). Anyone else would have given up on man long ago.

Kindness. We see the kindness of the Lord Jesus in the affectionate, sympathizing way in which He dealt with people. It was His great delight to bless them and to afford relief to those who needed it. His consideration of those He met endeared Him to them.

Goodness. Even His enemies credit our Lord with being good, showing kindness without partiality. He *"went about doing good and healing all who were oppressed by the devil"* (Acts 10:38). He thought of others, not of self. No one can ever match Him in showing kindness. He impoverished Himself to enrich others.

Faithfulness. He is faithful in keeping His promises, in performing His duty, and in loyal unswerving care for His people. There is no risk in trusting Him. No one has ever been disappointed in Him.

Gentleness. The mention of this word takes us back to the time when the disciples wanted to shoo the children away from Jesus. He said, *"Let the little children come to Me, and do not forbid them, for of such is the kingdom of heaven"* (Mt. 19:14).

Compassion. Christ had compassion on the multitude and sent the Twelve out into the harvest field (Mt. 9:36). He had compassion on the multitude and fed 5000 (Mt. 14:14). Again He had compassion on the multitude and fed 4000 (Mt. 15:32). Because of His compassion two blind men received sight (Mt. 20:34), a leper was healed (Mk. 1:41), a demoniac was delivered (Mk. 5:19), and a bereaved widow saw her son raised to life (Lk. 7:13). We see His compassion as the Good Shepherd (Lk. 15:4-7), as the Good Samaritan (Lk. 10:33), and as the father of the wayward son (Lk. 15:20). We see His tears of compassion at the grave of Lazarus (Jn. 11:35) and on the Mount of Olives as He wept over Jerusalem (Mt. 23:37-39). We have a compassionate Savior.

How we need that kind of compassion! How we need to pray:

Let me look on the crowd as my Savior did
Till my eyes with tears grow dim;
Let me view with pity the wandering sheep
And love them for love of Him. (Anon.)

Meekness. Any true portrayal of the Lord Jesus must reveal Him as One who is meek and lowly in heart. The word *"meek"* has the idea of broken. It is the word used to describe a young horse that has accepted the harness and patiently plods on, its head bobbing up and down, its eyes looking straight ahead.

Our meek Lord calls us to take His yoke and learn to be like Him. This will mean an uncomplaining acceptance of His will. When adverse circumstances come down on us, we will be able to say, *"Even so...for so it seemed good in Your sight."*

Jesus was humble in his cattle-shed birth, a birth that borrowed none of the glory of this world. He was humble in His life, with not a trace of pride or arrogance, not a fraction of a superiority complex. The supreme example of His humility was when *"He humbled Himself and became obedient to the point of death, even the death of the cross"* (Phil. 2:8).

Wast Thou, Savior, meek and lowly,
And will such a worm as I,
Weak and sinful and unholy,
Dare to lift my head on high? (H. F. Lyte)

He was a servant. Jesus was the true Israelitish bondslave who put His ear to the door and said, *"I love my Master; I will not go out free"* (Ex. 21:5). His whole life was one of serving His God and serving His fellows. Amazing! The Creator and Sustainer of the universe left the palace where He was served by myriads of angels, and came down to serve and to give His life a ransom for many. Paul vividly describes His self-abasement. Though He was personally equal with God, He didn't feel that positional equality with God the Father in heaven was something He had to hold onto at all costs. No. He emptied Himself of that position in heaven and became a Servant. He could say, *"I am among you as one who serves"* (Lk. 22:25-27). "There was not one act for self in all Christ's life; He was always at the service of others."

It brings a lump to our throat when we see Him donning the towel-apron of a slave and stooping to wash the disciples' feet.

> *We wonder at Thy lowly mind,*
> *And fain would like Thee be,*
> *And all our rest and pleasure find*
> *In learning, Lord, of Thee.*
> *Tho' in the very form of God,*
> *With heav'nly glory crowned,*
> *Thou didst a servant's form assume,*
> *Beset with sorrow round.* (Joseph Stennett)

He is still saying, as He said that fateful night in the upper room, *"I have given you an example, that you should do as I have done unto you"* (Jn. 13:15).

It is an authentic mark of Christlikeness when we stoop to serve.

Forbearance. We owed a debt we could not pay. Instead of demanding satisfaction from us, the Lord assumed the debt and paid it in full. What a wonderful Savior!

Forgiveness. His words, *"Father, forgive them, for they do not know what they do,"* ring down through the centuries. What further proof of His forgiving spirit is needed? Here is the God-Man dying in unspeakable torture and He prays that the Father will forgive His guilty murderers.

> *Thy foes might hate, despise, revile; thy friends unfaithful prove.*
> *Unwearied in forgiveness still, Thy heart could only love.* (Edward Denny)

But a word of caution must be added here. The fact that He asked for forgiveness for His assailants does not mean that they were automatically forgiven. Judas was not forgiven. Only those who come to Him in repentance and faith receive the benefit of that prayer.

Forgiveness presupposes repentance. Jesus said to the disciples,

If your brother sins against you, rebuke him; and if he repents, forgive him. And if he sins against you seven times in a day, and seven times in a day returns to you, saying, "I repent," you shall forgive him (Lk. 17:3-4).

Notice that forgiveness follows repentance.

There are some minor wrongs done against us that we can easily forget. They are not important enough to make an issue of them. But if there is a serious sin or offense, it is not righteous to forgive where there has been no repentance. It only encourages the culprit in his evil.

Where there has been repentance, our forgiveness must be unlimited. We have been forgiven millions; we should be willing to forgive what are comparable to a few cents.

How true that "forgiveness is the perfume that the trampled flower casts back on the foot that crushed it."

Courageous. I love the picture of Jesus on His final trip to Jerusalem and the cross. Luke tells us that *"He went on ahead"* (Lk. 19:28). He set His face as a flint to accomplish our redemption. The suggestion is that the disciples lagged behind, their feet dragging. They were hesitant to go.

Righteousness. One of the elements in the moral perfection of the Lord Jesus is His righteousness. He is scrupulously just and upright. He never stoops to anything that is dishonest, shady, or even questionable. His decisions are righteous and so are His actions.

Selflessness. Our Lord and Savior is the most selfless Man who ever lived. His whole career was one of self-abnegation, or putting the interests of others before His own. In lowliness of mind He esteemed others better than Himself (Phil. 2:3).

Consistency. The Savior of the world was always the same. His personal behavior perfectly matched His sublime teaching. Wild sweeps of temperament were foreign to Him. When He was angry (Mt. 23:33) or sorrowful (Jn. 11:35), it was always because the occasion called for it—never because He was swept away by His own feelings.

Single-mindedness. Jesus had one unifying and overriding purpose; that was to seek and save the lost. Did He not say, *"I have a baptism to be baptized with and how distressed I am till it is accomplished"* (Lk. 12:50)? He was referring, of course, to His baptism unto death at Golgotha when He would die for the sins of the world.

Class. When we say that Jesus had class, we mean that He acted elegantly, far above what would ordinarily be expected. Though He was omniscient and could read men's thoughts, He never needlessly embarrassed them. To Him everyone was special and must be treated with dignity.

Courtesy. Courtesy is a half cousin of charm. And the Lord Jesus was courteous. He was never rude, never crude. There was no situation where He was out of place. He had a perfect sense of propriety. No word or action of His ever caused Him embarrassment. He was always the perfect Gentleman.

Here is a characteristic that we can all emulate. It is hard for people to resist a courteous person. The gracious action, the appropriate word, wins fans for the One we represent.

Freedom from the love of money. Homeless and poor, our Lord apparently never carried money on His person. Certainly there is no mention of it. When He needed a coin to teach a spiritual lesson, He ordered Peter to retrieve one from the mouth of the first fish that he caught (Mt. 17:27). No one ever envied Him for His possessions. He left nothing but the clothes that He wore.

Obedience. In the volume of the book it is written of Him, He delighted to do the will of God His Father (see Ps. 40:8; Heb. 10:7).

Passion for souls. For one lost sheep, the Shepherd crossed deep waters, searched the waste desert, and climbed mountains wild and bare till He found one sheep that was lost (Lk. 15:1-7).

Friend of sinners. This title was meant to be an insult, but it is most lovely (Lk. 7:34). The Lord Jesus spent time with those who were outcast and looked down upon. The Lord bowed down to the gutter, visited them, and shared their food. He asked sinners to help Him. All this He did in a friendly way. They liked to be with Him and enjoyed His company.

Contentment. When the Savior met titanic unbelief, He contented Himself in the overruling plan and purpose of God, saying, *"Even so, Father, for so it seemed good in Your sight"* (Mt. 11:26).

Patience or Endurance. The writer to the Hebrews reminds us how Jesus endured great hostility of sinners against Himself (Heb. 12:3). The worst that Satan, demons, and men could do to Him did not deflect Him from going all the way to Calvary.

Zeal. Zeal is a word that is found only once in connection with the life of the Lord Jesus, that is, when He cast the money changers out of the temple courts. At that time, one of David's prophecies concerning the Messiah came alive to the disciples: *"Zeal for Your house has eaten Me up"* (Jn. 2:17). In other words, He was consumed with a burning passion for the things of God.

But this was not the only occasion. His whole life was marked by an earnest and ardent pursuit of the will of God. When His parents scolded Him for lagging behind in Jerusalem when they thought He should have stayed with them *en route* to Nazareth, He said, *"Did you not know that I must be about My Father's business?"* (Lk. 2:49).

Thankfulness. Here the verse that immediately comes to mind is

Matthew 11:25. He had just pronounced woes on the cities of Chorazin, Bethsaida and Capernaum. They had refused to accept Him in spite of the fact that most of His mighty miracles had been done there.

In spite of this towering unbelief, He turns to thankfulness to God the Father because He had *"hidden these things from the wise and prudent and revealed them to babes."*

That is a lesson for us. When things are grimmest in our lives, we should rise above the circumstances and raise our hearts and voices in gratitude to the Father.

Fanny Crosby lost her sight at age 3 through the malpractice of a physician. Years later when questioned about the incident, she said,

> Although it may have been a blunder on the physician's part, it was no mistake on God's. I verily believe it was His intention that I should live my days in physical darkness, so as to be better prepared to sing His praises and incite others to do so. I could not have written thousands of hymns…

A little boy in Grade 2 started out the morning by falling from the school bus and hitting his head on the concrete—requiring three stitches to close the gash! Recess proved a little unfortunate as he and another boy ran into each other—result: two of his teeth were loosened and a lip was cut. During the afternoon he fell and broke his arm. His principal decided to take the boy home immediately before anything else could happen. They were riding along a country road toward the boy's home when the principal noticed the little guy clutching something in his hand. "What do you have?" he asked.

"A quarter," answered the boy.

"Where did you get it?"

"I found it in the playground today," explained the little boy. Then he smiled and with an excited voice explained, "You know, Mr. Chapman, I've never found a quarter before. This is my lucky day."

> So much is dependent not on how the day looks to us—but at how we look at

the day. Some people miss seeing the roses behind a broken fence. Every day has its problems but faith can turn them into blessings. Each butterfly looks rather uneventful at its beginning—but what a difference a day makes.[17]

We should be thankful for memory, appetite, sight, hearing, health, soundness of mind, luxuries that Jesus didn't have on earth— an inner-spring mattress, running cold and hot water, a refrigerator, and a car.

He was Manly. Much modern art pictures Jesus as an effeminate Gentile. No so. He was the perfect specimen of humanity. All men would be like Him if sin had not entered.

He was a Man of prayer. Think of it! As the dependent Man, He prayed. As the Omnipotent God, He answered the prayers of others. He prayed when He was baptized by John (Lk. 3:21). He prayed all night before choosing the Twelve (Lk. 6:12). After healing the multitudes, He prayed (Lk. 5:16). And after healing and driving out demons in Capernaum (Mk. 1:35). The grave of Lazarus was the scene of His prayer (Jn. 11:41-42). He found time to pray after feeding the 5000 (Mt. 14:21, 23). When confronted with the unbelieving rejection of those He came to save, He found prayerful refuge in the sovereignty of God (Mt. 11:25-26). As High Priest, He prayed that His own people might be preserved from evil, live in separation from the world, be qualified for duty, and be brought home to heaven safely (Jn. 17). He prayed for Peter that his faith would not fail (Lk. 22:32). He prayed in the Garden of Gethsemane, submitting His will to His Father's (Lk. 22:41-44). And three of His last words on the cross were prayers (Lk. 23:34; Mt. 27:46; Lk. 23:46).

He did not judge by appearance but judged righteous judgment. He saw beyond the mite size of the widow's offering to its enormous devotion (Lk. 21:1-4). He distinguished between the repentant love of a sinful woman and the cold neglect of a self-

---

17   Babcock, Floyd C., *Quarterly News Letter, Winter 1991.*

righteous Pharisee (Lk. 7:36-48). He was not as impressed by Martha's fretful service as by Mary's quiet worship (Lk. 10:41-42). Outwardly the Pharisees seemed to be righteous but inwardly they were full of hypocrisy and lawlessness (Mt. 23). He rose above the natural tendency to think that just because a person or thing is beautiful, it must be good. How well He knew that "not all that glistens is gold." He was more concerned with inward qualities than with physical appearance.

We cannot help but think of the Lord's words to Samuel concerning Eliab: *"Do not look at his appearance or at the height of his stature, because I have refused him. For the Lord does not see as man sees; for man looks at the outward appearance, but the Lord looks at the heart"* (1 Sam. 16:7).

He was time efficient. The Master did not waste time. Every moment was precious to Him. Did He not say, *"I must work the works of Him who sent Me while it is day. The night is coming when no one can work"*? Every day had its allotted tasks. Even what might have seemed to be interruptions were part of the Father's will for Him.

Jesus condescended to men of low estate. He was always concerned with the last, the least, the lowest. Class distinctions were foreign to Him. He had a special love for those who were poor, weak, base, despised—for those who were nobodies as far as the world was concerned.

He endured. He endured untold hostility from sinners against Himself (Heb. 12:3). There was never the slightest thought of turning back. Endurance is not the fatalistic acceptance of circumstances but the steadfastness that carries on until the end.

It remains for us to think about the Savior's speech. What can we learn from Him in this area? How can we be more Christlike in the words that we say?

His speech was transparently honest. There was no deceit in His mouth. He never lied nor even shaded the truth. Never once did He resort to exaggeration. And He never stooped to flattery.

He was frank. Once He said to a woman, *"You have had five husbands, and the one whom you now have is not your husband"* (Jn. 4:18). At another time he said to a Pharisee, *"I entered your house; you gave Me no water for My feet...You gave Me no kiss... You did not anoint My head with oil"* (Lk. 7:44-46).

His speech was gracious. When He spoke in the synagogue at Nazareth, people *"marveled at the gracious words which proceeded out of His mouth"* (Lk. 4:22). Ever since then people have been wondering at them as they hear Him speaking through the written Word.

He did not complain. Our Lord knew that complaining would be an insult to the providence of God, the Father. It would mean that He doesn't know what He is doing. It would accuse Him of error or faulty judgment.

We should remember that whenever we are tempted to complain. Better to dismiss the thought or swallow the words, and say instead, *"As for God, His way is perfect"* (Ps. 18:30). After all, our Master does all things well.

His speech was edifying. Sometimes He did it by direct statements, sometimes by asking questions. He taught spiritual lessons using nature and everyday life.

> *He talked of grass, and wind, and rain,*
> *Of fig trees and fair weather,*
> *And made it His delight to bring*
> *Heaven and earth together.*
> *He spoke of lilies, vines, and wheat,*
> *The sparrow and the raven,*
> *And words so natural, yet so wise*

Were on men's hearts engraven—
Of yeast with bread, and flax, and cloth,
Of eggs, of fish, and candles.
See how the whole familiar world
He most divinely handles. *(Author Unknown)*

His speech was worthwhile. He talked about the things that matter. There was no idle chitchat—only what was helpful for this life and important for the life to come. He never gossiped.

His speech was appropriate. His mind was full of Scripture and He quoted it to fit the occasion. For instance, He answered Satan's temptations in the wilderness with three fitting portions from Deuteronomy.

Every answer was perfect. His silences were often more eloquent than His speech (Mt. 26:62-63; 27:12; Mk. 15:4-5; Lk. 23:9).

CONCLUSION

An author unknown to me has left these weighty lines:

How exhilarating it is to think that we can model the qualities of Christ to those who are searching for Him. By an exemplary lifestyle, the disciple can make his or her Lord attractive to others. In his letter to Titus, Paul urged him to teach slaves to work to please their masters *"so that in every way they will make the teaching about God our Savior attractive"* (Titus 2:10). People should not only hear truth worth hearing but also see lives worth emulating. The word Paul uses in that verse is rendered *adorn* in the King James Version—*"in every way adorn the doctrine."* That word is used of arranging jewels in such a way as to show off their beauty to the best advantage. This is our privilege.

What grace, O Lord, and beauty shone around Thy steps below!
What patient love was seen in all Thy life and death of woe.
Forever on Thy burdened heart a weight of sorrow hung;
Yet no ungentle, murmuring word escaped Thy silent tongue.
Thy foes might hate, despise, revile, Thy friends unfaithful prove;

Unwearied in forgiveness still, Thy heart could only love.

Oh, give us hearts to love like Thee, like Thee, O Lord, to grieve
Far more for other's sins than all the wrongs that we receive.
One with Thyself, may ev'ry eye in us, Thy brethren, see
That gentleness and grace that spring from union, Lord, with Thee.

(Edward Denny)

Thoughts of Thy sojourn in this vale of tears,
The tale of love unfolded in those years
Of sinless suffering and patient grace
We love again and yet again to trace.

(Author unknown)

O blessed renewing, O mercy unpriced
A growth to the stature and fullness of Christ.

(Anon.)

O patient, spotless One!
Our hearts in meekness train
To bear Thy yoke and learn of Thee,
That we may rest obtain.

(C. A. Bernstein)

FOURTEEN
BE KNOWN FOR YOUR LOVE

Love is not so much a matter of the emotions as of the will. It is not a fantasy state I fall into, but a deliberate action I determine to take. "Love is a decision that grows out of my will. I can choose to love. I can start right now—at home" (Author unknown).

It manifests itself in giving. *"God so loved the world that He gave ...."* (Jn. 3:16). *"The Son of God, who loved me and gave Himself for me"* (Gal. 2:20). *"Christ loved the church and gave Himself for it"* (Eph. 5:25). Since it is more blessed to give than to receive, the Lord always has the prerogative of being the more blessed.

It is the hallmark of Christians. *"By this all will know that you are My disciples, if you have love for one another"* (Jn. 13:35).

It goes out to the unlovable as well as the lovable, to the ugly as well as the handsome.

It repays every discourtesy with a kindness.

Without love all Christian service is futile. Love is better than the most spectacular display of the gifts of the Spirit (1 Cor. 13:1-3). Grace is more important than gift.

In cases of conflict, love does not announce a decision until it has heard both sides of the story (Prov. 18:13).

Love does not have a judging, critical spirit. When someone was condemning another because of what seemed to be a spiritual failure, Harry Ironside would quote these lines of Adelaide Proctor:

> *Judge not: the workings of his brain*
> *And of his heart thou canst not see.*
> *What looks to thy dim eyes a stain*
> *In God's pure light may only be*
> *A scar—brought from some well-worn field*
> *When thou would'st only faint and yield.*

It avoids condemning on the basis of circumstantial evidence alone. It avoids speaking negatively or critically of other people.

Love can be firm. It can condemn sin and punish disobedience (see Prov. 13:24). This is known as tough love.

First Corinthians 13 is the love chapter. In it Paul describes love as it is seen in the life of the Lord Jesus and as we should practice it. The theme that goes through the chapter is that love thinks of others, rather than self.

Love suffers long. It is neither impatient nor touchy.

It is kind. It is always looking for ways to show little acts that say, "I care."

It does not envy. It is not jealous of others. A loving person doesn't wish he were like someone else or owned what others possess.

It does not parade itself with prideful boasting.

It is not puffed up. It recognizes that it has nothing that it did not receive, and it can do nothing except the power be given to him.

It does not behave rudely.

It *"does not seek its own."* This may mean its own way or its own power, fame, wealth, or status. It is not selfish.

It is not provoked. It does not fly off the handle easily.

It thinks no evil. It does not, like Job's comforters, attribute a believer's plight to sin in his life.

It does not rejoice in iniquity, is never glad when people are treated unjustly, even if the people probably deserve it.

It does not keep a count of wrongs (v. 5, TEV).

It rejoices in the truth. Whenever truth scores a victory, it is glad, regardless of who gets the credit for it.

It bears all things. This may refer to bearing the burdens of others and of oneself. Love bears up under trials, persecutions, and sorrows with no thought of giving up.

It believes all things. It puts the best possible construction on things until evidence shows the contrary to be true. It doesn't mean that love is gullible or naive.

It hopes all things. It looks forward to a good outcome in spite of present difficulties and discouragements.

It never fails. Its power and effectiveness continue without lapse. It wins at last.

Love goes out to one's enemies, to those who hate us. It blesses those who curse us, and prays for those who spitefully use us. When struck, it turns the other cheek. It gives more than is asked, and lends without any thought of receiving anything in return.

It goes beyond natural behavior in loving the unloving, doing good to those who don't do good. This is not how you become sons of the Highest, but how you manifest yourselves as such.

Love is merciful just as God is in withholding deserved punishment. It is kind to the unthankful and evil. It is slow to judge or condemn but quick to forgive. It tries to see Jesus in other believers, even those who are unpleasant.

Our Lord is loving. He is love incarnate. We need an enlarged, improved vocabulary to describe His love. Our present dictionary is not adequate. There are not enough adjectives—simple, comparative, and superlative. Our language is utterly impoverished. Individual words are ashamed. We can go only so far; then we have to say, *"The half has not been told."* The subject exhausts all human language.

Let us begin, then, on a theme that cannot be finished.

His love is eternal, the only love that is unoriginated. It is age-abiding and unending. Our minds strain to comprehend a love that is ceaseless and unremitting.

It is immeasurable. Its height, depth, length, and breadth are infinite. Nowhere do we find such extravagance. Poets have compared it to creation's greatest expanses, but the words always seem to break under the weight of the idea.

His love to us is causeless and unprovoked. Our Lord could see nothing lovable or meritorious in us to draw out His affections, yet He loved us just the same. He did it because that's the way He is.

Our love of others is often based on ignorance. We love people because we don't really know what they are like. The more we get to know them, the more we become aware of their faults and failures, and then the less likeable they appear. But Jesus loved us even when He knew all that we would ever be or do. His omniscience did not cancel His love.

But there are so many people in the world—over six billion. Can the Sovereign love each one personally?

> *Among so many, can He care?*
> *Can special love be everywhere?*

Yes, with Him there are no nobodies. No one is insignificant. His affection flows out to every individual on the planet.

Such love is incomparable. Most people have known the love of a devoted mother. Or the faithful love of a selfless wife. David knew the love of Jonathan. And Jesus knew the love of John. But no one has ever experienced anything that can compare with the divine love. As a hymn reminds us, "No one ever cared for me like Jesus."

In Romans 8, Paul ransacks the universe for anything that might separate the believer from this love, but He comes up empty. Neither death, life, angels, principalities, powers, things present or to come, height, depth, nor any created thing can divorce the believer from it.

It is awesome to realize that the omnipotent One cannot love you or me more than He does at this moment. It is absolutely unrestrained and unreserved.

In a world of constant flux, it is assuring to find something that is unchanging, namely, the love of Christ. Our love moves in cycles. It is an emotional roller coaster. Not so with our Lord. His love never tires or varies.

And it is a pure love, utterly free from selfishness, unrighteous compromise, or unworthy motive. It is untainted and without a breath of defilement.

Like His grace, His love is free. For this we can be everlastingly thankful because we are paupers, beggars, and bankrupt sinners. And even if we owned all the wealth in the world, we still could never put even a down payment on a love so priceless.

Here is a love that is wonderfully impartial. It causes the sun to shine on the just and the unjust. It orders the rain to fall without discrimination.

And perhaps the most amazing thing about it is that it is sacrificial. It does not count the cost. It led the holy Son of God to Calvary to give its greatest demonstration.

> *Lord, e'en to death Thy love would go,*
> *A death of shame and loss,*
> *To vanquish for us every foe*
> *And break the strong man's force.* (H. L. Rossier)

At the cross we see a love that is stronger than death, that not even the billows of God's wrath could drown.

This unique love surpasses knowledge and defies the powers of utterance. It is sublime and matchless, the Everest of all affection.

We may search the earth for a better dictionary, a larger vocabulary to describe the Lord's love. But it is all in vain. Not until we reach heaven and gaze on incarnate Love will we see with clearer vision and understand with keener intellect the love of God that is in Christ Jesus our Lord. Hasten the day, O blessed Lord Jesus.

We cannot be Christlike without being loving. We are commanded to love God with all our affectionate powers, emotional powers, intellectual powers, and physical powers. We are to love our neighbor with the same intensity that we love ourselves. Husbands are to love their wives and wives their husbands. The household of faith, the world of lost mankind, even our enemies—these should all be recipients of our love.

We love when we give ourselves in service for others. We love when we give our money to those who are in genuine need. In fact, John tests our love by what we do with our money. *But whoever has this world's goods, and sees his brother in need, and shuts up his heart from him, how does the love of God abide in him?* (1 Jn. 3:17).

He also insists that genuine love means a willingness to lay down our lives for the brethren (1 Jn. 3:16). There is no greater love (Jn. 15:13). This is the way of the cross.

A mother's love is one of the great reflections of the Lord's love for us. A Christian mother was flown from Turkey in order to donate a kidney for her dying son. She thought that this would result in her own death. When the doctors asked, "Are you sure that you want to give a kidney for Kenan?" her answer was, "I am willing to give two kidneys."

It covers a multitude of sins. This does not mean that sins are atoned in this way, but that love throws a kindly veil over the faults and failures of others.

But love can be firm. It does not withhold correction when needed (see Prov. 13:24). When a bowl of apples is passed, love chooses the bruised apple so that someone else won't have to take it.

What else does love do?

• Love cleans the wash basin and tub after using them.

- Love gets more toilet tissue when the supply is gone.
- Love puts out the lights when they are not in use.
- Love sees work to be done and does it without being asked.
- It picks up random trash from the floor.
- It empties the garbage.
- It replaces gas and oil when it borrows a car.
- It doesn't keep people waiting, is punctual with appointments.
- It sees that food is passed to others at the table.
- It doesn't make fun of others or make sharp, cutting remarks.
- It takes the noisy baby out of meeting so he won't disturb others.
- It works in order to have money to give (Eph. 4:28).
- Love speaks loudly so the deaf can hear.

It forgives and doesn't hold grudges. George Washington Carver was refused admission to a college because he was black. Years later, when someone asked him the name of the college, he replied, "It doesn't matter."

When someone asked Clara Barton, "Don't you remember the nasty thing that woman said about you? she answered, "I not only don't remember. I distinctly remember forgetting."

It does not gloat over other men's sins (1 Cor. 13:6).

Love respects and obeys one's parents and cares for them in their old age. It does not fall into the trap of being nice to outsiders and unkind to Mom and Dad.

Love is thoughtful and courteous. It writes thank-you notes and in other ways expresses appreciation. It sends gifts to those who are largely forgotten.

> Do you know the world is dying for a little bit of love?
> Everywhere you hear them crying for a little bit of love.
> For the love that rights the wrong,
> For the love that brings the song;
> They have waited, Oh, so long, for a little bit of love. (Author Unknown)

FIFTEEN
HAVE COMPASSION FOR OTHERS

Christ and compassion go together; they are inseparable. We can be like Him in standing by people who are in a tragic situation and offer encouragement and hope. Jesus does this (Heb. 13:5-6). He is the Friend who sticks closer than a brother (Prov. 18:24).

We mistakenly think that all people are created equal and we tend to look down on those who don't fit our profile of what equal means. The truth is that not all are created equal. Some have greater intelligence than others. There are differences in physical attractiveness. And in differing talents. Some are born with serious impairments.

If I am compassionate, I will make allowance for these differences. My heart will go out to those that others despise. I will not rate people as the world does but will see them as precious, never dying persons for whom the Son of God died. I will value them as God does.

When an evangelist was returning to Britain, someone asked him what had impressed him most in the United States. He answered, "Seeing William Borden, that son of millionaires, with his arm around a bum at the city mission."

Fred Elliot would interrupt his morning devotions in order to go to the window and call out a cheery greeting to the garbage collector. To him neither activity was more sacred than the other.

At a summer Bible conference, Jack Wyrtzen ate with a seriously disabled man who was shunned by others because he could not hold the food in his mouth; some would invariably fall out on his newspaper bib.

J. N. Darby chose to stay in a humble cottage with an elderly couple rather than to accept accommodations accorded to a dignitary.

The compassionate disciple phones the elderly and the shut-ins. He visits those who are ill or injured. Or sends greeting cards to those who never receive one. Depend on him to bring food to the unemployed and to homes where death has struck. You will see him going out of his way to speak to that teenager in a wheelchair. He will be quick to befriend that fellow with a seeing-eye dog. He puts an arm around the little girl with Down's syndrome. All who are impaired or neglected, the lonely and sad love him because they know he cares.

Paul Sandberg had not followed his Master in vain. One day he entered a coffee shop and sat on a stool next to a fellow named Freddie. Paul faithfully witnessed to Fred and soon Fred entered the kingdom of God by the new birth.

When Fred was stricken with cancer some time later, Paul visited him regularly. Then in a sub-standard nursing home, Paul performed the duties that the nurses' aides should have done. The night Fred died, Paul was holding him in his arms, quoting verses of Scripture to him. I call that compassion!

In Western Michigan, a young fellow, only fifteen, began to receive treatment for cancer. Chemotherapy helped for a time, but it was nauseating. And it had another effect: It caused his hair to fall out. On top of the uncertainty of his disease, he had to bear the humiliation of returning to school with a head of patches and stubble.

But the first day back, he discovered an astonishing thing. A large number of his fellow students were completely bald! They had shaved their heads. With wise and ingenious grace these teenagers had thought of a way to ease their friend's pain and help him fit in.

How we need that kind of compassion! How we need to pray:

Let me look on the crowd as my Savior did
Till my eyes with tears grow dim,
Let me view with pity the wandering sheep
And love them for love of Him. (Author Unknown)

SIXTEEN
BE FILLED WITH THE SPIRIT
EPHESIANS 5:18

To many, the filling of the Holy Spirit is a vague, mystical subject. It does not convey a clear, distinct idea in people's minds. Add to that the fact that there is so much erroneous teaching on this work of the Spirit, and there is little wonder that Christians are confused.

First of all, the filling should be distinguished from other ministries of the Spirit. The filling is not the same as:

The indwelling. This means that the Third Person of the Trinity actually lives in the body of every believer. Our bodies are the temple of the Spirit.

The baptism. The baptism is that work of the Spirit that places a person in the body of Christ the moment he believes. He becomes a member of the universal church.

The seal. A seal is a mark of ownership and security. God the Spirit marks a believer as belonging to the Lord and kept safe by Him.

The earnest. This means a down payment or guarantee. Some compare it to an engagement ring. As sure as a person has the Spirit, so he will one day receive the full inheritance.

The anointing. In the Old Testament, kings and priests were anointed with oil as an inaugural rite. So the Spirit is our anointing as royal priests. The anointing has an additional meaning in 1 John 2:27. The teaching ministry of the Spirit enables us to distinguish between truth and error.

All these ministries of the Spirit take place the moment a person is saved. They are automatic. They do not require any cooperation on the part of the new believer. There are no conditions to be fulfilled. They are once-for-all experiences.

The filling of the Spirit is different. Actually there are two kinds of fillings in the New Testament.

First, there is a sovereign filling of a believer for some special work. Thus we read that John the Baptist was filled with the Holy Spirit from his mother's womb (Lk. 1:15b). In this way God prepared him to be the forerunner of the Messiah. Possibly this is how the word is often used in the book of Acts. Thus the disciples were filled with the Holy Spirit in preparation for the coming of the Spirit at Pentecost (Acts 2:4). Peter was filled to equip him for his convicting message to the rulers and people (Acts 4:8). Peter and John were filled in order that they might speak the Word of God with boldness (Acts 4:31). Saul was filled in order to preach Christ in Damascus (Acts 9:17, 22). Later Saul was filled in order to denounce Elymas, the sorcerer (Acts 13:9). At least some of these fillings were temporary and there were no conditions for the recipients to meet.

Then there is a filling that has conditions for us to meet. This is what we find in Ephesians 5:18. It is not something for which you pray; it is a command to be obeyed. It is clear in the original language of the New Testament that the meaning is "Be continually filled." It is an ongoing process, not an attainment. It is not an emotional experience as much as a consistent life of holiness.

Paul wrote, *"And do not be drunk with wine, in which is dissipation; but be filled with the Spirit."* But why did he mention anything as evil as drunkenness with the filling of the Spirit? It was probably because there are some similarities, and some glaring differences. First, the similarities. In both cases the person is under an outside control. In drunkenness, he is under the control of booze, sometimes called "spirits." The filling means he is under the control of the Holy Spirit. In both cases, you can tell by the way a person walks. The drunkard staggers haphazardly. The Spirit-filled person walks in separation from sin and the world. In both cases, you can tell by the way a person talks. The alcoholic's speech is garbled and profane. The believer's speech is Christ-exalting and edifying.

Then there are two dissimilarities. With drunkenness, there is a loss of self-control. With the filling there is none. With drunkenness, there is a lowered resistance to sin. With the filling, resistance is heightened.

I am reminded of the pungent words of James Stewart: "If it is a sin to be drunk with wine, it is a greater sin not to be filled with the Spirit."

As has been mentioned, the filling of the Spirit is the life of holiness. You find it in different clothing in these passages:

- It is the character of a citizen of the kingdom (Mt. 5:1-16).
- It is the abiding life (Jn. 15:1-17).
- It is the life of love (1 Cor. 13).
- It is the armor of the Christian (Eph. 6:10-20).
- It is the life of Christian character (2 Pet. 1:5-11).

Here are some of the essentials for being filled with the Spirit:

- Confess and forsake sin as soon as you are aware of it (1 Jn. 1:9; Prov. 28:13).
- Submit yourself to the Lord's control moment by moment (Rom. 12:1-2).
- Saturate yourself with the Word of God (Jn. 17:17). You can't be filled with the Spirit unless the Word of Christ dwells in you richly (Col. 3:16).
- Spent much time in prayer and worship (Rom. 8:26; 2 Cor. 3:18).

• Stay close to Christian fellowship, avoiding entanglement in the world's affairs (Heb. 10:25; 2 Tim. 2:4).

• Keep busy for the Lord (Eccl. 9:10).

• Say a resounding no to the unlawful appetites of the flesh (1 Cor. 9:27). Respond to sinful temptation as a dead person would (Rom. 6:11). In the moment of fierce temptation, call on the Lord (Prov. 18:10). Take rigorous action to avoid any sin (Mt. 18:8). Flee rather than fall (2 Tim. 2:22). He who fights and runs away, lives to fight another day.

• Control your thought life (Prov. 23:7; Phil. 4:8).

• Be Christ-centered, not self-centered (Jn. 16:14).

Now go about your work, believing that the Spirit is in control.

What will it be like—to be filled with the Spirit? Most of life will probably be the usual, routine, mundane hard work. Occasionally there will be mountain peaks. But you will notice that the gears of life mesh, that things happen that would not ordinarily happen. You will be conscious that the Lord is working in and through you. Your life will sparkle with the supernatural, and when you touch other lives something will happen for God.

Also there will be power (Lk. 24:49; Acts 1:8); boldness (Acts 4:13, 29, 31); joy (Acts 13:52); praise (Lk. 1:67-75; Eph. 5:19-20); and submission (Eph. 5:21).

A final caution. A person who is filled with the Spirit never says he is. The Spirit's ministry is to exalt Christ, not the believer. To boast as if one had already achieved is pride.

SEVENTEEN
TAKE THE LOW PLACE

Pride is the parent sin. It began in heaven when the handsome Lucifer sought to dethrone his Creator and God. Puffed up with pride, he fell into condemnation (1 Tim. 3:6). Christopher Marlowe called it "aspiring pride and insolence for which God threw him from the face of heaven." Not satisfied to bear the results alone, he wanted to share them, so he inveigled Adam and Eve to sin. Thus pride entered the human genes, and the sad result is that every one of us has enough of it to sink a fleet.

J. Oswald Sanders called pride a deification of self. "It thinks more highly of self than it ought to think. It arrogates to itself the honor which belongs to God only."

Any true portrayal of the Lord Jesus must reveal Him as One who is meek and lowly in heart. The word *meek* has the idea of broken. It is the word used to describe a young horse that has accepted the harness and patiently plods on, its head bobbing up and down, its eyes looking straight ahead.

Our meek Lord calls us to take His yoke and learn to be like Him. This will mean an uncomplaining acceptance of His will. When adverse circumstances crash in on us, we will be able to say, *"Even so...for so it seemed good in Your sight."*

Jesus was humble in His cattle-shed birth, a birth that borrowed none of the glory of this world. He was humble in His life, with not a trace of pride or arrogance, not a fraction of a superiority complex. The supreme example of His humility was when *"He humbled Himself and became obedient to the point of death, even the death of the cross"* (Phil. 2:8).

> *Wast Thou, Savior, meek and lowly,*
> *And will such a worm as I,*
> *Weak and sinful and unholy,*
> *Dare to lift my head on high?* (H. F. Lyte)

> *He humbled Himself to the manger*
> *And even to Calvary's tree;*
> *But I am so proud and unwilling*
> *His humble disciple to be.* (Anon.)

It is good for us to know our correct size. When George Washington was caught performing a menial task, a friend said, "General, you're too big a man to be doing that." "No, I'm not," he answered, "I'm just the right size."

> *Oh, I am so unlike to Christ whose likeness I would gain,*
> *I in His presence am so dim, comparison is vain.*
> *His humble, meek, and gentle ways I long to make my own,*
> *That brightly I may show His praise and live for Him alone.*

True humility does not consist so much in thinking badly of ourselves, as in not thinking of ourselves at all. I am too bad to be worth thinking about; what I want is to forget myself and to look to God, who is indeed worthy of all my thoughts (William Kelly).

Isaac Newton had one of the most brilliant minds of his age, and he was one of the most obvious geniuses our species has produced. Yet Newton said of himself,

I do not know what I may appear to the world, but to myself I seem to have been only like a boy playing on the seashore, and diverting myself now and then in finding a smoother pebble or a prettier shell than ordinary, while the great ocean of truth lay all undiscovered before me.

Compare that to Oscar Wilde's quip at the customs office in New York that "I have nothing to declare but my genius.

F. B. Meyer said of Dwight L. Moody, "Moody is a man who never seems to have heard of himself. No wonder God used him to wonderfully!"

A former Keswick speaker said, "There's nothing God cannot do if we keep our hands off the glory." Another preacher said, "It's all right if people praise you, so long as you don't inhale."

It's pride that keeps multitudes from confessing Christ and thus consigns them to an eternal hell. It's pride that makes it so hard for Christians to apologize when they have offended someone else. It's pride that makes it impossible for God to use us. It blocks the flow of spiritual power and witness. On the other hand, we can never be too small for Him to use.

J. N. Darby said, "Oh, the joy of having nothing and being nothing, seeing nothing but a living Christ in glory, and being careful for nothing but His interests down here."

Recognizing pride as his besetting sin, Robert Chapman left wealth and status to move to a skid-row dwelling. He said quaintly, "My pride never got over it."

We must deal resolutely with pride. William Law wrote, "Pride must die in you or nothing of heaven can live in you...Look not at pride only as an unbecoming temper, nor at humility as a decent virtue. One is all hell and the other all heaven."

The valet of a German kaiser said, "I cannot deny that my master was vain. He had to be the central figure in everything. If he went to a christening, he wanted to be the baby. If he went to a wedding, he wanted to be the bride. If he went to a funeral, he wanted to be the corpse."

Rabbi Simeone Ben Jochai said. "If there are only two righteous men in the world, I and my son are the two. If only one, I am he." Contrast with that what F. B. Meyer said of himself.

I am only an ordinary man. I have no special gifts. I am no orator, no scholar, no profound thinker. If I have done anything for Christ and my generation, it is because I have given myself entirely to Christ Jesus, and then tried to do whatever He wanted me to do.

The Christians desire should be:

> Keep me little and unknown,
> Loved and prized by Christ alone.—Charles Wesley

We should try to go through life anonymously. Actually we have nothing to be proud of. "The beginning of greatness is to be little; the increase of greatness is to be less; and the perfection of greatness is to be nothing." Darby was strong on this point. He said, "True greatness is to serve unseen and to work unnoticed."

In my files, I have a picture of an attractive young lady sitting at her vanity. A queen-sized mirror reflects her glamour. The vanity is covered with bottles of skin conditioners, fragrances, and tools of the beauty trade. But as you gaze intently at the picture, it seems to fade away and the form of a skull emerges.

It is good to remind ourselves of these pride busters:

A man can receive nothing unless it has been given to him from heaven (Jn. 3:27). *Without Me you can do nothing* (Jn. 15:5c). *So then neither he who plants is anything, nor he who waters, but God who gives the increase* (1 Cor. 3:7). *What do you have that you did not receive?* (1 Cor. 4:7).

> Would'st thou be great? Then lowly serve.
> Would'st thou go up, go down;
> But go as low as e'er you will,
> The Highest has gone lower still.

EIGHTEEN
BREAK ME, LORD

The Lord is near to those who have a broken heart, and saves such as have a contrite spirit (Ps. 34:18).

The sacrifices of God are a broken spirit, a broken and a contrite heart-these, O God, You will not despise (Ps. 51:17).

God resists the proud but gives grace to the humble (Jas. 4:6).

It would not be right to say that the Bible is full of references to brokenness. However, there are sufficient mentions to lead us to believe that it is a significant subject in the Christian life. Let us review some of them:

• Jacob's physical strength had to be broken before he could be clothed with spiritual power (Gen. 32:22-32).
• The earthenware pitchers were broken and the light shone out, terrifying the enemy (Jud. 7:18-19).
• Seven loaves of bread and two fish were broken and the multitude was fed (Mt. 14:19).
• The roof was broken and a paralytic was forgiven and healed. (Mk. 2:1-12).
• The jar was broken, the ointment poured out, and the house was filled with the fragrance (Jn. 12:3-5; Mark 14:3).
The Savior's body was broken and multitudes were redeemed (1 Cor. 11:24).

"When Jesus body was broken by the thorns, the nails, and the spear, redemption poured forth like a crystal stream, which cleanses the sinner and gives him life."

It is only as our earthen bodies are broken that blessing flows out to others (2 Cor. 4:7). "God uses for His glory those people and things that are the most perfectly broken."

THE BEGINNING OF BROKENNESS

True conversion is a form of brokenness. By nature we are wild colts, unfit for service. The Holy Spirit convicts us of sin, brings us to the place of repentance, until we say:

> Nay, but I yield, I yield,
> I can hold out no more;
> I sink by dying love compelled,
> And own Thee conqueror.

Then Jesus invites us to take His yoke upon us (Mt. 11:29). Just as yokes on the farm are for broken animals, so Jesus' yoke is for broken people. But His yoke does not chafe; it is lined with love.

When the Lord says, *"I am meek,"* the Spanish word is *manso*. That same word *manso is* used to describe a horse that has been broken in. It means docile.

SOME OF THE ELEMENTS OF BROKENNESS

Confession. True brokenness is seen in a readiness to confess our sins to God and to anyone we have wronged. David's confessions in Psalms 32 and 51 are classics that show what true confession is. It was the worst year of his life.

1. Confession should be prompt. True confession does not hide things under the table, waiting for time to heal them. David waited a year.

Many years ago, Christian professor Stuart Blackie of the University of Edinburgh was listening to his students as they presented oral readings. When one young man rose to present his recitation, he held his book in the wrong hand. The professor thundered, "Take your book in your right hand, and be seated!" At this harsh rebuke, the student held up his right arm. He didn't have a right hand. The other students shifted uneasily in their seats. For a moment the professor hesitated. Then he made his way to the student, put his arm around him, and with tears streaming down his face, said, "I never knew about it. Please, will you forgive me?" His humble apology made a lasting impact on that young man.

This story was told some time later in a large gathering of believers. At the close of the meeting a man came forward, turned to the crowd, and raised his right arm. It ended at the wrist. He said, "I was that student. Professor Blackie led me to Christ. But he never could have done it if he had not made the thing right."[18]

2. Confession should be individual. I, not we. "Father, if *we* have done anything wrong" is not genuine.

3. True confession is complete and forthright. Senator D'Amato of New York had mocked Judge Ito by simulating a Japanese accent. Later he said publicly, "It was a sorry episode. It was totally wrong. It was a poor attempt at humor. I am sorry for any offense I caused to Judge Ito. I offer my sincere apology."

4. It should be specific. Call the sin by its name. Gossip. Temper. Making a judgment before hearing both sides. Driving young people away by a critical spirit.

5. It should be unconditional. Not "If I have done anything wrong, I am willing to be forgiven" or "If you forgive me, I'll forgive you."

6. It should not trivialize the sin. "My behavior was inappropriate."

---

18   *Our Daily Bread,* Radio Bible Class, Grand Rapids, MI, October 18.

Then "My behavior was improper." Then "My behavior was wrong." Some call their sin a peccadillo or an indiscretion.

7. It should be accompanied by the intention to forsake the sin. A man's guilty conscience prompted him to send a letter to the Internal Revenue Service. The note read: "I haven't been able to sleep because last year when I filled out my income tax return, I deliberately misrepresented my income. I am enclosing a check for $150.00. If I still can't sleep, I'll send you the rest."[19]

When old Joe was dying, he remembered that he had had a falling out with Jim and he wanted to resolve the matter. So he called Jim to his bedside, told him that he was afraid to go into eternity without confessing his wrong, and he wanted to make things right. Everything seemed fine, but as Jim was leaving, Joe said, "But remember, if I get better, this doesn't count."[20]

8. It should not make excuses. "The devil made me do it." "It was my old nature." Dr. Ironside told this story on himself:

I remember when I was a young preacher, only a short time married, I had an idea that a preacher was entitled to indulge in the luxury of "nerves." I had seen others do it. I thought it a preacherified thing to go all to pieces. I got a lesson once; it takes a wife to give it to you sometimes! I had been preaching in San Francisco and had had a very full day. I went over early and had one meeting at 9 AM, then participated with a gathering of Christians in remembrance of the Lord at 11; then a meeting in the afternoon, and another later, and a street meeting, and then an inside meeting, and in all I preached five times. On my way home I was all in. I huddled in a corner of the streetcar...and was luxuriating in "nerves." My wife said something to me: I don't remember what it was. I answered her in that husbandly way that so many of us are familiar with!

She turned to me and said, "What do you mean, snapping at me like that, just after coming out of a meeting? You stand up on the platform and you look

---

19   Ibid. September 16.
20   Ibid. April 12, 1988.

so holy, you would think butter would melt in your mouth; and then you snap at me on the way home. I haven't done anything to deserve that. I just asked you a simple question. What would your congregation think of you now."

O dear, I was all down at once and humbled. I said, "My dear, I am so sorry, I didn't mean to snap at you, but you know I am all worn out. I preached five times today, and I am all unnerved."

My wife said, "Well, I have listened to you five times. I am just as tired as you are. If I can afford to be pleasant, you certainly can."

I had to apologize. I learned then not to excuse a bad temper and call it "nerves."[21]

9. We should not engage in self-defense. President Clinton confessed his sin: "Yes, it was wrong," but then in the next breath he said, "We are going to mount a vigorous defense."

10. It should not attack the one who exposed the sin. Mrs. Clinton defended her husband, saying, "Yes, it was improper, but the investigation was the result of a right-wing conspiracy."

It is far better to handle the situation as George Whitfield did. "At one point in his ministry, he received a vicious letter, accusing him of wrongdoing. His reply was brief and courteous: 'I thank you heartily for your letter. As for what you and my other enemies are saying against me, I know worse things about myself than you will ever say to me. With love in Christ, George Whitfield.'"[22]

EXAMPLES OF BROKENNESS IN CONFESSION

Paul the apostle was wrong in calling the high priest a white-washed wall, but when he was rebuked for doing it, he said, *"I did not know, brethren, that he was the high priest; for it is written, 'You shall not speak evil of the ruler of your people'"* (Acts 23:3-5).

---

21   Ironside, H. A., *The Keswick Convention*, London: Pickering & Inglis, 1939, p. 119.
22   *Our Daily Bread*, Radio Bible Class, Grand Rapids, MI, August 18, 1992.

One night, as he was closing a meeting, Dr. Donald Grey Barnhouse said, "As we sing the last hymn, will all the selfish people rush out in order to get one step ahead of the crowd, and will the unselfish people remain till the benediction in a couple of minutes." They had no more than begun to sing when a group of people at the front began to make their way out. Dr. Barnhouse realized in a minute that although he had been preaching in the Spirit, he had made that last comment in the flesh. He flashed a quick prayer to the Lord for cleansing from the sin of thoughtless unkindness. Then he flashed a signal to the organist at the end of the verse and apologized to the audience, hoping that someone would convey his apology to those who had left.[23]

When Canon Bill Butler was sent out to Rwanda by the Church of England to teach nationals who were being trained as pastors, he began to teach liberal theology, sowing doubts, denials, and drivel. Hearing that a group of "born again ones" (*abalokele*) had a prayer meeting on the campus every morning at 4 AM and that they were praying for him, he was incensed. One day he determined to set the leader straight and so he called him in and opened all his big guns of argument against him. The national took it graciously, saying only, "But you really do need help."

God began to work in Bill's life. He realized that what he had been teaching was false. When he went to the bishop and told him that he could no longer do it, the Bishop buried his head in his hands and said, "O Bill, now you can never become a bishop." Bill said, "Praise the Lord."

Then he realized he had to go to the Rwandan and apologize. How demeaning for a cleric of the Church of England! He got in the car and rehearsed all that he was going to say. When the national opened his door and saw Bill Butler, he said, "Hallelujah!"

---

23   *The Keswick Week* 1946, London: Marshall, Morgan and Scott, 1946, pp. 128-129.

Then the born again ones invited Bill to their 4 AM meeting. He had excuses, excuses. They said, "Well, would you try it for a week." He did and became deeply involved.

When the authorities heard about it, they transferred Bill to another school and forbade any meetings before 7 AM. The nationals felt that they had to obey God. As a result they were expelled just before graduation.

Later they contacted Bill and told him that he should go to the bishop and apologize for resentments and bad attitudes.

One day a member of Dr. Alexander Whyte's congregation came into the office with news that a preacher visiting the city had said publicly that one of Dr. Whyte's ministerial associates was not a Christian. Dr. Whyte blazed with indignation, irate that such a charge should be made against a faithful servant of the Lord. In a few well-chosen words, he expressed his anger against the one who had been guilty of this sin.

"That isn't all," the parishioner went on. "He even said that you are not a true believer."

At that Dr. Whyte slumped, then said, "Please leave the office so that I can be alone and examine my heart before the Lord."

THAT is brokenness!

Festo Kivengere admitted that he didn't like white people, and he didn't like the British who were ruling his country. The Lord told him to go to a British missionary and make things right with him. "He is your brother, white, English and all." He cycled fifty miles to ask for forgiveness. "I saw my brother. There stood before me a man whom Jesus loved, and we really had a wonderful time. I greeted him in the usual African way, embracing him. He didn't realize what had happened. And we stood there and I asked him to forgive me. We stood there, two of us in the presence of the Liberator, hearts beating in tune—not English and African but born again believers, set free by the Son of God. We talked, we prayed, we sang, we left each other. It is now thirty-three years, and I still love him very much."

"When love ceases to bleed, it ceases to bless."

WHAT HAPPENS WHEN WE REFUSE TO CONFESS

1. Fellowship with God is broken. God is still our Father, but communion with Him is interrupted.

2. Fellowship with fellow-believers is broken.

3. We lose the joy of God's salvation.

4. We lose our power.

5. We lose any effective testimony. Our lips are sealed. We are still saved through the merits of Jesus, but we are unfit for service on earth.

6. If the sin is of a public nature, we bring shame on the name of the Lord Jesus, and cause the Savior's enemies to blaspheme.

7. We are living a lie. Our actions cast doubt on the reality of our conversion. It's a case of high talk, low walk. We talk cream but live skim milk.

8. We lose our access to God in prayer.

9. Our works will be burned up, though not our souls.

10. We are in danger of making shipwreck of our lives. A single decision made by a backslider could put him on the shelf for the rest of his life as far as service for the Lord is concerned.

11. We may lose our physical life here on earth.

12. We may lose rewards at the Judgment Seat of Christ.

13. We live under a terrible sense of guilt.

In his book, *Finishing Strong*, Steve Farrar says:

Some of us have found ourselves chained to our past just like a circus elephant chained to a stake. This is one of the primary tools and schemes of the enemy to defeat Christians and to keep us from finishing strong. What does the enemy do? He simply mines the shadowy depths of our memory. He throws our past back at us. It may be one major sin from years past, and we still grieve over it and deeply regret it. Yes, we've been forgiven. Yes, we belong to Jesus Christ, but that failure keeps drifting back into our minds like a dark paralyzing fog whenever we seek to move out and do something significant for the Lord. We're like that elephant chained to the stake. That stake doesn't physically restrict that big old critter at all. He has the strength and resources to yank that thing out of the ground as if it were a toothpick. Yet the elephant remains chained by its memory. And so are many of us.

Maybe it was sexual immorality. Or lying to get your job. Or cruelty. Or neglect. Or a broken vow or pledge to God. Whatever it was, the enemy keeps throwing that one sin up in your face. The enemy uses it to paralyze you, and neutralize you. No, Satan cannot take away your salvation. But he can rob you of your joy. And all he has to do is bring up that one past sin.[24]

Regarding the chains of sin, Farrar quotes Robert Heffler:

There was a little boy visiting his grandparents on their farm, and he was given a slingshot to play with out in the woods. He practiced in the woods but he could never hit the target. And getting a little discouraged, he headed back to dinner. As he was walking back, he saw Grandma's pet duck. Just out of impulse, he let fly, hit the duck square in the head, and killed it. He was shocked and grieved. In a panic, he hid the dead duck in the woodpile...only to see his sister watching. Sally had seen it all, but she said nothing.

After lunch that day grandma said, "Sally, let's wash the dishes." But Sally said, "Grandma, Johnny told me he wanted to help in the kitchen today, didn't you, Johnny?' And then she whispered to him, "Remember the duck."

So Johnny did the dishes.

Later Grandpa asked if the children wanted to go fishing, and Grandma said, "I'm sorry but I need Sally to help make supper." But Sally smiled and said, "Well, that's all right because Johnny told me he wanted to help." And she whispered again, "Remember the duck." So Sally went fishing and Johnny stayed.

24   Farrar, Steve, Finishing Strong, Sisters, OR: Multnomah Books, 1995, p. 158.

After several days of Johnny doing both his chores and Sally's, he couldn't stand it any longer. He came to Grandma and confessed that he killed the duck. She knelt down, gave him a hug, and said, "Sweetheart, I know. You see, I was standing by the window and I saw the whole thing. Because I love you, I forgave you. But I was just wondering how long you would let Sally make a slave of you."[25]

The Lord sees every time we sin. But He waits to see how long it will be before we stop being slaves to guilt before we confess the sin.

The circle of confession should be as wide as the circle of the sin. An elder wrote to me:

Yesterday at the prayer meeting, a sister started talking in a disrespectful way about another sister who wasn't there. I exhorted her by telling her she should say these things directly to the sister involved. But I did it without love, in front of all the others. She started crying and went outside. It was now my turn to be exhorted. The others said I shouldn't have told her in such a hard way and in the presence of others. Feeling ashamed, I went to where she was and asked her to forgive me. Back in the meeting, I couldn't pray until I had confessed my sin to the Lord in front of all the others. Something like this had never happened to me before. One half-hour later she and I were totally reconciled, and the relationship restored.

Saintly F. B. Meyer tells how he lost his temper with a church official one Sunday night, just fifteen minutes before Meyer was to speak. Some of his assistants were coming in to pray with him before he entered the pulpit. He knew he was out of fellowship, and could not preach the gospel until the matter was made right. So he called the church official in and apologized for losing his temper. "The man looked more startled than pleased, but that did not matter. I had done what was right, and my soul shot into the blue of God's heaven again. God had brought me to the point of confession."[26]

25   Ibid. pp. 162-163.
26   Meyer, F. B., *The Christ Life for Your Life*, Chicago: Moody Press, n.d.,

RESTITUTION

Zacchaeus is the great New Testament example of a saved sinner who made restitution for past wrongs (Lk. 19:8). This should always be done in the name of the Lord, so He gets the glory.

W. P. Nicholson was a fiery, unconventional preacher in Northern Ireland years ago. At one time, he preached with such power that hundreds were saved. Their newfound salvation prompted them to return tools that they had stolen in the past. In fact, so many tools were returned that the machinery shops had to build sheds to store the tools. Finally, the companies had to issue a public statement, asking that no more tools be returned. There was no more space to house them.

There are cases where restitution is impossible. The best the Christian can do is confess his sins and leave the rest to the Lord.

FORGIVENESS

Brokenness involves not only asking for forgiveness, but also forgiving when someone apologizes to you. Corrie Ten Boom gives us a classic illustration of this. After World War II, when speaking on forgiveness at a church meeting in Germany, she saw a man in the audience who had been one of the cruelest guards in the concentration camp where her sister had died and where she herself had endured unspeakable humiliation and suffering.

At the end of the meeting, he approached her and said, "I have become a Christian. God has forgiven me. Will you?"

Then Corrie relived the past. She struggled to bring her hand out of her pocket. Finally, grace triumphed. She shook the hand of the repentant guard.

"I forgive you, brother!" she said. "With all my heart."

pp. 70-72.

There is a definite order in forgiveness:

1. First of all, when you have been wronged, you should forgive in your heart (Eph. 4:32). This takes the monkey off your back, but at this point you don't tell the offender that he is forgiven.

2. If he repents, you should forgive him orally and without number (Lk. 17:4). Tell him you forgive him. Don't trivialize what he has done. He wants to hear you say that he is forgiven.

God hates an unforgiving spirit. A serious rift had arisen between J. N. Darby and George Müller and it continued for years. Finally Darby went to the orphanage managed by Müller and asked to see him. The person at the door said that Mr. Müller was upstairs but that she would call him. When Müller came down, he said to Darby, "I have only ten minutes now free...you have acted so wickedly in this whole affair, that many things have to be looked into before we could be really united again."[27] Darby rose and left. That harsh outburst by Müller was the end of all hope of reconciliation. It was the last time the two men ever met—on earth.

In the early days of the church, a man was condemned to die for his faith. As the guards were leading him out to his execution, another Christian who had wronged the doomed man fell down before him and pled for forgiveness. The prisoner waved him aside and went on to be burned at the stake. That man's name is never found in any account of Christian martyrs. *"And though I give my body to be burned but have not love, it profits me nothing"* (1 Cor. 13:3).

ENDURING WRONG WITHOUT RETALIATION

Did you notice that the Lord Jesus never retaliated (1 Pet. 2:23)? For us sinful mortals, it's the most natural thing to do. We want to

---

27   Roger Steer, *George Mueller: Delighted in God*, Wheaton, IL: Harold Shaw Publishers, 1981, p. 136.

return tit for tat. But grace enables us to accept the wrong without trying to even the score (1 Pet. 2:19-20).

REPAYING EVIL WITH GOOD

Believers are called to reward every wrong with a kindness (Rom. 12:17, 20-21). An Indian was prodding his elephant to move faster along the street in Bombay. He was using a sharp, metal goad. Suddenly the goad fell to the pavement with a loud clanging. The elephant turned around, grasped the goad with its trunk, and held it out to the master.

The world is utterly struck speechless when they see a person who exhibits such brokenness.

HONORING OTHERS ABOVE SELF

Another proof of brokenness is when we esteem others better than ourselves (Phil. 2:3). This does not mean that they have better characters than ours. We esteem them better when we put their interests above our own. When Abraham and Lot came up from Egypt to the vicinity of Bethel, there wasn't enough pastureland to support the herds of both men. So Abraham told Lot to choose what he wanted, and he (Abraham) would take whatever was left (Gen. 13:1-13). He esteemed Lot better than himself.

When someone tried to nit-pick with H. A. Ironside over inconsequential matters, he would say, "Well, brother, when we get to heaven, one of us will be wrong and perhaps it will be me." He put the other man ahead of himself.

Several ministers were waiting in an anteroom to come out to the platform at the appointed time. When one of them, who was unusually loved and respected, emerged from the room, the audience broke out into applause for him, he quickly backed into the anteroom so that the clapping would appear to be for the others. He didn't want them to feel less loved.

PROMPT OBEDIENCE

Brokenness is visible in a person who is prompt in accepting and obeying God's will (Ps. 32:9). This is a lesson that Jonah had to learn the hard way. The colt on which Jesus rode into Jerusalem is a picture of the type of brokenness that God can use (Lk. 19:29-35)

When we are like clay in the hands of the divine Potter, He can mould and make us according to His will.

DEATH TO PUBLIC OPINION

We must come to the place where we are dead to the world's applause or frowns. When W. P. Nicholson was a young believer, he offered to serve with the Salvation Army. Those in charge sent him out with a sandwich board that said, "Dead to Public Opinion." He said he learned a great lesson that day. He was to fear man so little because he feared God so much.

KEEPING ONE'S COOL IN THE CRISIS

A broken person displays poise and equanimity in the crises of life. Delays, interruptions, mechanical breakdowns and accidents, schedule changes, and disappointments are all part of God's plan for him. There should be no frenzy, panic, hysteria, or ruffled feathers. The idea is to react instantly with calmness instead of impatience. A flat tire may be a blessing in disguise (see Rom. 8:28).

Here are some suggestions on how to handle interruptions. The first is from *Reader's Digest*:

> When you are exasperated by interruptions, try to remember that their very frequency may indicate the value of your life. Only the people who are full of

help and strength are burdened by other people's needs. The interruptions that we chafe at are the credentials of our indispensability. The greatest condemnation that anyone could incur—and it is a danger to guard against—is to be so independent, so unhelpful, that nobody ever interrupts us and we are left uncomfortably alone.[28]

The second helpful advice tells how a busy old man mastered the problem:

"Up to some time ago," he testified, "I was always annoyed by interruptions, which was really a form of selfishness on my part. People used to walk in and say, 'Well, I had just two hours to kill, and I thought I would come and see you.' That used to bother me. Then the Lord convinced me that God sends people our way. He sent Philip to the Ethiopian eunuch. He sent Barnabas to look up Saul of Tarsus. The same applies today; God sends people our way.

So when someone comes in, I say, "The Lord must have brought you here. Let us find out why He sent you. Let us have prayer about it."

Well, this does two things. It puts the interview on a different level because God is brought into it. Also it generally shortens the interview. If a person knows that you are looking for a reason why he is there, under God, if he doesn't have one, he soon leaves for greener pastures. So take interruptions from the Lord. Then they belong to your schedule, because God was simply rearranging your daily pattern to suit Him. To the alert Christian, interruptions are only divinely interjected opportunities."[29]

LIVING AS A BONDSLAVE (LUKE 17:7-10)

In his book *The Calvary Road,* Roy Hession describes the proper attitude a bondslave should take toward his servitude. He must be willing to have one thing on top of another put upon him, without

---

28   From *Points to Ponder, Anglican Digest,* Quoted in National Enquirer, quoted in Reader's Digest, Nov. 1977, p. 229.
29   Sanders, J. O. *Spiritual Leadership,* Chicago: Moody Press, 1975, pp. 90-91.

any consideration being given him. In doing this, he must be willing not to be thanked. Having done all this, he must not charge the other with selfishness. Having done all that, there is no ground for pride or self-congratulation, but we must confess that we are unprofitable servants, that is, we are of no real use to God or man in ourselves. The bottom of self is quite knocked out by the fifth and last step— the admission that doing and bearing what we have in the way of meekness and humility, we have not done one stitch more than it was our duty to do.[30]

WHAT BROKENNESS DOES NOT MEAN

The broken man is not a bland, spineless sort of jellyfish, a power-less cipher, exerting no influence on those around him. On the contrary, broken people are the most influential.

Meekness is not weakness. It is strength under control.

A meek man is one who accepts the will of God without resentment, who can afford to be gentle and mild because of inward strength, and who is under the perfect control of God.

Brokenness does not mean that a person is never angry. Jesus was angry with the money changers in the temple courts. We should be lions in God's cause, lambs in our own.

STEPS TO BROKENNESS

The question is, "How can I become a truly broken person?" The answer contains four steps:

1. Pray "Lord, break me" and really mean it.

2. Ransack your past for wrongs never righted, for unkind words, for words spoken in the flesh.

3. Confess them first to God, then to the person wronged.

---

30   Hession, Roy, *The Calvary Road*, Fort Washington, PA: Christian Literature, Crusade, n.d., pp. 58-59.

4. Share the humbling experience with others.

Unfaithful husbands and wives need to apologize to one another. An elder who had left his wife for another woman wrote this letter of apology:

After twenty two years of "riotous living," which I deeply regret, I have returned to God, asking His forgiveness for those years of sin and shame. In His mercy and love, He has drawn me back into fellowship with Himself and with His Son, Jesus Christ. I am now enjoying a peace and sense of well being that I have not experienced for many years. Praise His Name! The words of David in Psalms 32 and 51 have new meaning and joy for me: *"Blessed is the man whose transgressions are forgiven, whose sin is covered. Blessed is the man unto whom the Lord imputeth not iniquity." "I acknowledged my sin unto Thee and mine iniquity have I not hid. I said, I will confess my transgression unto the Lord, and Thou forgavest the iniquity of my sin. Selah."* And in the words of Psalm 51, He has *"restore[d] unto me the joy of Thy salvation."* I can hardly comprehend His grace.

I want to apologize to you and many of my brothers and sisters in Christ for the shame and hurt I have caused. I am sorry for my sin and wish there was some way to make it go away, but I can't do that, and I suppose the memory of those wasted years will haunt me for years to come. I know that many of you have been praying for me, and, to paraphrase Phil. 1:18b-19, *"I know that by means of your prayers and the help which comes from the Holy Spirit, I am free."*

I have written to all my family asking their forgiveness, and rejoicing with all of them in God's answered prayers.

I am now attending a Christian fellowship and have started going to a weekly Bible study. I feel the need of Christian fellowship and am thankful for these opportunities.

Think of what would happen if brokenness were practiced in business circles. One Christian employer wrote the following to his employees:

I spend almost all of my energies and priorities in forwarding my business and in the pursuit of personal pleasure. I practically never read the Bible. My sins in both thought and deed are grave indeed. The 10% I give to God's work is a mockery insofar as sacrificial giving is concerned. I am demanding and critical as a boss. All too often I am harsh and unloving as a husband. I don't attend church without fail like I did as a child.

When people praise me, you can see why I feel like such a fraud. That's why I feel compelled to reveal, with shame, what a miserable example of a Christian I am. Praise no one except ONE.

This letter was sent to 15 million people who received his catalog.

FULL TIME CHRISTIAN WORKERS SHOULD PRACTICE BROKENNESS

Bob Young, a missionary in Africa, had had a falling out with some of his fellow-workers. Then he and his wife came back to the States for the education of their children. Later they felt the Lord leading them to go back to Africa. But his wife suggested that before doing so, they write to the other missionaries and apologize for the way they had handled the doctrinal problem. He wrote a letter of true apology. The missionaries replied, "This is the kind of man we want to work with." The missionary couple returned to Africa, noticed a greater proficiency with the language than they ever had before, and saw blessing everywhere they went.

Oswald Sanders had just finished his message when a deacon rose and asked if he could speak:

"God has been speaking to me this evening," he said. "Most of you people know me, and I want to make a confession. When I am with you in public, I am always jovial and cheery and the life of the party, but at home I am a different person. I have been a street angel and a home devil. I have been bad-tempered and have given my wife and family a bad time. I have asked God to forgive me and to make me in private more like what I have tried to appear in public."[31]

---

31   Sanders, J. Oswald, *Shoe-Leather Commitment*, Chicago, IL: Moody Press, 1990, p. 139.

Think what would happen in our assemblies if all wrongs would be made right, if apologies could be made wherever needed, if grudges could be ended.

Children need to apologize to parents for stealing from their mother's purse, for lying when caught disobeying, and for talking back to parents.

Parents must sometimes apologize to children for unjust or excessive discipline, for being poor examples, and for angry outbursts.

There would be new joy, power, and effectiveness. There would be a tremendous weight lifted off shoulders. There would be better relations than ever existed before.

NINETEEN
KEEP YOURSELF PURE
**NOTE: This chapter discusses sexual issues frankly.
It should be read only by those struggling with these matters.**

The highway of Christian service is littered with the corpses of those who have been ruined by sexual scandal. They began the race with confidence and enthusiasm, but they subsequently fantasized about forbidden pleasures until finally they surrendered to them.

Dr. Howard Hendricks counted 246 men who started out in full-time ministry who experienced moral failure within a two-year period. Almost 250 men were castaways within twenty-four months of each other. That amounts to about ten a month who ended up set aside by the siren of illicit sex. Dr. Paul Beck estimated that a tenth of those who start out in Christian work at twenty-one are still preaching Christ at sixty-five. Nine out of ten fall out. "They're shot down morally, they're shot down with discouragement, they're shot down with liberal theology, they get obsessed with making money."[32]

None of us is safe from falling until we get to heaven.

The sexual drive is a gift of God, intended for procreation, pleasure, and purity. It is for use only in the marriage relationship. Notice the principles that Paul lays down in 1 Corinthians 6:12-20, especially the repetition of the word *"body"* and *"bodies"* eight times.

---

32   Farrar, Steve, *Finishing Strong*, Sisters, OR, Multnomah Press, 1995, p. 6.

Verse 12: God's gifts were not intended to be harmful to oneself or others or enslaving to oneself.

Verse 13: There is a difference between appetite for food and the sexual drive. Food and the stomach will be destroyed. They are temporal. The body is eternal. The body is for the Lord, not for sexual immorality. The Lord is for the body. He is interested in the welfare and holiness of the body.

Verse 14: God shows His interest in the body by the fact that He will raise it from the dead, just as He raised the Lord Jesus.

Verse 15: Our bodies are members of Christ. Think of the sacrilege of taking a member of Christ and joining it to a prostitute, or to any other person outside of marriage.

Verses 16-17: Sex with a harlot is a physical union. Union with the Lord is the deepest of all unions—the union of two spirits. A believer is in Christ and Christ is in the believer.

Verse 18: Sexual immorality is not something to be trifled with. We should flee it. It is the worst sin against the body. It has consequences in the body.

Verse 19: Our bodies are the temple of the Holy Spirit. He actually dwells in us. He is given to us by God. Our bodies are not ours to do with them as we please.

Verse 20: We were bought with a price, the precious blood of Christ. We should use our body and our spirit to glorify the One who owns them.

The sexual drive is admittedly one of the most powerful drives in the human body. Because of this, single men and some married men often give way to a form of self-abuse known as masturbation. It is a self-induced method of finding sexual release apart from intercourse. It is probably true that every normal, healthy young fellow has given way to it at one time or another. What is the scriptural teaching about this practice?[33]

---

33   Adapted from *Doing Time with Jesus* by the author, published by Em-

Strangely enough, the Bible does not deal specifically with the subject. The story of Onan in Genesis 38:1-11 has been often used to indicate God's displeasure with this practice. When Onan's brother died, the law of marriage in those days required that he marry the widow, that is, his sister-in-law, and raise children for his dead brother. Because the children would not be his own, Onan persistently refused and spilled his semen on the ground. For this disobedience, the Lord killed him. It was not because he masturbated but because he disobeyed. His sin was not sexual but selfish.

While there is no scripture dealing directly with the practice, there are several which provide instruction for the conscientious believer. Here are some of them:

Therefore, do not let sin reign in your mortal body, that you should obey it in its lusts. And do not present your members as instruments of unrighteousness to sin, but present yourselves to God as being alive from the dead, and your members as instruments of righteousness to God. For sin shall not have dominion over you, for you are not under law, but under grace (Rom. 6:12-14).

The emphasis here is that we should use the members of our bodies as instruments of righteousness rather than use them in ways that dishonor the Lord.

"But put on the Lord Jesus Christ, and make no provision for the flesh to fulfill its lusts" (Rom. 13:14). Our real purpose here in life is to represent the Lord Jesus and not to live for sexual gratification.

Or do you not know that your body is a temple of the Holy Spirit, who is in you, whom you have from God, and that you are not your own, for you were bought with a price; therefore glorify God in your body (1 Cor. 6:19-20).

The Third Person of the Trinity actually dwells in the body of every believer. Knowing that He is present all the time should keep us from stooping to such an unworthy act.

The wife does not have authority over her own body, but the husband does. And

maus Bible College, Dubuque, IA, pp. 23-25.

likewise the husband does not have authority over his own body, but the wife does" (1 Cor. 7:4).

The basic thought here is that neither spouse should refuse the marriage act when the other one desires it. But beyond that, the fact that a person does not have authority over his own body rules out such self-serving behavior.

"Therefore, having these promises, beloved, let us cleanse ourselves from all filthiness of the flesh and spirit, perfecting holiness in the fear of God" (2 Cor. 7:1). Masturbation is a defilement of both body and mind, and we should cleanse ourselves from it.

"That each of you know how to possess his own vessel in sanctification and honor" (1 Thess. 4:4). The word *"vessel"* here may mean a person's own body. In that case, it means that we should use it only for holy and honorable purposes.

"Flee also youthful lusts; but pursue after righteousness, faith, love, peace with those who call on the Lord out of a pure heart" (2 Tim. 2:22). *"Beloved, I beg you as sojourners and pilgrims, abstain from fleshly lusts which war against the soul"* (1 Pet. 2:11). While such lusts are associated with youth, they are not confined to young people. The Bible says to flee from it and pursue more noble goals. Since this act is often connected with unclean fantasies and lustful thoughts, it should be avoided in accordance with Matthew 5:27-28. There Jesus said that the thought of sin is synonymous with the act. Sin begins in the mind. If we think about it long enough, we will commit it eventually. We should discipline ourselves to think positively and in purity: *"Whatever things are pure...meditate on these things"* (Phil 4:8).

As already mentioned, the general teaching of Scripture is that the only proper use of sex is within the marriage relationship. Since masturbation does not meet this requirement, it is an abuse of a God-given faculty.

Someone has said that the main harm of self-abuse is found "in its insult to self-respect, self-discipline, the power to make strong decisions, and a general sense of fitness." The practice often leaves a tremendous sense of guilt and uncleanness that paralyzes a person as far as Christian service in concerned.

Having said that, we should balance the subject by admitting that the seriousness of the practice has been greatly exaggerated. Even church leaders have issued solemn warnings that it causes sexual impotence, insanity, and nervous breakdowns. These statements are not supported by competent medical evidence.

This battle is one of the most difficult that a young believer has to wage. His strongest resolutions end in failure. His most urgent prayers seem to go unanswered. The struggle seems to be as futile as it is unrelenting. Yet we must not say that there is no hope for victory. That would mean that the Holy Spirit is not powerful enough to enable us to win. We certainly don't have the power to overcome but He does.

Whenever there has been failure, we should remember that there is forgiveness and cleansing through confessing and forsaking the practice (1 Jn. 1:9; Prov. 28:13).

The more we memorize scriptures, and meditate on the pure Word of God, the more we will experience victory in this area. The practice will dwindle down to isolated acts.

Here is the way of deliverance from the power of indwelling sin:
• Present your body daily to the Lord as a living sacrifice (Rom. 12:1-2).
• Spend much time in the Word of God. *"Your word I have hidden in my heart, that I might not sin against You"* (Ps. 119:11).
• Pray in season and out of season. Here are some suggested prayer requests:
      —Keep me from sin.
      —May I never bring dishonor on the Name of the Lord Jesus

by falling into sexual sin.

—Take me home to heaven rather than allowing me to fall.

—May the temptation to sin and the opportunity to sin never coincide.

—Keep me from doing it even if I want to do it.

• Practice sublimation by redirecting the physical drive into paths that are morally, ethically, or spiritually higher. You can do this by keeping busy for the Lord. Too much sleep is not helpful. A better policy is to work yourself to death, then pray yourself alive again. The times of greatest temptation are when you are over-fed and over-slept. King David didn't practice sublimation. He indulged the flesh when he should have been on the battlefield (see 2 Sam. 11:1-27).

In 1 Corinthians 9:27, Paul shares in rather a restrained way how he found victory: *"I discipline my body and bring it into subjection, lest, when I have preached to others, I myself should become disqualified."* In other words, he did not pamper his body with much food, rest, and relaxation. He kept too busy for God during the day to engage in sinful activities and too tired at night to entertain lustful fantasies. When he went to bed, he fell asleep quickly.

• Control the thought life. Be careful what you feed on. TV, pornography, books and magazines that glorify sexual sin are often the open sesame to moral failure.

• Be occupied with Christ (2 Cor. 3:18).

• In the moment of fierce temptation, call on the name of the Lord (Prov. 18:10).

SECTION III
CHRISTIAN LIFE

TWENTY
TOTAL COMMITMENT

All Christians must agree that the atoning work of the Lord Jesus on Calvary's cross is of such enormous significance and value that it requires His followers to be committed to Him. There is no question about the necessity of commitment; that is a foregone conclusion and one that is generally accepted. But there are two unanswered questions: To what extent should we be committed to Him? And how can this be worked out in everyday life?

Ideally we should be *totally* committed. Nothing less than a complete sacrifice of ourselves—spirit, soul, and body—is a fitting response for His sacrifice for us. Many of our hymns express this eloquently. "Love so amazing, so divine, demands my heart, my life, my all." "How can I do less than give Him my best and live for Him completely after all He's done for me?" "How can I make a lesser sacrifice when Jesus gave His all?"

However, there may be a valid question whether any believer is ever *totally committed* to the Savior. Even the apostle Paul had to admit that he had not already attained or was already perfect (Phil. 3:12). When we think of our sins, our failures, our self-centeredness, and our mixed motives, we hesitate to claim that our dedication to the Lord is what it should be.

And yet that need not stop us from striving toward the ideal. Even if we have not arrived, we can press toward the goal. Even if we can't sing, "All to Jesus I surrender" as our present experience, we can sing it as the aspiration of our heart.

So that leads us to examine the whole subject of commitment in scriptural detail. What is commitment? Commitment is giving your life to the Lord to do with it whatever He pleases. It is a definite, well-considered act by which a person chooses Christ's will instead of his own. It is losing your life for His sake and the gospel's. It is giving Him the devotion of your heart and the love of your soul.

> *Whether sickness or health*
> *Whether poverty or riches.*
> *Whether at home or abroad.*
> *Whether single or married.*
> *Whether unknown or well known.*
> *Whether a short life or a long one.*
> *Take me as I am, Lord,*
> *And make me all Thine own.*
> *Make my heart Thy palace*
> *And Thy royal throne.*
> (Author unknown)

Certain words are not in the vocabulary of commitment: "Not so, Lord." "Let me first…" "Not now, but later."

THE RATIONALE OF COMMITMENT

There are weighty reasons for full commitment to Jesus Christ:

1. The mercies of God demand it. "It seems an insult to that love which gave ALL for us, to say that we love, and yet stop to calculate about giving all to Him when our all is but two mites. His all is heaven, earth, eternity, Himself. Better not to love at all. Better to be

cold than lukewarm" (Lady Powerscourt).

"There is a lack of sincerity in committing the eternal soul to God for salvation and then holding back the mortal life. We dare to trust Him to save us from hell and to take us to heaven but we hesitate to let Him control our lives here and now" (R. A. Laidlaw).

2. The only reasonable response to the fact that God the Son died for me. It is our only reasonable service, the most sane, sensible thing we can do in view of the mercies of God. If He died for me, the least I can do is give up my life for Him. "If Jesus Christ is God and died for me, then no sacrifice can be too great for me to make for Him" (C. T. Studd).

"The cross of Christ will never mean anything to you until it takes your breath away and becomes the most important thing in your life" (Harold St. John).

3. It is the sure way to know the guidance of God (Rom. 12:2).

4, Gratitude demands it.

5. We are not our own. At enormous cost, the Lord Jesus purchased us at the cross of Calvary. We belong to Him. If we take our lives and use them the way we want, we are thieves.

> I had known about Jesus dying for me, but I had never understood that if He died for me, then I didn't belong to myself. Redemption means buying back, so that if I belong to Him, either I had to be a thief and keep what wasn't mine, or else I had to give up everything to God. When I came to see that Jesus had died for me, it didn't seem hard to give up all for Him (C. T. Studd).

A village organist twice refused a visitor permission to play the church organ. Finally, he yielded, and the stranger began to play. It was as if the whole church was filled with heavenly music. The organist asked him, "Who are you?"

In modesty the stranger replied, "My name is Mendelssohn."

"What!" said the man, now covered with mortification. "Did I refuse *you* permission to play on my organ?"[34]We should give God credit for knowing how to play our organ better than we can.

6. Jesus is Lord. If He is Lord, He has a right to all. *"To this end Christ died and rose and lived again, that He might be Lord"* (Rom. 14:9).

7. He knows what's best for us better than we do. He knows options of which we are ignorant.

8. It saves us from wasted lives, from trivia. It saves us from being people whose only work is selling balloons on parade days or dark glasses on days when there is a complete eclipse of the sun. Or from rearranging deck chairs on the Titanic or straightening pictures on the walls of a burning house.

One day Steve Jobs, head of Apple Computer, was talking to John Scully, president of Pepsi-Cola. He felt that Scully could better use his ability in the exploding computer industry. Jobs said to Scully, "When are you going to stop selling sweetened water and do something that will change the world?" Scully accepted the challenge.

After the resurrection, Peter said to the other disciples, *"I am going fishing"* (Jn. 21:3). Incredible. He had the message of the world's redemption, and Peter was going fishing.

9. The love of Christ constrains us (2 Cor. 5:14-15). David Livingstone said it "compels us."

10. Christ gives us a new sense of values, of what is important.

Once any man has looked into Christ's eyes and felt the magnetism of His way of life, he is never going to be content with the secular ideals and standard that may have seemed adequate enough before Christ came. Christ has spoiled him for anything else. The old standards of values have become cinders, ashes, dust. Thank God for that.[35]

In his book *Biblical Preaching,* Haddon Robinson quotes Ernest

34   Sanders, J. O., *Shoe Leather Commitment*, Chicago, IL: Moody Press, 1990, pp. 56-57.
35   Stewart, James S. *King For Ever*, Nashville, TN: Abingdon, 1973, pp. 60-61.

Campbell as saying:

> I was struck the other day by Leonard Woolf's view of his life's work. "I see clearly," he said, "that I have achieved practically nothing. The world today and the history of the human anthill during the past 5-7 years would be exactly the same as if I had played Ping-Pong instead of sitting on committees and writing books and memoranda. I have therefore to make a rather ignominious confession that I must have in a long life ground through between 150,000 and 200,000 hours of perfectly useless work."[36]

The cross is of such significance that for the believer who understands it, it has to be everything or nothing.

Failure to commit our lives to Christ is tantamount to yawning in His face. It is saying to Him, "You haven't done anything that merits my allowing You to run my life."

EXAMPLES OF COMMITMENT

Christ (Isa. 6; Heb. 10:7). Our Lord was consumed by zeal for His Father's affairs. His single pure desire was to please Him.

Abraham (Gen. 22:1-19). This man had an unflinching determination to obey God, even if it meant sacrificing life's dearest treasure, his only son, Isaac.

The burnt offering (Lev. 1:13b). The prominent feature of the burnt offering is that it was totally consumed for God. The offering expressed the offerer's desire to live wholly for Him.

The Hebrew bondslave (Ex. 21:2-6; Deut. 15:11-18). When a Jewish slave became eligible for freedom. He could choose to be his master's slave forever.

Ruth (Ruth 1:16-17). This Gentile maiden expressed her commitment in these undying words:

---

36   Haddon W. Robinson, *Biblical Preaching*, Grand Rapids, MI: Baker Book House, 1980, p. 144.

Entreat me not to leave you or to turn back from following after you; for wher-ever you go, I will go; and wherever you lodge, I will lodge; your people shall be my people, and your God, my God. Where you die, I will die, and there will I be buried. The Lord do so to me, and more also if anything but death parts you and me.

Esther (Esther 4:16). At a time when her Jewish people were threatened with extinction, this queen risked her life to plead for them, saying, *"I will go to the king, and if I perish, I perish."*

Shadrach, Meshach, and Abednego (Dan. 3:17-18). Their loy-alty to God caused them to brave a furnace of fire rather than com-promise their faith. To the then-world ruler, they said,

Our God whom we serve is able to deliver us from the burning fiery furnace, and He will deliver us from your hand, O king. But if not, let it be known to you, O king, that we do not serve your gods, nor will we worship the gold image which you have set up.

Thomas Cranmer and the hand that signed the recantation. In a moment of weakness, Bishop Cranmer had signed a recantation of his convictions, but then he reconsidered. Before being burned at the stake, he thrust the hand that had signed the evil document in the fire, saying, "Perish this unworthy hand." He wanted it to be the first part of him to burn.

John Nelson Darby. During a productive life of unflagging devo-tion and service, Darby lived out of a suitcase. One day he sat in a cheap Italian boarding house and sang, "Jesus, I my cross have taken, all to leave and follow Thee." It was true.

C. H. Spurgeon. The "Prince of Preachers" wrote:

In that day when I surrendered myself to my Savior, I gave Him my body, my soul, my spirit. I gave Him all I had and all I shall have for time and eternity. I gave Him all my powers, my faculties, my eyes, my ears, my limbs, my emotions, my judgment, my whole manhood, and all that could come of it.

A. T. Pierson said of him: "Of all the mind he had and all the chance God gave him, he made the most."

William Borden. This son of wealth expressed his dedication like this: "Lord Jesus, I take hands off as far as my life is concerned. I put Thee on the throne in my heart. Change, cleanse, use me as Thou shalt choose. I take the full power of Thy Holy Spirit. I thank Thee."

Betty Stam. Betty meant it when she wrote at the front of her Bible:

Lord, I give up my own purposes and plans, all my own desires, hopes, ambitions, and accept Thy will for my life. I give myself, my all utterly to Thee, to be Thine forever. I hand over to Thy keeping all of my friendships, my love. All the people whom I love are to take second place in my heart. Work out Thy whole will in my life at any cost, now and forever. To me to live is Christ.

George Müller. When Arthur T. Pierson asked George Müller, "What is the secret of your great work and the wonderful things that God has done through you?" Müller looked up for a moment, then bowed his head lower and lower until it was almost between his knees.

He was silent a moment or two and then said, "Many years ago there came a day in my life when George Müller died. As a young man, I had a great many ambitions, but there came a day when I died to all those things, and I said, 'Henceforth, Lord Jesus, not my will but Thine,' and from that day God began to work in and through me."

General Booth. The founder of the Salvation Army said, "When I was a lad of seventeen, I determined that God should have all that there was of William Booth."

Bishop Taylor Smith. He used to kneel by his bed every morning and pray, "Lord Jesus, this bed your altar; myself your living sacrifice."

WHAT HINDERS OUR COMMITMENT?

1. Fear of God's will—of what He might ask. The first thing that comes to people's mind is the mission field. Snakes, scorpions, spiders, swamps, suffocating heat and humidity. But God has a variety of wills for His people. And His will is always good, acceptable, and perfect. "The God of infinite love and wisdom wants only the best for His people."

A young lady said to Graham Scroggie, "I am afraid to make Christ Lord, afraid of what He will ask of me." Wisely Dr. Scroggie turned to the story of Peter at Joppa. The Lord told Peter to rise and eat. Three times Peter responded, *"No, Lord."* Tenderly Scroggie said, "You can say 'No' and you can say 'Lord,' but you can't say 'No, Lord.' I'm going to leave my Bible with you and this pen. You go into another room and cross out the word *No* or *Lord."* The woman returned weeping quietly. Peering over her shoulder, he saw the word *No* crossed out. She was saying, "He's Lord. He's Lord." Such is the stuff of holy obedience.[37]

He doesn't drag reluctant draftees. He wants volunteers. He works in us both to will and to do (Phil. 2:13).

2. Fear of what God will take. This is totally unfounded. Our God doesn't come to take but to give. What's more, His will is good, acceptable and perfect. To be afraid of it is to be afraid of a blessing.

3. Fear of God's denials. We fear He might not want us to get married. (That's not likely. Marriage is His will for most of the human race. If He wants you to be single, He'll give you grace for it and you'll learn that it's better to be single than to be married to the wrong person.) We fear that His will might jeopardize our chance for a lucrative career, a nice home in the suburbs, children, and two cars. Won't it be enough to give our retirement years to Him?

He doesn't want the tail end of a wasted life. He wants the best.

---

37   Foster, Richard, *Freedom of Simplicity*, London: Triangle, SPCK, 1981, pp. 94-95.

Lord, in the fullness of my might
I would for Thee be strong;
While runneth o'er each dear delight,
To Thee should soar my song.
I would not give the world my heart
And then profess Thy love;
I would not feel my strength depart,
And then Thy service prove.
I would not with swift winged zeal
On the world's errands go;
And labor up the heavenly hill
With weary feet and slow.

O not for Thee my weak desires,
My poorer, baser part;
O not for Thee my fading fires,
The ashes of my heart.
O choose me in my golden time,
In my dear joys have part;
For Thee the glory of my prime,
The fullness of my heart. (Thomas H. Gill)

4. Fear of loss of independence. His will might interfere with our love of doing our own thing and doing it our own way. This means giving the best of life to the world, the hands of which are stained with the blood of Christ.

5. Fear of the unknown. When Abraham moved away from home in obedience to the Lord, he learned that it's better to walk in the dark with God than to walk alone in the light. It was better to trust God's eyesight than his own.

6. Fear of loss of security. We fear that we might not have a visible means of support, that we might have to go on welfare. When will we learn that God is our only security, and that if we put Him first, we will never lack the necessities of life.

7. Fear of hardships. Loss of comforts. We think that full surrender means loss of comforts. We will be doomed to outside toilets. We wouldn't be able to take a shower every day. We would have to wear hand-me-down clothing and use early Salvation Army furniture and second hand everything. Those fears are laughable.

8. Fear of inadequacy. People say, "I am not gifted enough for God to use. I am a nobody with no special talents." These folks forget that God loves to use the foolish, weak, base, and despised believers (1 Cor. 1:26-28). If they qualify for any of these titles, God can use them. Then when something happens for God, He gets the glory.

9. Fear of loss of status. We think ourselves too big for Christian service. It's a step down the social ladder. This is nothing but rotten, stinking pride. Consider the following: We may climb the ladder of success and then when we have reached the top, we may find that the ladder was leaning on the wrong wall.

We may barter God's best for His second best.

What are the alternatives to a life of total surrender?
• A life devoted to trivia.
• A saved soul and a lost life.
• An entrance into heaven empty handed.

Cornelius Plantinga Jr. described it like this: "Right now you are making a career of nothing—wandering through malls, killing time, making small talk, watching TV programs until you know the characters better than you know your own family."

DEFECTIVE COMMITMENT

There are at least three clear examples of defective commitment in the New Testament.

1. Ananias and Sapphira (Acts 5:1-11). They pretended to give all

but kept back a part for themselves.

2. Peter's three refusals (Mt. 16:22; Jn. 13:6, 8; Acts 10:13-14). The apostle said, *"Not so, Lord."* You can say, *"Not so,"* and you can say *"Lord,"* but you can't say, *"Not so, Lord."*

3. The men who said, *"Me first"* (Lk. 9:57-62). Three men said they wanted to follow Christ, but they put their own interests ahead of His.

FULL SURRENDER

It's a crisis. There has to be a first time when we put our lives on the altar in total commitment. There may be an enormous struggle. *"Being in an agony, He prayed more earnestly, and His sweat was as it were great drops of blood falling down to the ground."*

"Give Him all there is of you. No half measures, no broken pieces, no reservations, no keeping part of the gift and no pretending that the part is the whole. There is an impressive unity and simplicity about the life that undistractedly loves and serves God with the whole heart. Such a life will not be easily seduced from its first love" (Anon.).

"There is something fitting about young people with talents and potential laying it all at the Savior's feet" (Author unknown).

There may be no necessary emotional experience. No lights, bells, or shivers in your nervous system. But there will be a sense of only giving up what you have ceased to love.

David Livingston said, "It's a pity I don't have more to give."

> *Poor is our sacrifice whose eyes*
> *Are lighted from above.*
> *We offer what we cannot keep,*
> *What we have ceased to love.*

Isaac Watts wrote:

> *Forbid it, Lord, that I should boast*
> *Save in the death of Christ my God;*
> *All the vain things that charm me most,*
> *I sacrifice them to His blood.*

Homer Grimes asked and then answered:

> *What shall I give Thee, Master?*
> *Thou who hast died for me.*
> *Shall I give less than all I possess*
> *Or shall I give all to Thee?*
> *Jesus, my Lord and Savior,*
> *Thou hast given all for me.*
> *Not just a part, or half of my heart,*
> *I will give all to Thee.*

Charlotte Elliott put it this way:

> *Just as I am, Thy love unknown*
> *Has broken every barrier down;*
> *Now to be Thine, yea, Thine alone,*
> *O Lamb of God, I come, I come.*

E. H. Swinstead answered yes:

> *Jesus, Lord and Master, love divine has conquered,*
> *I will henceforth answer Yes to all Thy will.*
> *Free from Satan's bondage, I am Thine forever;*
> *Henceforth all Thy purposes in me fulfill.*

This is the way Cecil J. Allen verbalized his full surrender:

> *His hands, and feet, and heart, all three*
> *Were pierced for me on Calvary,*
> *And here and now, to Him I bring*
> *My hands, feet, heart an offering.*

J. Sidlow Baxter saw the reasonableness of total commitment:

O Christ, Thy bleeding hands and feet,
Thy sacrifice for me,
Each wound, each tear demands my life
A sacrifice for Thee.

Baxter also wrote:

Dear Cross, I hear Thy pleading voice.
To spurn I cannot move.
My heart is conquered, take my all
For less insults Thy love.

Frances Havergal offered herself to be Christ's forever:

Take my love, my God I pour
At Thy feet its treasure-store.
Take myself and I will be
Ever, only, all for Thee.

In another poem, Frances expressed it like this:

In full and glad surrender, I give myself to Thee
Thine utterly and only and evermore to be.
O Son of God who lovest me, I will be Thine alone,
And all I am and all I have shall henceforth be Thine own.

Thomas O. Chisholm also yielded his life for Jesus alone:

O Jesus, Lord, and Master
I give myself to Thee
For Thou in Thine atonement
Did'st give Thyself for me.
I own no other master,
My heart shall be Thy throne.
My life I give henceforth to live
O Christ, for Thee alone.

Betty Daasvand's logic drove her to write:

> *After all He's done for me,*
> *After all He's done for me,*
> *How can I do less than give Him my best*
> *And live for Him completely*
> *After all He's done for me.*

Isaac Watts saw total commitment as the only proper response to Calvary love:

> *Thus might I hide my blushing face*
> *While His dear cross appears;*
> *Dissolve my heart in thankfulness,*
> *And melt my eyes to tears.*
> *But drops of grief can ne'er repay*
> *The debt of love I owe;*
> *Dear Lord, I give myself away*
> *'Tis all that I can do.*

One final verse from Avis B. Christiansen:

> *Only one life to offer—take it, dear Lord, I pray;*
> *Nothing from Thee withholding, Thy will I now obey.*
> *Thou who hast freely given Thine all in all for me,*
> *Claim this life for Thine own to be used, my Savior,*
> *Every moment for Thee.*

All these poets would agree with Henry Bosch when he wrote: "Instead of charting your own future, seek God's direction. Because His will is based on His infinite love and wisdom, you may be sure that your highest joy and greatest fulfillment will be found in doing what He wants you to do."

Total commitment is not only a crisis, a first time experience. It is a process. We must renew the commitment day by day. Then we go about, doing the things that our hands find to do. We kill ourselves with work, then pray ourselves alive again. God guides us when we are in motion. He does not reveal the blueprint all at once. It's an unfolding scroll.

We must stay close to the Word. Commitment to Christ involves giving a major place to the Bible. I cannot be devoted to the Living Word without being devoted to the written Word, and spending time in the Word every day shows this devotion. It is shown also in studying, memorizing, meditating on, and obeying what we read. God's Word will be in our hearts: we will teach it to our children; we will talk about them when we sit in our house, when we walk by the way, when we lie down, when we rise up; we will bind them as a sign on our hands (our actions) and as frontlets before our eyes (our desires); we will write them on the doorpost of our house and on our gates (see Deut. 6:6-9). In other words, the Bible will permeate every area of our lives.

In our hectic world it takes tons of discipline to turn off the claims of social life and to put away the *TV Guide* and the remote control in order to devote ourselves to the consecutive, systematic study of the Word, but it's part of the price to be paid if we are going to give our utmost for His highest.

We must spend much time in prayer. The dedicated disciple is a person of prayer. Commitment involves communion, and communion means spending time with the Person we love. The Savior does not have first place in my life if my contacts with Him are occasional, spasmodic, brief, and hurried. On the other hand, the more I love Him, the more I will want to fellowship with Him at the throne of grace. There is no pat answer to the question, "How much time should I spend in prayer?" That depends on our work schedule, our home responsibilities, the length of our prayer list, and the prayer burdens that the Lord lays on our heart. In addition to regular prayer times, we can practice extemporaneous prayer. And even insomnia can be harnessed for prayer.

I want my life so cleared of self
That my dear Lord may come
And set up His own furnishings
And make my heart His home.
And since I know what this requires,
Each morning while it's still,
I slip into that secret room,
And leave with Him—my will.
He always takes it graciously,
Presenting me with His;
I'm ready then to meet the day
And any task there is.
And this is how my Lord controls
My interests, my ills;
Because we meet at break of day
For an exchange of wills. (Anne Grannis)

Harold Wildish had this advice pasted in the front of his Bible:

As you leave the whole burden of your sin and rest upon the finished work of Christ, so leave the whole burden of your life and service, and rest upon the present inworking of the Holy Spirit. Give yourself up morning by morning to be led by the Holy Spirit, and go forth praising and at rest, leaving Him to manage you and your day. Cultivate the habit all through the day of joyfully depending on and obeying Him, expecting Him to guide, to enlighten, to reprove, to teach, to use, and to do in and with you what He wills. Count upon His working as a fact, altogether apart from sight or feelings. Only let us believe in and obey the Holy Spirit as the Ruler of our lives, and cease from the burden of trying to manage ourselves. Then shall the fruit of the Spirit appear in us, as He wills, to the glory of God.

What will life be like when you turn over control of your life to the Lord? You will notice that the gears mesh. Life will sparkle with the supernatural. There will be a marvelous converging of circumstances.

You will sense you are smack in the middle of God's will, and you wouldn't want to be anywhere else, or doing anything else. You will be radioactive with the Holy Spirit. You will know that God is working in and through you, and that when you touch other lives something will happen for God. But it happens without making you proud.

There will be occasional mountain peak experiences, but most of life will be routine and sometimes humdrum. God's plan will emerge step by step.

THE CHALLENGE OF COMMITMENT

In describing the coronation of a monarch in Westminster Abbey, John Stott said that one of the most moving moments was just before the coronation, just before the crown was placed on his or her head. The Archbishop of Canterbury calls four times toward the four points of the compass in the Abbey, "Sirs, I present to you the undoubted king of the realm. Are you willing to do him homage?" And not until a great affirmative shout had thundered down the nave of Westminster Abbey four times was the crown brought out and placed on his head.

Ladies and gentlemen, I present unto you the Lord Jesus Christ as your undoubted Lord and Savior. Are you willing to do Him homage by turning your life over to Him?

There is a sense in which the call of Christ comes to every man and woman, every young man and young woman. If we refuse to follow Him for any reason, He will get others to do so—others who are as good as we are, or better. But we will never get a better Christ to serve.

At a conference in Ben Lippen, North Carolina, a young woman was giving testimony to her call to service. In the course of her message, she held up a blank piece of paper, saying that it contained God's will for her life. The only writing on it was her signature at the bottom. Then she said, 'I have accepted

God's will without knowing what it is, and I am leaving it to Him to fill in the details.' She was a true disciple, and she was on safe ground. With such a yielded will, the Holy Spirit would be able to guide her mental processes as she moved along the path of life.[38]

Theodore Monod describes the road to full surrender as it unfolded in his life:

Oh, the bitter shame and sorrow
That a time could ever be,
When I let the Savior's pity
Plead in vain, and proudly answered,
"All of self, and none of Thee."

Yet He found me; I beheld Him,
Bleeding on the accursed tree;
Heard Him pray, "Forgive, them, Father";
And my wistful heart said faintly,
"Some of self and some of Thee."

Day by day His tender mercy,
Healing, helping, full and free,
Sweet and strong and, oh, so patient,
Brought me lower, while I whispered,
"Less of self, and more of Thee."

Higher than the highest heavens,
Deeper than the deepest sea,
Lord, Thy love at last has conquered,
"None of self and all of Thee."

---

38   Sanders, J. O., *Shoe Leather Commitment*, Chicago, IL: Moody Press, 1990, p. 31.

TWENTY-ONE
YOU CAN KNOW FOR SURE

It hardly needs mentioning that before anyone ventures to disciple someone else, he should have assurance of his own salvation and should be able to explain how it is obtained. God wants His people to enjoy their salvation, but you can't enjoy it if you don't know you have it, nor can you explain the biblical way of assurance to others.

Paul knew he was saved (2 Tim. 1:12). The Ephesian believers knew it (Eph. 2:8). So did John and Peter (1 Jn. 3:2; 1 Pet. 1:3-5). We should, too.

Let's come right to the point. Assurance of salvation comes first and foremost through the Word of God. For instance, we read in John 5:24 that if you hear His word and believe on the One who sent Him, you have eternal life. You will not come into judgment. You have passed from death to life.

Who is the Speaker here?
It is Jesus (see v. 19).
Can He lie?
No.
Can He deceive?
No.
Can He be deceived?
No.

If He said it, is it true?

Yes.

All right. He says, *"He who hears My Word."* This means more than hears with the ears. It means hears and responds. It means hears and believes. So ask yourself, Have I believed on Jesus as my Lord the best way I know how?

You answer, "Yes."

What else does Jesus say?

He says I must believe on the One who sent Him.

Who sent Jesus?

God the Father sent Him.

Why did He send Him?

He sent Him to pay the penalty for my sins.

Do you believe that?

Yes.

What does the Lord say next?

He says, *"has everlasting life."*

Do you have eternal life?

At this point some will say no.

Why do you say no?

Because I don't feel any different.

Read it again. Does it say you will *feel* you have eternal life?

No.

What does it say?

It says, *"has eternal life."*

Do you have eternal life?

Yes.

How do you know?

Because Jesus says so in the Bible.

It's just as simple as that—hearing, believing, having. God wants us to base our salvation on the surest thing in the universe—His

Word. Assurance of salvation does not come through feelings. Members of the Mormon Church say, "I know it's true because I have a burning in my bosom." But such feelings are unreliable. Feelings are fickle and changeable. And they can be controlled by the devil.

Ask the thief on the cross: **Are you saved?**
Yes.
Do you feel that you are saved?
No, all I feel is pain.
Do you know you are saved?
Yes.
How do you know?
Because I heard the Lord say to me, *"Today you will be with Me in paradise."*

He got his assurance of salvation through the oral words of Jesus. Today we get it through the written Word.

An unknown writer said,

> *God does not ask the soul to say,*
> *"Thank God I feel so good,"*
> *But turns the eye another way*
> *To Jesus and His Word.*

When an acquaintance asked Martin Luther if he felt that his sins had been forgiven, he replied, "No, but I'm as sure of it as that there's a God in heaven."

> *For feelings come and feelings go,*
> *And feelings are deceiving.*
> *My warrant is the Word of God.*
> *Naught else is worth believing.*
> *Though all my heart should feel condemned*
> *For want of some sweet token,*

There is One greater than my heart,
Whose word cannot be broken.
I'll trust in God's unchanging word,
Till soul and body sever,
For though all things shall pass away,
His word will stand forever.

It was Dr. Ironside who said, "I don't know I'm saved because I feel happy, but I feel happy because I know I'm saved."

Dr. C. I. Scofield of *Reference Bible* fame said, "Justification takes place in the mind of God and not in the nervous system of the believer." God reckons us righteous when we believe. We don't necessarily feel it, but we know it because the Bible says so.

George Cutting, the author of *Safety, Certainty, and Enjoyment,* helps us by saying: "It's the blood that makes us safe. It's the Word that makes us sure."

John Wesley wrote,

Frames and feelings fluctuate.
These can ne'er your Savior be!
Learn in Christ yourself to see.
Then be feelings what they will,
Jesus is your Savior still.

Isaac trusted that he was feeling the hairy arm of Esau, but it was Jacob's arm. He was deceived.

We said earlier that assurance comes first and foremost through the Word—but not exclusively. As a person grows in the Christian life, his assurance is confirmed in many ways. He is aware that God is producing changes in him.

- He has a desire to obey the Lord (1 Jn. 2:3-6, 17).
- His life becomes righteous (1 Jn. 2:29).
- He begins to hunger and thirst after purity, goodness, and truth (Gal. 5:22-24).

- He loves the brethren (1 Jn. 3:11, 14).
- Prayer is instinctive for him (Gal. 4:6).
- He loves the Word of God (1 Pet. 2:2).
- He hates sin (Ps. 97:10).
- He has a desire to share his faith with others (Acts 4:20).
- He has an awareness of temptation and opposition (1 Cor. 10:13; 1 Jn. 3:13)
- He patiently endures (Heb. 10:36; 12:5-11).
- He is addicted to good works (Tit. 2:14; James 2:14-26).

Is it presumption for a person to say that he is saved? If salvation were by works, then it would be presumption. In that case, salvation would be either earned or deserved. But salvation is a free gift. To accept that gift by faith does not involve human merit or attainment, and leaves no room for boasting.

The real presumption is in calling God a liar (1 Jn. 5:10). God says, *"He who has the Son has life"* (1 Jn. 5:12). To disbelieve that verse is saying that God isn't telling the truth.

Someone may ask at this point, "But how do I know if I have believed in the right way?" The answer is easy. If trusting the Lord Jesus Christ is your only hope for eternal salvation, then you have believed in the right way and are as saved as God can make you.

Another problem! I don't know the day and the hour when I first trusted Christ. That is possible. Some people can point to the exact time when they first accepted the Lord Jesus. Others (including me) do not know. The important thing is to know at this moment that Jesus died for your sins at Calvary and that you are trusting Him as your Lord and Savior. God knows the moment when you first reached out and touched the hem of Christ's garment, but if you don't know and want to, why don't you do it now?

A sensitive soul asks, "If I were saved, would I have the thoughts that I have, say the things that I say, or do the things that I do?" We still have the old nature after we are saved. It is not improved. We have within us the seed of every sin. But we have the indwelling Spirit. He gives a greater awareness of indwelling sin than we ever had before. Although we are capable of every sin, we have the power not to commit them. We are not sinless, but we do sin less. Satan often sows doubts in our mind concerning our salvation. At such a time, the remedy is to quote the Word, just as Jesus did in His temptation in the desert.

One final question: I have trusted Christ but I don't have the witness of the Spirit. Shouldn't I have the witness of the Spirit? Yes, you should, but what do you think the witness of the Spirit is? If you think it is some mysterious feeling that sweeps over you, some ringing of bells, flashing of lights, and tingling in your nervous system, then I understand your difficulty. But the witness of the Spirit is not a feeling. He witnesses through the Word of God.

Let me illustrate from 1 John 5:13: *"These things I have written unto you that believe in the name of the Son of God, that you may know that you have eternal life..."* Take the verse phrase by phrase:

"These things." John is referring primarily to his first epistle.

"I have written." The *"I"* is the apostle John. But in a wider sense the writer is God since He inspired the Scriptures. So when we read *"These things I have written..."* we can hear God referring to His authorship of the Bible.

"To you that believe in the name of the Son of God." When we read that, we ask ourselves, "Have I believed in the name of the Son of God?" We answer, "Yes, I am trusting solely on the merits of Christ for eternal life."

"That you may know that you have eternal life." It is not a question of feeling. It does not say "that you may feel." Possession of eternal life is something you can know. Since you have believed, the Spirit witnesses to you on the authority of God's Word that you have eternal life. In other words, the Spirit witnesses through the Bible, the infallible Word of God.

TWENTY-TWO
ETERNAL SALVATION

If your disciple is truly saved, then he should know that he is saved forever. Not only so, he should be able to prove this from the Bible.

First of all, there are positive statements to this effect. Take John 10:27-29, for example:

My sheep hear My voice, and I know them, and they follow Me. And I give them eternal life, and they shall never perish; neither shall anyone snatch them out of My hand. My Father, who has given them to Me, is greater than all; and no one is able to pluck them out of My Father's hand.

Jesus said that no sheep of His will ever perish. If that ever happened, then Jesus said something that isn't true. In that case He is not God and our faith is futile.

There are numerous other verses that say that our salvation is eternal. Here are a few:

For God so loved the world that He gave His only begotten Son, that whoever believes in Him should not perish but have everlasting life (Jn. 3:16).

He who believes in the Son has everlasting life; and He who does not believe the Son shall not see life, but the wrath of God abides on Him (Jn. 3:36).

Jesus answered and said to her, "Whoever drinks of this water shall thirst again. But whoever drinks of the water that I shall give him will never thirst. But the water that I shall give him will become in him a fountain of water springing up into everlasting life (Jn. 4:13-14).

Most assuredly, I say to you, he who hears My word and believes in Him who sent Me has everlasting life, and shall not come into judgment, but has passed from death into life (Jn. 5:24).

Most assuredly, I say to you, he who believes in Me has everlasting life (Jn. 6:47).

And this is eternal life, that they may know You, the only true God, and Jesus Christ whom you have sent (Jn. 17:3).

There are other ways by which we can know that we will never perish. The moment we are saved we receive the seal of the Spirit (Eph. 1:13b). The Holy Spirit is the seal. He is a mark or pledge of ownership and of security. He is our seal for the day of redemption, that is, until we reach heaven (Eph. 4:30).

The Holy Spirit is also given to us as a guarantee, sometimes called an earnest or a down payment (Eph. 1:14). He is *"the guarantee of our inheritance until the redemption of the purchased possession, to the praise of His glory."* This means that just as surely as we have the Holy Spirit, we will one day have the full inheritance, including the glorified body.

Here is another proof of our eternal security. We are *"in Christ."* God sees us *"in Christ"* and accepts us, not because of who we are or what we are, but because we are *"in Him."*

God would have to find some sin or imperfection in Christ before He could condemn us. This is clearly impossible.

We are also members of the body of Christ (1 Cor 12:13). It is inconceivable that Christ should spend eternity in heaven with missing members.

But now we must face the question, "What happens when a Christian sins? Doesn't he lose his salvation?" To find the answer consider the following facts:

When we are saved, we are forgiven as far as the eternal penalty of all our sins, past present and future. They were all future when Jesus died for us. God will never remember them again.

At that time, a new relationship is formed. We become children of God by faith in Jesus. Nothing can break a relationship. You cannot cease being the child of your earthly father. And it is true also of your heavenly father.

When we sin, our fellowship with God is broken. Not out relationship, but our fellowship. Relationship is an unbreakable chain, whereas fellowship is a tender thread. The happy family spirit remains broken until we confess our sins.

Notice this carefully. We receive forgiveness of the eternal penalty of our sins when we believe on the Lord Jesus Christ. That is a once for all forgiveness. We receive forgiveness of our sins as believers when we confess and forsake them (1 Jn. 1:9). This takes place constantly in the Christian life. In John 13:10, Jesus taught that there is one bath of regeneration but many washings.

There is a difference between occasional sin and the practice of sin. We all sin (1 Jn. 1:8, 10; 2:2b) but we do not practice sin. We are not sinless but we do sin less. Sin dominates the life of a sinner (1 Jn. 3:4-9). In this passage, John uses the present continuous tense. Read it like this: "Whoever practices sin also practices lawlessness. Whoever abides in Him does not go on sinning. Whoever practices sin has neither seen Him nor known Him. He who practices righteousness is righteous. He who goes on sinning is of the devil, for the devil has sinned from the beginning. Whoever has been born of God does not sin habitually."

The Bible makes distinctions which, if observed, prevent a person from believing that a believer can be lost.

There is the difference between a true believer and a pretender. A person can say he is a Christian even if he has never been born again.

185

In the parable of the wheat and tares (Mt. 13:24-30), the wheat pictures genuine believers whereas the tares are clearly pretenders. Tares look like wheat but that's as far as the similarity goes.

There is a difference between a backslider and an apostate. A backslider is a child of God who is out of fellowship with the Lord. An apostate is a person who once professed to believe but then completely abandoned the Christian faith. Peter was a backslider but Judas was an apostate. Four passages that describe apostates are Hebrews 6:4-8, 10:26-31, and 1 John 2:18-28; 5:16.

There is a difference between reformation and regeneration. Two passages that describe reformation are Matthew 12:43-45 and 2 Peter 2:18-22.

We must be careful to distinguish the root and fruit of salvation. Faith is the root; we are saved by believing in Christ. Good works are the fruit.

Many people have been disturbed by passages with an unsettling "if" in them:

> ...if indeed we suffer with Him, that we may also be glorified together (Rom. 8:17).

> Moreover, brethren, I declare to you the gospel which I preached to you, which also you received and in which you stand, by which also you are saved if you hold fast that word which I preached to you—unless you believed in vain (1 Cor. 15:1-2).

> Yet now He has reconciled [you] if indeed you continue in the faith, grounded and steadfast, and are not moved away from the hope of the gospel (Col. 1:21, 23).

What follows each of these "ifs" is a description of what true believers are like, not how they were born again.

But doesn't James say we are justified by works? Yes, he does (Jas. 2:24). But he does not mean works rather than faith, or even faith plus works. He is insisting that we are saved by the kind of faith that results in good works. Faith is invisible. Works make it visible. Abraham's good work was willingness to slay his son. Rahab's good work was willingness to betray her city. They were only valuable in that they demonstrated real faith that was already there. Without faith they would have been bad works.

Then we must distinguish whether a passage is speaking of salvation or service. In 1 Corinthians 9:27 Paul is speaking of service: *"But I discipline my body and bring it into subjection, lest, when I have preached to others, I myself should become disqualified."*

He did not fear losing his salvation, but he feared being disqualified as a servant of the Lord. He did not want to be put on the shelf.

We must see the difference between salvation and fruitbearing. John is speaking of the latter in John 15:1-8. Be careful in reading verse 8. It does not say that God casts out a non-abiding Christian and casts him in the fire. It says the indefinite "they." In other words, men do it. The world has nothing but contempt for a Christian who is not living the abiding life. They take the testimony of such a person and cast it in the fire.

Be aware of the difference between salvation and discipleship. A disciple may be unfit for service in the kingdom (Lk. 9:62) and yet be fit for heaven through the merits of the Lord Jesus. The following passages deal with discipleship rather than the way of salvation: Luke 9:23; 14:26, 33; John 12:25.

In Galatians 6:8 Paul writes, *"For he who sows to the flesh will of the flesh reap corruption, but he who sows to the Spirit will of the reap everlasting life."* Does this teach that a Christian can lose his salvation? Not at all. Here everlasting life means life in its fullness. There will be degrees of enjoyment of everlasting life in the future state. Everyone will be happy but some will have a greater capacity for enjoying heaven than other. Faithful stewardship of money is one way of determining that capacity.

In handling the subject of eternal security, it is of first importance to assemble clear statements that say that the believer has life that is everlasting and that he can never perish. There are many other passages that require eternal security even though they do not say it in so many words. Finally it is of great importance to see controversial verses in their context. Are the verses speaking about salvation or about some other subject? Finally, we must not build our doctrine on human experience ("I knew a man who...").

The Word of God is our authority.

For a more in depth treatment of this subject, a disciple should refer to the book *Once in Christ, In Christ Forever* by the same author.

TWENTY-THREE
BE BAPTIZED

In discipling another person, you want to be sure that he understands the meaning of baptism and that he himself has been baptized. You should lead him through the following questions and answers step by step.

WHAT IS BAPTISM?

Christian baptism is a ceremony by which a new believer publicly declares himself to be a follower of the Lord Jesus Christ. He is saying goodbye to his former way of life. In figure, he is testifying that he died with Christ, was buried with Christ, and rose to walk in newness of life.

Baptism is a pledge of allegiance to Jesus as Lord. It is a symbolic burial of the old self. It is also a commitment to live in obedience to Christ.

WHO SHOULD BE BAPTIZED?

Everyone who claims to have been born again through faith in Christ should be baptized. This ceremony is not a guarantee that the person has actually been saved. That will be demonstrated to others by the evidence of a transformed life as time goes on. Baptism is on the basis of a person's profession that he has trusted Christ for salvation.

WHEN SHOULD IT BE DONE?

In the New Testament, the church practiced instant baptism. As soon as a person repented and believed on the Savior, he or she was baptized. There was no waiting period.

BY WHOM SHOULD IT BE DONE?

In the Great Commission (Mt. 28:19), Jesus taught His disciples to baptize those who embraced the Christian faith. Nowhere is it even hinted that only those who have been "ordained by men" can administer the ordinances of the church.

HOW SHOULD IT BE DONE?

The early church practiced baptism by immersion, that is, by momentarily lowering the person completely under water, then raising him or her up. In later years some churches adopted the practice of daubing, sprinkling, or pouring water on the head.

Jesus baptized in Aenon because there was much water there (Jn. 3:23). When Philip baptized an Ethiopian eunuch, they both went down into the water, both Philip and the official, and they both came up out of the water (Acts 8:38-39). Only immersion pictures the real meaning of baptism; it is the burial of the old man and the rising of the new person in Christ (Rom. 6:4). Only immersion symbolizes the truth of being planted together in the likeness of [Christ's] death (Rom. 6:5).

SHOULD BABIES BE BAPTIZED?

You will search the Scriptures in vain for any reference to infant baptism. The Bible is silent on the subject. Some church rituals actually say that baptism makes a baby a member of Christ and an inheritor of the kingdom of God. This unbiblical teaching is not only a denial of the true gospel but is disproved by the subsequent lives of many who were baptized as babies.

IS BAPTISM NECESSARY?

It is not necessary for salvation. Over 150 times in the New Testament, salvation is stated to be a free gift to those who put their trust in the Person and work of the Lord Jesus.

If baptism were necessary for salvation, why did Jesus never baptize anyone (Jn. 4:1-2)? Or why did Paul rejoice that he had baptized only a few? (1 Cor. 1:14-16). How did the thief who was crucified with the Lord go to heaven without being baptized (Lk. 23:43)? If Christ finished the work necessary for our salvation (Jn. 19:30), why is it necessary to add baptism to His finished work? When the household of Cornelius believed, they received the Holy Spirit and were thus saved. It was after this that they were baptized (Acts 10:44).

But baptism *is* necessary for obedience. It was commanded in the Gospel of Matthew, practiced in the book of Acts, and expounded in Romans 6. It is one of the two ordinances of the Christian church (the other is the Lord's Supper), and is therefore important. A person may go to heaven unbaptized, but he will be unbaptized for all eternity. It is something we can do on earth to please the heart of Christ that we won't be able to do in heaven.

WHAT ABOUT VERSES THAT ARE OFTEN USED TO TEACH THAT BAPTISM IS NECESSARY FOR SALVATION?

John 3:5: *"Jesus answered, 'Most assuredly, I say to you, unless one is born of water and the Spirit, he cannot enter the kingdom of God.'"* There is no mention of baptism here. Water is sometimes used as a type or symbol of the Word and of the Holy Spirit but never of baptism. The Jews did have what was known as proselyte baptism for Gentiles who converted to Judaism, but Jesus could not be talking to

Nicodemus about this because Nicodemus was not a convert; he was not only a born Jew but also a ruler of the Jews. Jesus could not be talking about Christian baptism because the Christian church did not come into being until later at Pentecost.

Ephesians 5:26: *"That He might sanctify and cleanse it with the washing of water by the Word."* There is no mention of baptism here. The washing of water is by the Word, not by baptism.

Titus 3:5: *"...according to His mercy He saved us, through the washing of regeneration and renewing of the Holy Spirit."* There is no mention of baptism here. *"The washing of regeneration"* means the cleansing that is produced by the new birth.

Mark 16:16: *"He who believes and is baptized will be saved; but he who does not believe will be condemned."* Here baptism is not the means of salvation but the expected public confession that follows. The last half of the verse shows that faith alone is the means of salvation.

Acts 2:38: *"Then Peter said to them, 'Repent, and let every one of you be baptized in the name of Jesus Christ for the remission of sins; and you shall receive the gift of the Holy Spirit.'"* This was spoken to the men of Israel (Acts 2:22), the nation that was guilty in a special way of the death of the Son of God (Acts 2:23). By being baptized, believing Jews separated themselves from that guilty nation. They saved themselves from that perverse generation (Acts 2:40). Only then would the Lord send the Holy Spirit on them.

This applies also to Acts 22:16. By being baptized as a Christian, Saul of Tarsus washed away his sins connected with the death of Christ and the persecution of His people. Only Jews were ever told to be baptized for the remission of sins.

Acts 2:38 could also mean "be baptized because your sins have been forgiven as a result of your repentance." When we see a poster "Wanted for Murder," it does not mean "Wanted in order to commit murder" but "Wanted because a murder has been committed." The word *"for"* in verse 38 could mean "because of."

1 Peter 3:21: *"There is also an antitype which now saves us, namely baptism (not the removal of the filth of the flesh, but the answer of a good conscience toward God), through the resurrection of Jesus Christ."* The deliverance of Noah and his family is a picture of our salvation. Notice the following: The ark is a picture of Christ. The flood is a symbol of the judgment of God. The ark was the only way of salvation from God's judgment. The ark was baptized in the water. Those who were in the ark were saved by the baptism of the ark. Those who were in the water perished.

Now notice the antitype: Christ is the only way of escape from God's judgment. He was baptized in the water of divine wrath. He likened His death to a baptism. *"I have a baptism to be baptized with, and how distressed I am till it is accomplished"* (Lk. 12:50. See also Ps. 42:7 and Mt. 20:22).

Those who are in Christ, that is, who believe on Him are saved. Those who were literally baptized in the waters of the flood perished. So the passage cannot be used to teach salvation by baptism.

We are saved, not by our own baptism, but by Christ's baptism to death at Calvary.

With regard to these verses that are used to teach salvation by baptism, it needs to be repeated that no few verses can contradict the mass of verses that teach salvation by faith alone.

Spurgeon was right when he wrote:

You might hold a man in an everlasting shower but you could not make him a "member of Christ" thereby. Or you might drag him through the Atlantic Ocean, and if he survived the immersion, yet still he would not be one jot the better. The door is not baptism, but Christ. If you believe on Christ, you are a member of His church. If your trust is stayed upon Christ, who is God's great way of salvation, you have evidence that you were chosen by Him from before the foundation of the world—and that faith of yours entitles you to all the privileges which Christ has promised in His Word to believers.

TWENTY-FOUR
THE LORD'S SUPPER
LUKE 22:7-20; 1 CORINTHIANS 11:23-34

On the night of His betrayal, the Lord Jesus instituted what has come to be known as the Lord's Supper, a meeting designed to constantly remind His people of His death for them. By partaking of bread and the fruit of the vine, they remember that God the Son gave His body and shed His blood for their redemption.

It is an act of obedience to the clear request of the Savior, *"This do in remembrance of Me"* (1 Cor. 11:25). And it is one of the ways we have to please Him that we only have in this life.

When we gather to remember Him in this way, we can claim Matthew 18:20 that He is there with us. For us this is one of the greatest possible privileges. We appropriate His presence by faith.

Vernon Schlief illustrates this well in his book *Our Great Adventure in Faith.*

One Lord's Day morning, when the Christians were gathered together to remember the Lord, my great-grandmother happened to lift up her head to glance out of the window and was startled to see their barn in the distance burning, with great flames licking at the roof. She nudged her husband and whispered excitedly in his ear, "John, our barn's on fire." Without so much as lifting His head, he whispered back to her, "Hush, we're in the presence of the Lord."[39]

Remembrance of the Lord leads inevitably to worship, thanksgiving, and praise. At such a time, a person achieves his highest destiny—the worship of God. He satisfies the desire of God for worshipers (Jn. 4:23). And he saves himself from being a cleansed leper who fails to return to give thanks (Lk. 17:12-19).

The Bible does not say how often we should observe the Lord's Supper. Jesus said, *"as often as"* (1 Cor. 11:26). The disciples did it every Lord's Day (Acts 20:7). We can show the measure of our love for Him by following their example. There is no danger of its becoming commonplace. Calvary provides reason for ceaseless adoration.

Faithful attendance at the Lord's Supper has a sanctifying influence on a believer. He or she confesses and forsakes all known sin before participating (1 Cor. 11:27-32). In partaking of the bread and wine, the worshiper has a vivid reminder of what his sins cost the Savior, a powerful deterrent to go on in sin. Added to that is the fact that we become like what we worship. The more we gaze upon Him, the more we are changed into His image by the Spirit of the Lord (2 Cor. 3:18).

We have an appointment with the Lord, and He misses us when we are not there. We know this from Luke 7:45-46. If He missed the Pharisee's kiss and the anointing of His feet with fragrant oil, certainly He misses the love we could have lavished on Him but didn't.

---

39   Vernon Schlief, *Our Great Adventure in Faith*, Grand Rapids, MI: Beeline Books, 1976, P.13.

TWENTY-FIVE
NOW CONCERNING GUIDANCE

The most important factor is determining the guidance of God is a person's own spiritual condition. Notice!

As for me, being on the way, the Lord led me (Gen. 24:27).

The humble He guides in justice, and the humble He teaches His way (Ps. 25:9).

Trust in the Lord with all your heart, and lean not on your own understanding; in all your ways acknowledge Him, and He shall direct your paths (Prov. 3:5-6).

I beseech you therefore, brethren, by the mercies of God, that you present your bodies a living sacrifice, holy, acceptable to God, which is your reasonable service, And do not be conformed to this world, but be transformed by the renewing of your mind, that you may prove what is that good and acceptable and perfect will of God (Rom. 12:1-2).

These verses are saying in different ways that you have to be near to hear. It was to the disciple who leaned on Jesus' breast that God gave the Revelation of Jesus Christ. It is to those who abide in Christ that He reveals His mind and will.

God has a plan for each of our lives. We don't have to make it. All we have to do is find out what it is, then do it. Here are some important steps:

1. Desire earnestly to know God's will. He doesn't show it to spiritual dilettantes, to dabblers who have nothing more than a superficial interest.

2. Acknowledge that you don't know which way to go. *"O Lord, I know that the way of man is not in himself; it is not in man who walks to direct his steps"* (Jer. 10:23). As we have already seen in Proverbs 3:5, we must not lean on our own understanding.

3. Trust the Lord fully in the matter. He has promised to reveal His will; now believe that He will. *"Who among you fears the Lord? Who obeys the voice of His Servant? Who walks in darkness and has no light? Let him trust in the name of the Lord and rely upon his God"* (Isa. 50:10). God has something better for you than you could ever think. He knows options that you could never dream of.

4. Commit yourself to Him without any reservation (Rom. 12:1-2). This means having no will of your own, to be wholly yielded to Him. As someone has said, "No reserve, no retreat, no regrets." This makes you available to the Lord.

5. Confess sin as soon as you are aware of it in your life (1 Jn. 1:9). This keeps you clean. If you are available and clean, then it is God's responsibility to show you His will.

6. Pray continually for a revelation of His will. *"Teach me Your way, O Lord, and lead me in a smooth path, because of my enemies"* (Ps. 27:11). In major matters, I ask the Lord to confirm the guidance in the mouths of two or three witnesses (Mt. 18:16). If He gives me two or three clear evidences of His will, I won't miss it.

7. Put yourself in a position to receive this revelation by spending much time in the Word of God. *"Your word is a lamp to my feet and a light to my path"* (Ps. 119:105).

8. If there are different possibilities, get as much information about each one as possible. The more information I have, the easier

it seems for the Lord to guide me. List the pro's and con's on a sheet of paper. This sometimes brings things into focus.

9. Seek the advice of godly elders or other mature believers whose spiritual judgment you respect. Don't ask those who will probably tell you what you want to hear.

10. Resist the temptation to manufacture your own guidance.

Look, all you who kindle a fire, who encircle yourselves with sparks: Walk in the light of your fire and in the sparks you have kindled—This you shall have from My hand; you shall lie down in torment" (Isa. 50:11).

11. Be willing to wait. This is often the hardest step in the process. Wait until the guidance is so clear that to refuse would be positive disobedience. If you become impatient, remember the thirty years Jesus spent in Nazareth. *"Whoever believes will not act hastily"* (Is. 28:16). God is seldom in a hurry. If you are trusting Him, you don't have to be. C. I. Scofield said, "Faith rests upon the confident assurance that God can speak loudly enough to make a waiting child hear. Our part is to wait quietly until we are sure."

If you are praying for guidance and no guidance comes, God's guidance is for you to stay where you are. Darkness about going is light about staying. Remember the pillar cloud in Exodus 40:36. Only move when the cloud moves.

While waiting for guidance, keep busy for God. *"Whatever your hand finds to do, do it with your might"* (Eccl. 9:10). "It is our duty to do our duty. This simple fact takes care of a large area of life for which no further guidance need be sought" (J. Oswald Sanders).

Now we go a step further to face the question. How does God guide?

1. He guides through the Bible. His general will is set forth in the sacred Scriptures. He will never guide in a way that is contrary to the Word. But He often speaks through a specific passage or verse of Scripture. As you read the Word, a verse may jump out at you as if

God were speaking to you orally. It might not seem clear to someone else, but to you it is a definite indication of the will of the Lord.

2. God also guides through the advice of others. *"Listen to counsel and receive instruction, that you may be wise in your latter days"* (Prov. 19:20). Usually the best advice comes through saints of spiritual stature. But don't rule out the possibility that an unsaved person, not knowing of your search for guidance, may unthinkingly say just the right word to answer your perplexity.

Here let me warn you that when the call of God comes to a person, there are often voices that say a discouraging word. When God called the cricket champion, C. T. Studd, some of his friends whined, "You're mad, leaving your cricket and going to be a missionary. Couldn't you wait until you've finished your cricketing days? Couldn't you make more of an impact for God as a cricketer? Why go as a missionary to a place where they have never even heard of cricket?" If God is really talking to you, you will treat such talk as drivel.

3. God sometimes speaks through the marvelous converging of circumstances—the timing of a letter or a phone call, for instance.

4. He also speaks through the subjective witness of the Holy Spirit. He can work on your intellect, your emotions, and your will so that you are convinced that you know His will. We have to be extra careful when the guidance is subjective, but the fact remains that God can and does speak by molding our thoughts and desires, by laying burdens on our heart. *"For it is God who works in you both to will and to do for His good pleasure"* (Phil. 2:13). Someone has said, "It is folly to act when the dove of peace has flown from the heart."

5. The Lord can guide by hindrances. Notice!

Now when they had gone through Phrygia and the region of Galatia, they were forbidden by the Holy Spirit to preach the word in Asia. After they had come to Mysia, they tried to go into Bithynia, but the Spirit did not permit them" (Acts 16:7).

What kind of leading was this? It was leading by impediment. It was guidance by prohibition. It was the ministry of the closed door. There came to the apostle what the Friends (Quakers) would describe as "a stop in the mind." His thought was resisted and had no liberty. He felt that his purpose was secretly opposed by an invincible barrier. In certain directions he had no sense of spiritual freedom, and therefore he regarded that way as blocked. *"The angel of the Lord stood in the way for an adversary."* I think it is very needful to emphasize this; God sometimes leads us by negations. The closed door is the indication of His will. We attempt to go, but the Spirit suffers us not.[40]

6. And finally he can guide by the example of Christ. What would the Lord Jesus do? "God will never lead us in any course that does not fit the character and teaching of Christ" (J. O. Sanders).

Some people are adamantly set against putting out the fleece, as Gideon did (Jud. 6:37-40). This means that we ask God to guide us by meeting or failing to meet some condition which we have set. There is always the danger of putting out the fleece so that what we want is practically assured. However, if a person is yielded to God's will and sincerely willing to do it, I don't like to limit God. He can accommodate Himself to our weakness. He has done it for me.

One of the old preachers used to advise young people to "pour water on the sacrifice." He was thinking of the day when Elijah was about to call down fire from heaven. Before doing so, he commanded his men to pour four barrels of water on the sacrifice and the wood. The command went out a second time. And a third. Elijah didn't want a chance spark to ignite the sacrifice. He arranged things so that when the fire fell, it could only be the work of Jehovah. So in seeking guidance we should arrange things so that the guidance could only be the Word of the Lord.

Sometimes guidance is very clear. Sometimes it is not so clear. God

---

40   Sanders, J. O., *On to Maturity*, Chicago, IL: Moody Press.

leads one step at a time. He doesn't show the complete picture.

But I believe this. No one who really desperately wants God's guidance will ever fail to get it.

His will is good and acceptable and perfect. It is not as some think—dangerous, unpleasant, and the thing we don't want to do.

TWENTY-SIX
KNOW YOUR BIBLE

All Scripture is given by inspiration of God, and is profitable for doctrine, for reproof, for correction, for instruction in righteousness, that the man of God may be complete, thoroughly equipped for every good work (2 Tim. 3:16-17).

Think of the wonder of this Book, the Bible. Imagine! It is the Word of God! Our most precious earthly possession, the Holy Bible. We should be men and women who have convictions about this. There is a lot of mealy-mouthed talking about the Bible today. There are people in ecclesiastical circles who can talk out of both corners of their mouth about it. They don't hesitate to speak about the authority of the Bible, but they don't say God-breathed or the "inspired" Word of God. We want to be men and women who have convictions, who know what we believe about the Scriptures and are willing to stand and be counted.

The Bible is one of the few things that we have on earth that we'll have in heaven. Isn't that wonderful? *"Forever, O Lord, Thy Word is settled in heaven"* (Ps 119:89). *"Heaven and earth may pass away, but My Word shall never pass away"* (Mt. 24:35). Here it is, the textbook of eternity. What a challenge!

In this Book we have truth. Jesus said, *"Sanctify them through Thy truth. Thy Word is truth"* (Jn. 17:17). Sometimes I think we hear this so much, it fails to have an impression on us. It's enough to make angels gasp! The Bible, the truth of God.

The writer of Psalm 119 could think of almost a hundred and seventy-six good things he could say about the Word of God. How many can you and I think of? It's a challenge, isn't it? The psalmist just goes on and on without repeating himself, and tells all that this precious Word means to him.

Let us be committed men and women. Let us be committed to the inspiration of the Scriptures. *"All Scripture is inspired of God."* All Scripture is God-breathed. When men sat down to write, they wrote as the Holy Spirit of God moved them. We don't understand all the mechanism of that. It's not necessary for us to understand. It's just enough to know that the Bible is not only authoritative, it is inspired of God.

We want to be committed not only to the general inspiration of the Scriptures, but to the verbal inspiration of the Scriptures. I turn to 1 Corinthians 2 for that. In this chapter, the Apostle Paul is giving us three things. He is giving us revelation (v. 10). Then he goes on to the subject of inspiration (v. 13a). Finally he deals with illumination (v. 13b). Please look at verse 13. In dealing with inspiration, Paul is speaking about himself, not you and me. He is speaking about himself and the other apostles and prophets of the first century who gave us the New Testament. *"These things we also speak, not in words which man's wisdom teaches, but which the Holy Spirit teaches..."*

Now you have to supply a word between *but* and *which*. It is implied. And what is that word?" It is *words*. Now read the verse again. *"These things we also speak, not in words which man's wisdom teaches, but [words] which the Holy Spirit teaches."* This says that the very words of Scripture are inspired. The Bible is verbally inspired. God didn't say to Isaiah, "Isaiah, here's the general outline and you just word it the way you think best..." Isaiah sat down and wrote the very words that God by the Holy Spirit gave him—words which the Holy Spirit teaches.

Then Paul deals with illumination. *"Comparing spiritual things with spiritual."* This is admittedly a difficult clause. I suggest that it means "conveying spiritual truths with Spirit-given words." This describes how he conveyed the truth to us. He taught spiritual doctrines with inspired words.

Let us be committed to the *verbal* inspiration of the Scriptures. Let us also be committed to the *plenary* inspiration of the Scriptures. This Book is inspired from Genesis through Revelation. The Lord Jesus said that inspiration extends, not just to the words, but to the jots and tittles. The tittle wasn't a word or ever a letter. It was a stroke. It was a stroke of a letter. It would be equivalent to the bottom stroke on a capital "E" which the capital "F" doesn't have. The Lord said that not a jot or tittle would pass away till all of these things would be fulfilled.

Inspiration also extends to the difference between the singular and plural of a noun. In Galatians 3:16, Paul notes the distinction between seeds and Seed. *"Now to Abraham and his Seed were the promises made. He does not say, 'And to seeds,' as of many, but as of one, 'and to his Seed,' who is Christ."*

We should be committed not only to the inspiration of the Scriptures but to the fact that the Bible is God's final revelation to man. In verse 3 of his epistle, Jude speaks of *"the faith which was once for all delivered to the saints."* Once for all! Nothing can be added to it.

We also want to be committed to the sufficiency of the Bible. Peter reminds us of this in 2 Peter 1:3: *"As His divine power has given to us all things that pertain to life and godliness, through the knowledge of Him who called us by glory and virtue."* Notice that expression, *"all things that pertain to life and godliness."*

We believe in the sufficiency of the Word of God. Not the Word of God plus the book of Mormon. Not the Word of God plus *Science and Health with the Key to the Scriptures*. Not the Word plus Roman Catholic tradition, or even contemporary culture. Not the Bible plus experience. Not the Bible plus *The Believer's Bible Commentary*. Not the Bible plus psychology or philosophy or any of those things. The Bible itself is sufficient. And I love what I read in 2 Timothy 3:17, *"That the man of God may be complete."* That word, *"complete"* really means adequate. Isn't that wonderful? That means that a person who reads, studies, meditates on, memorizes, and obeys the Word of God becomes the adequate person.

Then, we want to be committed to the infallibility of the Scriptures as well. The Lord Jesus said in John 8:31-32, *"If you abide in My Word, you are My disciples indeed, and you shall know the truth."* No true finding of science will ever conflict with the true interpretation of the Scriptures. It would be impossible for them to do it because God is the Author of both books. He is the Author of the Bible and He is the author of true science as well. Today we hear people quibbling about this. You even hear the suggestion that the Bible contains error. A teacher in one of the so-called evangelical seminaries in the United States said, "We know the Bible contains error. Jesus said that the mustard seed is the smallest of all seeds. We know that the mustard seed is not the smallest of all seeds, therefore, the Bible contains error." It's really pathetic to think of a professor in a seminary coming across with something like that, as if the Lord Jesus were giving a scientific sermon on mustard seed. That wasn't the point at all. I can just see those people going through the marketplace and seeing all the spices arrayed on the stands for sale, or maybe the woman looking through the cabinet at home at the spices she has, and the mustard seed was the smallest. You see, when he said that, it isn't that the Bible contains errors, that Jesus Christ is capable of error. Let's have conviction concerning the infallibility of the Word of God.

Years ago, I came across this quote by B. H. Carroll, and it made me chuckle. I've been thinking about it ever since. He said, "When I was a boy, I found one thousand contradictions in the Bible. I marked them. I had nearly one thousand more contradictions then than I do now. Now I have a half a dozen things in the Bible that I can't explain satisfactorily to myself, but I've seen nine hundred and ninety-four out of a thousand coalesce and harmonize like two strings mingling." And he said, "I'm inclined to think that if I had a little more sense, I could reconcile the other six." That's it! That's exactly right. Let's be committed to the infallibility of the Word of God.

Let's be committed to read the Word of God. This is very important. A special blessing is pronounced, on those who read the Word of God. This is especially true of the book of Revelation, but it applies to the whole Bible. *"Blessed is he who reads and those who hear the words of this prophecy, and keep those things which are written in it; for the time is near"* (Rev. 1:3).

It's not enough to just read the Bible. Let us be committed to study the Word of God. I remember that as a young fellow, it dawned on me that I wasn't going to know everything when I got to heaven. I had always thought I was going to be omniscient in the glory land so why study the Bible now? But then I read Ephesians 2:7, *"That in the ages to come He might show..."* God would show. I thought that if God is going to show, I'm going to be learning. I thought, well if I'm going to be learning, then heaven is going to be a school, God is going to be the Teacher, the Bible is going to be the textbook, the term will be eternity. Up until then, I thought that business is the main thing in life. So I studied business and became a banker. But then I thought, hmmm. And at the age of thirty it really came to me. I thought, this is the book of eternity. And some day I'm going to sit down with the patriarchs, Abraham, Isaac, and Jacob in the kingdom of the Father. *"Many shall come from the east and the west, sit down with Abraham and Isaac and Jacob in the kingdom of the Father"*

(Mt. 8:11). And we're going to converse! But how intelligently will I be able to converse? Especially if I sit next to Obadiah or Zephaniah! Would you believe that that started me on a diligent study of the Word of God? I thought, well, it's an awful big job, MacDonald. Sixty-six books. I thought, well I know, but a big job is made up of many little jobs. I can't do a big job, but I can do many little jobs. I started the systematic, verse by verse study. Some days I didn't do more than five verses. It took me thirty years to get through. I studied each verse, asking what is God saying in this? I came to difficult passages where great and godly men have different interpretations. I thought about those interpretations. Which one is the best? Which one fits in best with the context and with the rest of the Bible?

Yes, this is the textbook of eternity. You say, everybody is going to be happy in eternity. I know, but some people will be happier than others. Everybody's cup will be full, but some people will have bigger cups than others. Everyone will enjoy the Lord Jesus, but some will have a greater capacity for enjoying Him than others. And we're determining that capacity down here by what we do with the Word of God. We'll all enjoy heaven but we're determining our capacity for enjoying the glories of heaven by what we do right now with this Word. When I saw that, it took me out of the world of ticker tape and started me on the way to higher dividends. I hope it will be a challenge to you.

I know what some of you are thinking. A baseball game or a TV documentary is far more exciting than Bible study. But it's only more exciting if you look at it through the eyes of flesh. If you look through the eyes of faith, the Bible is more important because what you do with this book counts for eternity. Put on your faith glasses. See through the eyes of faith, and you'll realize that only that which is eternal really matters. The score of that football game is going to be quickly forgotten.

A worthy goal is to become a diligent student of the Word of God, to become proficient in the English Bible. And even if you only do a few verses a day, just let them accumulate, and you'll be surprised at the progress you'll make. There are all kinds of Bible study helps. Make use of them.

In studying the Word of the God, take it literally wherever you can. We believe in the literal interpretation of the Scriptures. That's why we believe in a pre-tribulation Rapture. That's why we believe in a pre-millennial return of Christ, because if the first sense makes sense, you don't look for any other sense. It's the first rule of Bible interpretation.

And don't try to explain away difficult passages that you don't like. That's a temptation. There are a lot of hard words of Jesus in the New Testament. And it's a terrible temptation when you come to them, to just try to explain them away. For instance, the "cultural argument." "Well, that was just for the culture of that day." You hear this all the time.

Erwin Lutzer of Moody Church wrote, "We've been so caught up with the spirit of the age that, like a chameleon, we've changed colors to blend in with the latest worldly hue." When the gay rights activists argue that homosexuality is only an alternate sexual preference, we find certain evangelicals writing books agreeing. They say that the Bible doesn't really condemn homosexuality after all.

When the feminists press their demands for equality, some preachers have re-studied the New Testament only to find that Paul didn't mean what he said. Or even more frightening is the conclusion of one evangelical that Paul was just plain wrong on the subject of feminism.

And so we accommodate the Scriptures to whatever winds happen to be blowing. We become so absorbed by our culture, that we have nothing to say to it. In our zeal to be relevant, we've lost our prophetic voice. Every time we make a doctrinal compromise, the enemies of Christianity are strengthened.

Here is an illustration of how far the cultural argument can go.

Episcopal Bishop John Spong of Newark, New Jersey, said in an article that "traditional concepts of the resurrection and ascension of Jesus as well as famous Old Testament passages cited to condemn homosexuality cannot be taken literally and must be placed in the context of the times in which they were written." The Bible speaks to all ages and to all cultures as well. *"Forever, O Lord, Thy word is settled in heaven"* (Ps. 119:89). Don't be swayed by the "cultural argument."

Don't be swayed by the "tradition argument," "We've never done it that way." When the Lord Jesus was on earth, He had occasion to condemn that type of thinking. Here's an old Jewish father, and he's destitute. He goes to his son who has become very wealthy, very successful in business and has a lot of money, and he says, "Son, we raised you and here we are at the end of life, and we have nothing." There was a tradition among the Jews that all that son had to do was say, "Corban," and that released him from any obligation to his father. Corban meant that "anything that you might be profited by me has been dedicated to the Temple." It didn't mean that the Temple ever got his money. It was just a tradition of men, a verbal formula.

Then there's the "non-literal argument." People say, "Jesus didn't mean that literally." *"So likewise, whoever of you does not forsake all that he has cannot be My disciple"* (Lk. 14:33). He couldn't have meant that literally! He knows I have to live, doesn't He? A young man said that to Spurgeon once who was pressing the claims of Christ on him. He said, "Well, I have to live, don't I?" And Spurgeon said, "I don't grant that. We have to obey God." That's it. We have to obey God even if it runs against the grain of human nature.

Don't be swayed by the "exception argument." I hear this frequently. It goes like this: "I know what the Bible says, but in my case, the Lord wants to make an exception." Have you ever heard that? These are ways in which we nullify the commandments of God. God is looking for men and women, young men and young women who will tremble at His Word. That's what He is looking for, people who will bow their brains to the Word of God. Men that love the Word of God, and women that love the Word of God. People who have the attitude, "If God says it, I will obey it."

I like to tell about a young fellow who was a student at Emmaus years ago. He called himself the Emmaus dropout. I wish we had more dropouts like him. He had a simple, uncomplicated faith. Before he was saved, he was so self-conscious, he couldn't talk to people. Then he got saved in Fayetteville, NC, and he became a power for God. And he had that attitude when he'd go to the Word of God. He'd say, "I don't care if no one else is doing it; if that's what the Lord says, that's what I want." And I've been with that young fellow in France going door to door; he speaks fluent French. He preaches in the open air in Germany today. He learned a lot of an Indian dialect. He speaks Polish and a little Russian. How did he do it? It wasn't his great IQ. It was just that attitude. "I want to do what the Word of God tells me to do."

And then there's the "prudence" or "common sense" argument. Jesus said,

> *Do not lay up for yourselves treasures on earth, where moth and rust destroy, and where thieves break in and steal, but lay up for yourselves treasure in heaven, where neither moth nor rust destroys, and where thieves do not break in and steal* (Mt. 6:19-20).

Well, you have to use common sense, don't you? You have to provide for a rainy day, don't you? You see, you're using common sense. There's something better than common sense, and that's divine revelation. If we went by common sense, we'd never have the gospel of the grace of God. I tell you, the truth of God transcends common sense or prudence. And when the Lord said that we should not lay up treasures on earth, He meant exactly what He said.

I remember when George Verwer was first saved, and Dale Rhoton was discipling him. Dale would come to some of those difficult portions and ask, "What does that mean, George?"

George would answer, "Either the Bible means what it says, or we ought to throw it away." God honored that attitude. Those two students started to live those principles, and the reverberations have been felt throughout the world.

I can remember praying with Ray Lentzsch in a little town in Belgium. I remember him saying, "Lord, common sense is rat poison!" He was more right than wrong. When it comes to the interpretation of the Scriptures, get beyond common sense. The Word of God is divine revelation.

And then, of course, there is the "never offend" argument. You wouldn't want to do it if you'd offend somebody, would you? Friends, it seems that everything we do as Christians offends somebody. The gospel is offensive, isn't it? The gospel doesn't leave man a leg to stand on. It just cuts the ground right out from under him. It tells him he's a sinful wretch! It tells him the best thing you can say about him is no better than filthy rags, and the worst you can say about him is that he murdered his God! Don't talk to me about the "never offend" argument. If the Bible says it, we do it. And we can't help whether it offends people or not!

I can remember being asked to take a funeral in Chicago. The lady in charge said, "Now, one of my sisters is married to a Jew, and a brother is married to a Roman Catholic, and we're Lutherans, and I wouldn't want you to say anything to offend."

I said, "Well, you'd better get somebody else to preach the message."

"No, no, no, we want you to preach the message!"

"Well, you better get somebody else if you're worried about offending somebody." We did preach it. We preached the gospel. I can't say that no one was offended.

There is also the "hyper-dispensational" argument. Let me just pause here and say that I am a dispensationalist. I don't think I could understand the Bible if I didn't see dispensations. I'd be offering

212

animal sacrifices if I weren't a dispensationalist. I think that a lot of people who fight against dispensationalism are in fact dispensationalists. They have a Bible that's divided into two dispensations, Old and New Testaments. But then there is a *hyper*-dispensationalism that robs you of the Sermon on the Mount, robs you of the Gospels, and robs you of all but the Prison Epistles. I don't want that. I want to extract honey from all the Word of God, don't you? Stick to your dispensations, but avoid hyper-dispensationalism.

There is the "friendship argument." E. J. Carnell wrote a book called *The Case for Orthodoxy*. Actually it was a frontal attack against fundamental Christianity. You'd never suspect that from the title, *The Case for Orthodoxy*. Carnell wrote, "Adam could well have received his body from a previously evolved ape so that Genesis could be non-historical and non-scientific." The book argues against fundamentalism and the inerrancy of Scriptures.

When John Whitcomb, who was then the president of Grace Seminary in Indiana, was criticizing Carnell's book to George Elden Ladd, Ladd replied, "Well, you don't know him personally as I do. He is a gracious gentleman, a godly man."

I ask, "What has that got to do with it? He's arguing against the inspiration of the Scriptures. Many of the most militant modernists and liberals are gracious people. They have a reputation of being that way. It doesn't affect matters at all." It makes me think of the carpenter's shop that had a sign out front, "All kinds of twistings and turnings done here."

When things happen in our own family and some member has to be disciplined by the local church, it's amazing how people can twist the Scriptures to excuse the guilty. Blood is still thicker than water. We can take verses of Scripture and twist them if they're really hitting somebody in our family. The Word of God applies to everyone, not just for those outside our family circle.

In addition there is the "science" or "scholarship argument." A young man said to me not long ago, "I find it difficult fitting the Bible into science." He is saying that science is right and the Bible has to be accommodated to it. Why does he say this? Sometimes it is the desire for intellectual or scholarly respectability. That can be deadly when it comes to the handling of the Word of God.

And then, of course, there is the "God is too good" argument. "God is too good to sustain an everlasting hell." This is strong in evangelical circles today, the denial of the eternal punishment of the wicked. The Bible teaches it. The Bible says, *"The smoke of their torment ascends forever and ever"* (Rev. 14:11). It says, *"Where their worm does not die and the fire is not quenched"* (Mk. 9:44). Yet men say that God is too good to sustain an everlasting hell. They forget that God never built hell for men. They forget that God Incarnate died to save men from hell. They don't realize God is looking for the slightest excuse to save man and bring him home to heaven. If he'll just repent and receive the Lord Jesus Christ as his Savior, he'll never have to go to hell.

We should not only be committed to study the Word of God. We should commit ourselves to memorize it.

Wherewithal shall a young man cleanse his way? By taking heed thereto according to Thy word. Thy word have I hid in my heart, that I might not sin against Thee" (Ps. 119:9, 11).

We memorize verses or passages of Scripture so that the Holy Spirit has something to draw from in the great moments of life. The sword of the Spirit is the Word of God. Here the Word of God means just the appropriate verse for that particular occasion. But the Spirit can't do it if we don't have the Word stored in our heart.

We should also be committed to meditate on the Word. I fear that meditation is a lost art. We are so busy. But "God never asks of us such busy labor as leaves no time for sitting at His feet. The patient

attitude of meditation He often counts as service most complete."
You ask, "How do you meditate?"

You take a verse of Scripture, and just as a cow chews the cud, you mull it over. Here is an example. I have a text on the wall in front of my bed with the words, *"Worthy is the Lamb who was slain to receive power and riches and wisdom, and strength and honor and glory and blessing!"* (Rev. 5:12). That puzzles me. How can the Lord Jesus receive any more of these things than he already has? *"Worthy is the Lamb who was slain to receive power..."* He's got all power. How could He receive any more? And then it says, *"riches."* He owns the cattle on a thousand hills. I don't see how He can get any more riches than He's got now. And then, *"To receive wisdom and strength and honor and glory and blessing..."* Then it hits me. He can receive my power (talents). He can receive my riches (my earthly treasures). He can receive my wisdom (the finest of my intellectual powers). He can receive the best of my physical strength, the best of my praise and worship. In short, He can receive all that I am and have. He is worthy of my all. I can come and lay all at His blessed feet. Now the verse has taken on new meaning! I'm not saying that's the right interpretation, but that's what it says to me as I lie there and meditate on it. Let's be committed to meditate on the Word of God.

Be committed to obey the Word of God. I already talked about Larry Smith, my friend in Germany, who had a great desire to obey the Word of God. Obedience is the organ of spiritual knowledge.

Think about that. Obedience is the organ of spiritual knowledge. Do you want to know more about the Bible? Obey what you know. God will give you more. That's the way it works. It's interesting to think that you can reach a certain stage and then you come to a block. There's something there that you don't want to obey, and you plateau, or even go downward. *"For whoever has, to him more will be given; but whoever does not have, even what he has will be taken away from him"* (Mk. 4:25). Let us commit ourselves to obey the Word of God.

"On this one will I look, on him who is poor and of a contrite spirit, and who trembles at My word" (Isa. 66:2). And the Lord Jesus said, *"If you abide in My word, you are My disciples indeed. And you shall know the truth, and the truth shall make you free"* (Jn. 8:31-32).

Let's be committed to teach and preach the Word. *"Be ready in season and out of season. Convince, rebuke, exhort with all long-suffering and teaching"* (2 Tim. 4:2). It doesn't say preach psychology. It doesn't say preach philosophy. It doesn't say preach self-esteem. It doesn't say preach health and prosperity. It says, *"Preach the Word."* It is the Word of God that has power. A single verse of Scripture is worth a thousand arguments. Let that message ring through your heart. Preach the Word. There never will come a time in the history of the earth when God's method will not be preaching the Word of God.

We should be committed to test everything by the Word of God. I received a letter from a young fellow recently in which he asked, "What is your scriptural authority for saying this?" I say, "Praise the Lord for that young fellow." He is a Berean (Acts 17:30). He wanted to know the scriptural authority for it. We need more like that. *"To the law and to the testimony! If they do not speak according to this word, it is because there is not light in them"* (Isa. 8:20). I wrote him a letter commending him for his attitude. The great test is, "What does the Bible say?" Many of us were brought up with this question: "What says the Word? Test everything by the Word of God."

If the Bible isn't the Word of God, we have nothing. We might as well pack up our bags and go home. But the Bible *is* the Word of God. The Bible is God's Word to us in which He has told us all that we need for life and godliness. If the Bible is not the Word of God,

Christ is not risen and the gospel is uncertain. But the Bible *is* the Word of God.

At the coronation of a British monarch, the Bible is delivered to him or her with these words:

> We present you with this Book, the most valuable thing the world affords. Here is wisdom. Here is the royal law. These are the living oracles of God.

I say to you: "I present you with this Book, the most valuable thing the world affords. Here is wisdom. This is the royal law. These are the living oracles of God." I charge you, each one reading this book, be committed to the Word of God. Have convictions about the Word of God. And in a day of declension and denial, stand fast for the Word of God.

TWENTY-SEVEN
STUDY TO BE APPROVED

Every believer should be a Bible student. Too many Christians think that serious study of the sacred Scriptures is just for their pastor or minister. It is a colossal mistake. Every child of God should diligently make the Word his own.

A second mistake is that to study the Bible you need a seminary training. Wrong! Charles Haddon Spurgeon never had formal Bible training. Neither did G. Campbell Morgan or Harry A. Ironside.

> They were devoted students of the Word, learning its deeper truths through hours of study, meditation, and prayer. The first step toward fullness of life is spiritual intelligence—growing in the will of God by knowing the Word of God.[41]

Set aside a definite time and place where you can study without distraction. Many Christians find the early morning hours to be the best. Every time you keep this appointment, it strengthens the habit. Every time you miss, it weakens the habit.

You can also discipline yourself to utilize spare time to resume your study where you left off.

---

41   Wiersbe, Warren W., *The Bible Exposition Commentary*, Vol. 2, Wheaton, IL: Victor Books, 1989, p. 111.

Motivation is tremendously important. The greatest incentive to study the Bible is the fact that it is the Word of God. In it, you hear God speaking to you. When you live with this realization, studying it becomes a joy, not a task.

Another motivation is having to prepare for a Sunday School class or a Bible class. When you know you have to explain a passage or answer questions about it, you have a very practical incentive. Consider yourself blessed if you have the privilege of teaching the Word in a class.

Still another experience that drives us to the Word is witnessing to the unsaved, especially members of cults. Often they bring up arguments that we are not able to answer. We are embarrassed so we go home and study the Bible until we are able to answer them convincingly. In this sense, cultists are our friends. Christians who witness grow faster in the knowledge of the Word.

You should not think that Bible study is going to be easy. Be prepared to dig, to search, to compare, and to research.

Begin with prayer. Ask the Holy Spirit to speak to you as you read. Ask Him to show you wonderful things out of God's Word (Ps. 119:18). Submit to Him as your Teacher.

You will then decide what book of the Bible you are going to study. This will depend in part on where you are in the Christian life—whether you are a new believer or whether you already have some background in the Scriptures.

Don't try to do too much at any one time. It's better to take a few verses and get something out of them than to take a chapter and quickly forget what you have read. Generally speaking, a chapter is too much.

Read the passage over and over until it becomes a part of you. Close familiarity with the very words of the Bible is invaluable.

Write down questions that you don't understand. When people ask me how I study the Bible, I say, "With a question mark for a brain."

That doesn't mean that I have questions with regard to the truth of the Word. I just keep asking myself, "What does that mean?" In *Disciples Are Made—not Born,* Walter A. Henrichsen wrote,

> What does it say that I do not understand? Write down all the problems that you have with the passage. When I first began Bible study, I thought that the fewer problems I had, the better I understood the passage. The more I study the Scriptures, the more I realize that the converse is true. The deeper I probe into the passage, the more problems I have—that is, the more things in the chapter I realize I do not understand.[42]

Write down your own commentary on each verse. You really haven't grasped the meaning until you can explain it in simple, understandable words. Strive for that goal. A teacher named Russell L. Ackoff wrote:

> I once had a brilliant student, now a well-known professor, who wrote a highly technical thesis. I asked him to assume that I was an ordinary corporate manager. Would he explain his thesis briefly?
>
> He went to the blackboard and began to cover it with mathematical symbols. I stopped him to remind him that I was an ordinary manager, not a mathematician. After a long pause he said, "I don't understand what I've done well enough to explain it in non-technical language."[43]

Unless people can express themselves well in ordinary English, they don't know what they are talking about.

Get help from dependable commentaries, Bible dictionaries and encyclopedias, reputable versions of the Bible, paraphrases, word-study books, and other reference works. I take beneficial help wherever I can get it.

Keep looking for answers to your questions. "Some of the questions you have will be answered in the course of your Bible study,

---

42   Henrichsen, Walter A., *Disciples are Made—Not Born,* 1974: Victor Books, p. 100.
43   Quoted in *Reader's Digest,* July 1993, p. 149.

some will be answered as you talk with others about it, and some may never be fully answered."[44]

Sometimes events of daily life cast light on the Scriptures. Believers in a concentration camp see treasures in the Bible that the rest of us miss.

Welcome opportunities to share the result of your studies. This spreads the blessing and delivers you from living in a world of trivia.

TWENTY-EIGHT
PRAYING ALWAYS

A person never comes closer to omnipotence than when he prays in the name of the Lord Jesus. Actually man will never be all-powerful, not even in heaven. But when he prays in the Savior's name, it's the same as if the Lord Jesus was making the request to the Father. In that sense, the one who prays has extreme power at his command.

Prayer changes things. An old English bishop said, "When I pray, things happen. When I don't pray, they don't."

If Christians only knew it! They hold the balance of power in the world. They might seem like a helpless minority, but with God, they can influence the destiny of nations. Think of the following:

Prayer has divided seas, rolled up flowing rivers, made flinty rocks gush into fountains, quenched flames of fire, muzzled lions, disarmed vipers and poisons, marshaled the stars against the wicked, stopped the course of the moon, arrested the rapid sun in its great race, burst open iron gates, recalled souls from eternity, conquered the strongest devils, and commanded legions of angels down from heaven. Prayer has bridled and changed the raging passions of man, and routed and destroyed vast armies of proud, daring, blustering atheists. Prayer has brought one man from the bottom of the sea, and carried another in a chariot of fire to heaven. What has not prayer done?.[45]

The best prayer comes from a strong, inward necessity. When all is calm and well in our lives, we don't feel the need of prayer. But when we find ourselves at wit's end corner, between a rock and a hard place, with no way to look but up, then we can storm the gates of heaven in torrents of entreaty. "It is fervent prayers that wing their way to the throne of God."

Cold prayers are as arrows without heads, as swords without edges, as birds without wings; they pierce not, they cut not, they fly not up to heaven. Cold prayers always freeze before they get to heaven. (Thomas Brooks)

It is not the arithmetic of our prayers, how many they are; nor the rhetoric of our prayers, how eloquent they be; nor the geometry of our prayers, how long they be; nor the music of our prayers, how sweet our voice may be; nor the method of our prayers, how orderly they may be; nor even the theology of our prayers—how good the doctrine may be—which God cares for. Fervency of spirit is that which avails much (Bishop Hall).

Think about this. God seldom if ever does anything except in answer to prayer. Spurgeon agrees:

Prayer is the forerunner of mercy. Turn to sacred history and you will find that seldom ever did a great mercy come to this world unheralded by supplication. Prayer is always the preface of blessing.

R. A. Matthews adds his testimony to this truth:[46]

God has limited certain of His activities to responding to the prayers of His people. Unless they pray, He will not act. Heaven may will something to happen, but heaven waits and encourages earth's initiative to desire that will, and then to will and pray that it happens. The will of God is not done on earth by

---

45   Author unknown.
46   R. A. Matthews, *Born for Battle*, Bromley, Kent, England: STL Books, 1978. p. 14.

an inexorable, juggernaut omnipotence "out there" overriding or ignoring the will of man on earth. On the contrary, God has willed that His hand be held back while He seeks for a man, an intercessor to plead "Thy will be done on earth" in this or that specific situation.

Dr. Moberly put it this way: "He bids His own work wait on man's prayers."

Prayer moves God to do things that He would not otherwise have done. This is clear from James 4:2; 5:16: *"You do not have because you do not ask." "The effective, fervent prayer of a righteous man avails much."*

This explodes the notion that all that prayer accomplishes is that it brings us into submission to what God would have done anyway.

God always answers prayer in exactly the way we would answer it if we had His wisdom, love, and power. Sometimes the answer is the precise thing we asked for. Sometimes the Lord says, "Wait." And sometimes He says, "No, that would not be good for you." The saying is true: "God nothing does, nor suffers to be done but what thou would'st thyself if thou but knew the end of all He does as well as He."

Someone may object, "What about the salvation of loved ones? We pray for them but they don't get saved." I believe that when I pray for an unsaved person, God speaks to him in some way. Perhaps someone passes him a tract. Or speaks to him about the Lord. Perhaps he hears a Christian program on the radio or TV. Or God mysteriously jiggles his conscience. God speaks, but He doesn't save people against their will. In His sovereignty He decided to allow man to have a will in the matter. He is not going to populate heaven with people who don't want to be there.

The work of God is done more in prayer than in any other way. We appeal to R. A. Matthews for a brilliant commentary on this:[47]

---

47   Op. Cit., p. 72.

Prayer is the cutting edge in any work for God. It is not a supplemental spiritual rocket to get some well-meaning effort off the ground. Prayer is the work and the working power in any spiritual ministry. It should be the central thrust. The spiritual history of a mission or a church is written in its prayer life. The expression of corporate life is not measured in statistics but in prayer depth. The program of preaching, teaching, serving, the goal-setting, the adoption of new, twentieth-century techniques, seminars on time management and administrative procedures are all good but effective and productive in God's economy only as they are subject to prayer.

Prayer should be a joy for us. It was for the apostle Paul. In Philippians 1:4, he said, *"Making request for you all with joy."* This is not the prevailing attitude to prayer, according to Donald English.

How different it is from many textbooks on prayer—prayer as duty, as discipline, as routine, as ritual. Paul says, "Pardon me, I happen to enjoy it." What's wrong with *enjoying* prayer? I know there are times when it has to be a discipline, a routine; but are we not allowed that warmth of the Spirit as we pray, which enables it to be a joyous activity?

Prayer leads a person to heights that make reason dizzy. It often deals in the realm of the impossible and accomplishes it.

> *Prayer makes the darkest clouds withdraw.*
> *It climbs the ladder Jacob saw,*
> *Gives exercise to faith and love,*
> *Brings every blessing from above.*
> *Restraining prayer we cease to fight.*
> *Prayer makes the Christian's armor bright.*
> *And Satan trembles when he sees*
> *The weakest Christian on his knees.* (Wm. Cowper)

Someone has said "I measure my effectiveness by the number of people I pray for and the number of people who pray for me."

Prayer goes to the Father through the Son (Eph. 2:18). In Revelation

8:1-4, the Lord Jesus is seen as an Angel with a golden censer. When our prayers reach Him, He adds incense to them and offers them on the golden altar before the throne. The incense is the fragrance of His Person and work. When our prayers reach God, all impurities have been removed and the prayers are absolutely perfect.

Prayer is more important than service. "God sets more value on prayer and communion than on labor. The Heavenly Bridegroom is wooing a wife, not hiring a servant" (Author unknown).

We honor God by the greatness of our prayers. A beggar asked Alexander the Great for a farm for himself, a dowry for his daughter, and an education for his son. When reproached by his aides for granting all these requests, Alexander said, "I get tired of these people who come asking for a gold coin. That saucy beggar treated me like a king; he asked big." We should ask big:

> *Thou art coming to a King.*
> *Large petitions with thee bring.*
> *For His love and power are such*
> *You can never ask too much.* (John Newton)

Too often our prayers are puny, as suggested in this poem:

> *If you had been living when Christ was on earth*
> *And had met the Savior kind,*
> *What would you've asked him to do for you,*
> *Supposing you were stone blind?*
>
> *The child considered and then replied,*
> *"I suppose that without doubt,*
> *I'd have asked the Lord for a dog with a chain*
> *To lead me daily about."*
>
> *How often thus in our faithless prayers,*
> *We acknowledge with shamed surprise,*

We have only asked for a dog with a chain
When we might have had opened eyes. (M. Calley)

When we get to heaven, we'll wish we had prayed more.

TWENTY-NINE
YOUR DAILY TIME WITH JESUS

The daily quiet time, also known as the QT, is a definite period each day when a believer holds communion with the Lord through reading the Bible and in prayer. He feeds upon the Scriptures as the necessary bread of God and holds audience with the mighty God as friend with Friend.

Usually it is scheduled as the first thing each morning, since that is considered the best time of the day, and the best belongs to the Lord. But if, for any reason, it is not possible to do that, we don't need to be legalistic about it or spend the day with a guilt complex. There is no law against having it later in the day.

There is no best way of holding the quiet time. Each one must determine which method is best for him. However, the following suggestions might be helpful.

As with all habits, every time you do it, you strengthen the habit. Every time you miss, you weaken the habit.

It is best to have a designated time and place, as free from distractions as possible. If your communion is interrupted by the memory of something you have to do that day, write it down on a slip of paper, then continue with the Word.

Begin with prayer, asking the Lord to speak to you through the Word, whether in devotion, instruction, comfort, correction, or guidance.

Limit yourself to a short portion of the Bible. It's better to read five verses and get something out of them than to read a chapter and retain nothing. Too often believers try to do too much, get discouraged, and quit.

After reading your passage for the day, ask yourself the following questions:

- Is there something about the Lord Jesus in the passage?
- Is there some command for me to obey?
- Is there some sin to confess/avoid?
- Is there a promise to claim?
- Is there some problem verse or passage which I don't understand and for which I should seek an answer? (Confession! I personally find it difficult to enjoy something I don't understand.)
- Is there something that I can translate into praise and worship?
- Is there something for which I am reminded to pray?
- Is there a verse that I should memorize?
- Is there some spiritual blessing for which I should be thankful?

Some find it helpful to jot down their thoughts in a notebook.

After you have studied the passage carefully, don't hesitate to consult a good commentary for answers to your problems or for new light on the verses.

There are other ways to have a quiet time.

One is to use *Daily Light on the Daily Path.* The Bagster family who compiled it wrote,

It is a book of selected passages from the Bible, with readings for every day of the year, one for the morning and one for the evening. A headline text at the top of the page sets the theme. Then from other parts of the Holy Scriptures, God's precious words are brought together for the further illumination of that verse.

In a miraculous way, the passages selected…have exactly fitted the needs of Christians in every kind of trying circumstance. Hundreds of thousands of Christians throughout the world, to its remotest corners, are each day reading the same page with its message of comfort and help.

The Bagster family prayed earnestly over every verse before including it.

Another excellent daily devotional book is *Morning and Evening Readings* by C. H. Spurgeon. His comments on single Bible verses are instructive, interesting, and sometimes humorous. He brings out truths that we would probably never see, if left to our own devices.

There are many other books, booklets, and calendars with readings for each day. They are helpful for beginners and enjoyable for mature saints. Some suggest readings that take you through the Bible in a year.

Be sure to end your QT with prayer, thanking the Lord for what you have learned and asking for strength to obey.

Try to share your meditations with others during the day. This fixes the lessons more deeply in your own mind, and permits others to share the blessings with you (Mal. 3:16).

Stephen Olford says devotional time with God "is absolutely vital to a life of sustained spirituality, effectiveness, and love." Think about that!

THIRTY
BE A WORSHIPER

That is the reason for our existence—we were made to worship God. The Father seeks worshipers who will pay homage to Him in spirit and in truth. This means that their worship is not a matter of going through certain rituals and reciting prepared prayers by rote. Rather it is in spirit, that is, inspired by the Spirit and empowered by the Spirit. And it is in truth, that is, sincere and from the heart.

Worship is the outpouring of praise to the Lord for His person and work. It is ascribing worth to Him for who He is and for what He has done. It may include adoration and thanksgiving. It is a love song to the triune God. In real worship, self is absent except when we express the marvel that He should care for us.

The first mention of worship in the Bible occurs when Abraham took his only son, Isaac to offer him as a burnt offering to God (Gen. 22:5). The chief act of worship in the New Testament is the presentation of our bodies to the Lord as a living sacrifice, holy, acceptable to Him (Rom. 12:1-2). The body here stands for the spirit, soul, and body—all that we are as persons.

Preaching is not worship. It may inspire worship in the hearts of listeners, but preaching is the conveying of a message to an audience.

Giving a testimony is not worship although, once again, it may stir up worship. Worship is addressing God directly.

Worship is directed to the Father and the Son in the Bible, but for some reason not given, it is never addressed to the Holy Spirit.

Critics of the Bible might think that it is selfish of God to want worship. They don't understand. It is for our good, not God's. We become like what we worship (2 Cor. 3:18):

> *But we all, with unveiled face, beholding as in a mirror the glory of the Lord, are being transformed into the same image from glory to glory, just as by the Spirit of the Lord.*

HOW CAN WE STIMULATE WORSHIP?

The Psalms provide much fuel for worship. The attributes of God are a favorite theme, as well as the care of the Lord in history and prophecy. Contemplating God's gift of His Son, as pictured in Abraham's offering of Isaac, lifts our hearts in praise. The Savior's life and work are fuel for ceaseless adoration—His incarnation, His perfect life here below, His atoning sacrifice, His resurrection, His ascension and present ministry at God's right hand, His coming again, and the blessings that have flowed to us through Him.

David and the other writers of the Psalms were worshipers. They had great thoughts of God. The marvels of His creation swept them away in rapturous song. When they considered His greatness, goodness, and grace, their minds strained to take it all in. They thought of Him as the Upholder and Controller and were confounded.

The writer of the closing psalms was so overwhelmed that he called on all creation, animate and inanimate, to sing the praises of the Lord. All people great and small, old and young, kings and princes, yes, all angels, together with beasts, birds, and creeping things should form a universal choir. He enlists the accompaniment of all kinds of instruments—harps, trumpets, cornets, timbrels, cymbals, and organs. His subject is so amazing that he summons the sun, moon, and stars to join the anthem. The heavens, earth, sea, hills, mountains, and waters must not be silent. Fire, hail, snow, and stormy winds have their part. The subject is so breathtaking that the Lord is worthy of total worship.

Yet these psalmists did not have a Bible. They did not know how the Son of God would come down to Planet Earth and be born in a cattle shed, His crib an animal's feed box. They did not know that wise men would see their God "contracted to a span, incomprehensibly made Man." Nor did they know that in that manger would lie the One "who built the starry skies." Hidden from their eyes was the truth that the Babe in the manger would be "the Eternal Word that spoke the worlds out of the womb of nothing, that the tiny arms of this helpless child were hands of Him who laid the timbers of the universe"[48]

They did not know that the Architect and Maker of the universe would one day wear a Carpenter's apron in a place called Nazareth. Or that He would "wander as a stranger in the world His hands had made." They would have gasped at the thought of God having no place to lay his Head, or that He would sometimes sleep under the stars while His followers went to their homes.

Did they realize that God would actually come to earth and heal the sick, give sight to the blind, restore limbs to the maimed, cast out demons, and raise the dead? Or that in spite of all His kindness, He would be insulted, ridiculed, and driven out of town?

It would have been incredible to them that He, the Judge of all, would be betrayed by one of His own, arrested, and put on trial. The civil authorities would find Him innocent, but He would be scourged until His back was like a furrowed field and He was no longer recognizable as a man.

---

48   Macpherson, Ian, *The Burden of the Lord*, Nashville, TN: Abingdon, 1951, p. 14.

The psalmists did not know in great detail what we now know. At a place called Calvary men would nail their God to a cross of wood.

It would be unimaginable to these Old Testament poets. They would have shaken their heads to think that the brightness of God's glory, the express image of His person, the Maker and Upholder of the universe, would be there on a cross, purging man's sins (Heb. 1:1-3). Frail creatures would take the One who is high and lifted up in glory and lift Him up on a pole of shame. The heaven of heavens cannot contain Him, yet He was bound by nails. It was the Immortal who was dying.

Imagine the torrent of heavenly harmony that the psalmist's massed choir of the redeemed would have raised if they could have sung in the words of Charles Wesley:

> *Amazing love! How can it be*
> *That thou, my God, should die for me?*

Or Isaac Watts hymn that says:

> *Forbid it, Lord, that I should boast*
> *Save in the death of Christ my God.*

They saw through a glass darkly. At times they had brief glimpses of what would happen, but the full revelation was not for them to know. The thought is this: If they, with the limited knowledge they had, could have poured out such torrents of praise, worship, adoration, and thanksgiving to the Lord, how much more should we with what we know about Calvary and of the One who died there for us extol Him?

Once we grasp the truth of what our God has done for us, of the sacrifice He made to save us, we will be spontaneous and compulsive worshipers. No one will have to coax or cajole us to praise the Lord. Our tongues will be the pen of a ready writer. Our lives will be one unending psalm of praise to Him. In the words of Charles

Wesley again, we will "dissolve our hearts in thankfulness and melt our eyes in tears." We will be "lost in wonder, love, and praise," and "drowned in love's mysterious deep." Like the psalmist we will call on all creation to join us in singing the excellencies of Him who called us out of darkness into His marvelous light.

To me, there is nothing that makes me a worshiper as much as the fact that the One who died on the cross of Calvary for me is my Creator and the Sustainer of the universe. As preparation for the Lord's Supper on Sunday, I like to spend quiet time with the Bible and the hymnbook on Saturday evening. Many of the old hymns express the marvel of Calvary better than I could ever do and give much fuel for prayer.

Evangelism and service then become an outgrowth of worship.

THIRTY-ONE
LOVE CHRIST'S ASSEMBLY[49]

To me, who am less than the least of all the saints, this grace was given, that I should preach among the Gentiles the unsearchable riches of Christ, and to make all people see what is the fellowship of the mystery, which from the beginning of the ages has been hidden in God who created all things through Jesus Christ; to the intent that now the manifold wisdom of God might be made known by the church to the principalities and powers in the heavenly places, according to the eternal purpose which He accomplished in Christ Jesus our Lord (Eph. 3:8-11).

The assembly is tremendously important in the mind of God and in the Word of God. Let me just mention a few things in connection with it.

It's important because it is the only society on earth to which God has promised perpetuity. Jesus said, *"On this rock I will build My church, and the gates of Hades shall not prevail against it."* That is not valid for any other group.

The importance of the assembly is seen by the prominent place that it is given to it in the New Testament. I think we are justified in

---

49   The word *assembly* is generally used in this book in preference to *church*. An *assembly* is a gathering of people whereas *church* commonly means a building.

judging the importance of a subject by the amount of the New Testament that is devoted to it. Vast tracts of the Scripture cover this subject. In Ephesians 1:19-23, Paul wrote:

> What is the exceeding greatness of His power toward us who believe, according to the working of His mighty power which He worked in Christ when He raised Him from the dead and seated Him at His right hand in the heavenly places, far above all principality and power and might and dominion, and every name that is named, not only in this age but also in that which is to come. And He put all things under His feet, and gave Him to be head over all things to the church, which is His body, the fullness of Him who fills all in all."

How is His body the fullness of Him who fills all in all? I hold in my hand a little 3" by 5" index card. I'm going to tear it in half to illustrate. One piece represents the Lord Jesus Christ. The other represents the body of Christ, the church. Now I hold them together again. In a sense, the church is the complement of Christ. It is as if the Lord Jesus doesn't consider Himself complete without the church, His body. And His body is His vehicle on earth for expressing Himself to the world. When I see this, I realize the church is important. The assembly is important; we must have convictions concerning it. And we should be enthusiastic about it, not apologetic. I'm afraid some of us get hesitant when we come to the subject. We're afraid to sound out the truth about it.

The church is spoken of as an object lesson to angelic beings. We read that in Ephesians 3:10,

> *To the intent that now the manifold wisdom of God might be made known by the church to the principalities and powers in the heavenly places.*

Just think of angelic beings, or celestial beings at least, looking down on the earth and seeing what God has done with the church. He took the Jew and the Gentile, and brought them together, believing Jew and believing Gentile. With all kinds of different personalities, all kinds of wart and wrinkles, and all the rest, He brought them together He made one new man out of them.

Speaking at the Keswick Conference in England, Jonathan Lamb read the following quote:

> Christ died that humans of every type be reconciled to God and to one another. The genius of Christianity is that it makes possible on-going fellowship between people who could not otherwise tolerate, let alone enjoy one another. Christ gets refined socialites hobnobbing with migrant farm workers, middle-aged squares weeping with rebels and swingers, Blacks, Indians, Jews, and Whites praying earnestly together, and management and laborer sharing each other's problems. In a world divided by class, commerce, race, education, politics, the generation gap, and a million clashing interests, Christ alone can make incompatibles mesh.[50]

This came home to me very powerfully some years ago when I was in Haifa. There is an assembly in Haifa in which believing Jews and believing Arabs break bread together. It is really a beautiful exhibition of what we have here in the Word of God. Celestial beings look down and marvel at the wisdom of God.

Paul speaks that the truth of the assembly as the capstone of scriptural revelation. In Colossians 1:25 he writes, *"Of which I became a minister according to the stewardship from God which was given to me for you, to fulfill the Word of God."*

To fulfill or complete the Word of God? Actually, Colossians wasn't the last book of the New Testament to be added. And yet, as far as the revelation of new, important doctrines, it was the capstone of scriptural revelation, particularly the revelation of the church.

In 1 Timothy 3:15 we read that the assembly is the unit on earth that God has chosen to propagate the faith: *"But if I am delayed, I write so that you may know how you ought to conduct yourself in the*

---

50   Lamb, Jonathan, *Truth on Fire*, Keswick Ministry 1998, Carlisle, England: OM Publishing, 1998, p. 240.

house of God, which is the church of the living God, the pillar and ground of the truth." In Bible times, pillars were often used to post news or declarations. The church is the pillar to placard the truth.

God loves the assembly. God had this secret in His mind from all eternity, that in the fullness of time, He was to form a new society with a heavenly calling and a heavenly destiny, and that He was going to send His Son down to this world to seek a bride, and at enormous cost.

I found this tidbit in *Choice Gleanings* calendar some time ago:

> If we could but realize that the dearest object in this world to our Lord Jesus is His church, we would spend lest time in peripheral activities and concerns. Our efforts would then be directed toward the up-building of the local church where we fellowship, and our love would reach to every member of His body. Thus we would be caring for that which He loves most in the world.

God loves the assembly. Christ loves the assembly. The apostle Paul loved the assembly. He says in Ephesians 3:8:

> *To me, who am less than the least of all the saints, this grace was given, that I should preach among the Gentiles the unsearchable riches of Christ, and to make all people see what is the fellowship of the mystery, which from the beginning of the ages has been hidden in God who created all things through Jesus Christ.*

Now, to some young believers, that might just seem like a jumble of holy words, but let me seek to simplify it. In those verses, the apostle Paul is saying that he had a two-fold ministry. Can you see it? What was the two-fold ministry of the apostle Paul? First of all, *"That I might preach among the Gentiles the unsearchable riches of Christ...."* That's the gospel, isn't it? But he doesn't stop there. He says *"And to make all men see what is the fellowship* [or administration] *of the mystery."* That's the church. And I can't say that He loved one more than the other. He kept those things in balance.

Sometimes I think we are more enthusiastic about gospel work than we are about the local assembly. Paul wasn't. Paul's great desire was to preach the gospel, to see people saved, to see them brought into the fellowship of the local church, and see them grow in the things of the Lord so that they become reproducing Christians. It's a great vision, isn't it? And I would challenge you. Where do you stand on this two-fold ministry? You're probably an aggressive soul-winner. I thank God for that. It's wonderful, but don't stop there. Have the two-fold ministry that the great apostle Paul had.

God loves the assembly. Christ loves the assembly. Paul loved the assembly. Could I just bring my squeaky voice in and say, "I love the assembly, too"? It's my mother. I owe a lot—I owe every-thing, in a way—to the local assembly. It's in that assembly that I heard the gospel preached. It's in that assembly I came under the convicting power of the Holy Spirit of God. It's in the assembly I was taught the Word of God. It wasn't very spectacular to outward view. It wasn't very dramatic. It was Christians sitting around, holding conversational Bible reading and going through the Bible book by book. The first conversational Bible reading I remember as a young lad was going through the book of Isaiah. Imagine! Deep stuff! That was my background. That was my training. I thank God for it today. I love the assembly. I really do. And I'm enthusiastic about it.

I want to go over with you some of the truths of the assembly found in the Word of God. Let me just say this, there shouldn't be any assembly distinctives. Does that shock you? Well, there shouldn't be any. Look, the truth is there for all the people of God, isn't it? It's all there in the Bible. The only thing that makes it distinctive is that some people practice it and others don't. But the principles are there for all God's people to believe and practice.

ONE BODY

The first principle I love is that there's only one body. I love Ephesians 4:4, *"There is one body and one Spirit, just as you were called in one hope of your calling; one Lord, one faith, one baptism."* This is the death knell of denominationalism. I hate, loathe, despise, and abominate sectarian titles. That's just a gentle, subtle way of saying I don't like them! I don't like the title, "Plymouth Brethren." "Brethren" is universal, "Plymouth" is rather local. It makes me think of "Roman Catholic." "Catholic" means universal, and Roman means not universal—it means Roman. I don't like those titles. I don't even like the title "Christian Brethren" because all of God's people are Christian brethren, and I don't want anything that sets me apart from other members of the body of Christ.

When H. A. Ironside was asked what denomination he belonged to, he'd reply in the words of Psalm 119:63, *"I am a companion of all those who fear You and of those who keep Your precepts."* Isn't that lovely? That's the right denomination to belong to. And if somebody comes to you and says, "What denomination do you belong to?" just say, "The same one that Paul did," and that will make a Bible student out of him. He'll have to go to the Word of God to see what denomination Paul belonged to. It will open his eyes. It really is a glorious truth. One body here on earth, made up of all true believers in the Lord Jesus Christ.

But people want to get you into a pigeonhole, don't they? If you ever want to get others uncomfortable, just answer like this when they say, "What are you?"

"Well, I'm a Christian."

"Of course, we're all Christians. What else are you?"

"I'm a disciple of the Lord Jesus."

"I know you're a disciple of the Lord Jesus, but what church do you belong to?"

"I belong to the church which is His body."

They're never happy until they can put you in some denominational slot. Don't yield to it!

CHRIST THE HEAD AND GATHERING CENTER

Christ is the Head of the church. *"For the husband is the head of the wife, as also Christ is Head of the church; and He is the Savior of the body"* (Eph. 5:23). No man is the head of the church, be he pope, archbishop, or president. Even the elders are not the head of the church. Christ is the head and the only One.

Christ is not only the head of the church, He is the gathering center of His people. This is a wonderful truth. I wish it were more appropriated today. When we meet together, we don't meet to a man. We don't meet to a church in the denominational sense. We meet to Christ. Christ is the gathering-center, and we go there because we believe the Lord Jesus Christ is there. We appropriate that by faith because He said, *"Where two or three are gathered together in My name, there I am I in the midst of them."* You say, I don't see Him, I'm not conscious of Him. Well, sometimes you go to meetings, and I tell you, the heavens come down very low and the priests can't minister because of the glory of the Lord, and I want to be there at those times, don't you? Christ is the gathering-center of His people.

All believers are members of the body of Christ (1 Cor. 12:12-13):

For as the body is one and has many members, but all the members of that one body, being many, are one body, so also is the Christ. For by one Spirit we were all baptized into one body—whether Jews or Greeks, whether slaves or free— and have all been made to drink into one Spirit.

I'd like you to notice something at the end of verse 12. It says,

As the body is one and has many members, but all the members of that one body, being many, are one body, so also is Christ [lit., the Christ].

There's a very unusual use of the word Christ here. It refers to Christ the Head plus the church His body. Amazing, isn't it? Sometimes we become so used to these verses we don't realize how breathtaking they are. It's mind-boggling that the Spirit of God would use the words *"the Christ"* to describe Christ the Head plus the church, His body. All believers are members.

I love all believers in the Lord Jesus. I love all of those who have been redeemed by precious blood. They're my brothers and sisters in Christ, fellow members of the body. I can learn something from every one of them. There's no believer in the Lord Jesus that I can't learn something from. And not only that, I should pray for all believers, not just those in my own local fellowship, but all believers, because we are fellow members of that body. And I should rejoice when they preach Christ. I might not agree with the way they cross their t's or dot their i's, but I can rejoice like Paul did in Philippians 1:18 that Christ is preached.

But that doesn't mean that I can do everything that they do. This is where we have to be careful. I can love them. I can learn from them. I can learn zeal and love and dedication to the Lord Jesus, but I can't do a lot of the things they do. My conscience, like Luther's, must be captive to the Word of God. I have to go by what the Word of God teaches me. For instance, it doesn't mean that I can cooperate with other believers in crusades where converts are sent back to an apostate church. It makes me think of what Moody said: "I wouldn't put live chicks under a dead hen." He was right on when he said that.

THE PRIESTHOOD OF ALL BELIEVERS

All believers are priests. We're holy priests and we're royal priests.

Coming to Him as to a living stone, rejected indeed by men, but chosen by God and precious, you also, as living stones, are being built up a spiritual house, a holy priesthood, to offer up spiritual sacrifices acceptable to God through Jesus Christ (1 Pet. 2:4).

But you are a chosen generation, a royal priesthood, a holy nation, His own special people, that you may proclaim the praises of Him who called you out of darkness into His marvelous light" (1 Pet. 2:9).

Male believers are priests. Female believers are priests. All believers are. And all believers have the function of offering up the sacrifices of their person, their possessions, their praise, and their service to the Lord. But the Spirit of God puts controls on the public exercise of the priesthood. We shouldn't be surprised at that. Think of the controls that the Spirit puts on the use of tongues in an assembly (1 Cor. 14). If anybody speaks in tongues, there must be an interpreter. Not more than three may speak in tongues in any one meeting. They must speak one at a time. What they say must be edifying. The women must remain silent. All things must be done decently and in order. And so it is with regard to the public use of the priesthood of the believer. *"I desire that the men* (lit. *males*) *pray everywhere"* (1 Tim. 2:8). *"I do not permit a woman to teach or to have authority over a man, but to be in silence"* (1 Tim. 2:12). We shouldn't be surprised at these controls. If the Spirit of God can put controls on the public use of gifts in the assembly, why can He not do it on the priesthood of believers as well?

A PLURALITY OF ELDERS AND FUNCTIONING SAINTS

A local assembly is made up of saints, elders, and deacons. Philippians 1:1 makes this clear: *"Paul and Timothy, servants of Jesus Christ, to all the saints in Christ Jesus who are in Philippi, with the bishops* [the elders] *and deacons…"*

That was the makeup of the church in Philippi. They gathered together for the apostles' doctrine and fellowship, for the breaking of bread, and for prayer (Acts 2:42). And I think if you bring those verses together, you have a definition of a local assembly. It's a group composed of saints, elders, and deacons, who gather together for the apostles' doctrine, fellowship, the breaking of bread, and prayer.

A great truth of the assembly is that there's no such a thing as a clerical system. There is no one man officiating. This is a glorious truth. It is the saints who are to do the work of the ministry. The gifts were given *"for the equipping of the saints for the work of ministry, for the edifying of the body of Christ"* (Eph. 4:12). It's because of this portion of the Word of God that I fellowship in an assembly today. I was out in Honolulu when the Spirit of God came to me in a very real way and asked, "Why are you in an assembly? Would you be just as happy in a denominational church? Or a Bible church? Are you in the assembly because your father was in the assembly? Is that why you're there?" And I said, "That does it! I'm going to go to the Word of God and see what it teaches." I really believe that the Spirit of God led me to this passage of Scripture. I saw that every believer is a minister, that is, a servant.

Because of centuries of tradition revolving around the clerical system, it seems hard to believe that the idea of one man officiating in a church, doing most, if not all, of the preaching, is not the New Testament pattern. Yet the whole idea of dividing an equal brotherhood into clergy and laity is completely without scriptural support. It's foreign to the New Testament. There is no biblical warrant for anyone to speak of "my pastor" or for any preacher to speak of "my church." It just isn't found in the Word of God. Nowhere in the New Testament is any reference ever made to a one-man minister in the church. I'm going to read you some quotes from men, many of whom held the office of a cleric in a church, and they're all going to say the same thing: it's not right.

Barnes, the noted Bible commentator, wrote:

There is no allusion to anyone who is to be superior to the elders and deacons. If Paul supposed there was to be an order of prelates in the church, why is there no allusion to them? Why is there no mention of their qualifications? If Timothy was himself a prelate, was he to have nothing to do in transmitting the office to others? Were there no peculiar qualifications required in such an order of men which it would be proper to mention? Would it not be respectful at least of Paul to have made some allusion to such an office if Timothy himself held it? There was none.[51]

People say, "Well, Paul himself was a minister." Listen, the longest Paul ever stayed in one place at one time was two years at Ephesus. During his total ministry, he stayed three years there. But at any one time, he only stayed there for two years. And his strategy was to see people saved, to see them built up in the faith, and to move on. As a gift to the church, he considered himself expendable.

What about Timothy? Was he a minister?" The old Bibles used to have a postscript saying that he was the first bishop of the church at Ephesus. Thank God they've removed that now from the epistles to Timothy. Timothy wasn't a minister in a church. He was an itinerant troubleshooter for the apostle Paul, not a settled cleric in a church. The New Testament teaches plurality of elders but not a one man ministry.

Alexander Maclaren wrote,

I cannot but believe that the present practice of confining the public teaching of the church to an official class has done harm. Why should one man be forever speaking, and hundreds of people who are able to teach sitting dumb to listen, or pretend to listen to him? I hate forcible revolution, and do not believe that any institution, either political or ecclesiastical, which need violence to sweep them away, are ready to be removed, but I believe that if the level of spiritual life were raised among us, new forms would naturally be evolved in which the great principle of the democracy of Christianity is founded, namely, "I will pour out My Spirit on all flesh, and on my servants and on my handmaidens, I will pour out in these days of My Spirit, and they shall prophesy.[52]

---

51   *Barnes on the New Testament*, Vol. VIII, Thessalonians–Philippians, p. 155.

52   *The Expositor's Bible, Colossians and Philemon*, London: Hodder & Stoughton, 1903, pp. 328-330.

J. I. Packer adds his testimony. He says,

By clericalism, I mean that combination of conspiracy and tyranny to which the minister claims and the congregation agrees, that all spiritual ministry is his responsibility and not theirs, a notion that is both disreputable in principle and Spirit-quenching in practice.[53]

In his book, *God's New Society*, John R. W. Stott says this:

What model of the church, then, should we keep in our minds? The traditional model is that of the pyramid, with the pastor perched precariously on the pinnacle, like a little pope in his own church, while the laity are arrayed below him in serried ranks of inferiority. It is a totally unbiblical image, because the New Testament envisages not a single pastor with a docile flock, but both a plural oversight and an every-member ministry.[54]

This is not written by somebody who opposes the clerical system. It's written by a man who was a cleric in the Church of England.

Donald Gray Barnhouse was the pastor of the Tenth Presbyterian Church in Philadelphia. He said:

By the close of the first century, there was a party within the church organization that had gained a victory over the laity by exalting itself to a place of dominance, even though Peter had warned against it. As seen in the letter to the church at Ephesus in the second chapter of the book of Revelation, there was in the first century a party called the Nicolaitans, who, as their name in Greek indicates, had gained supremacy over the laity. There it is stated that God Almighty hates the works of those who advocate and enforce rule over others within the body of Christ.[55]

Evangelist Leighton Ford wrote in the *Christian Persuader*, "Our

---

53   *Keep in Step with the Spirit*, Old Tappan, NJ: Fleming Revell Co., 1984, p. 29.
54   *God's New Society, The Message of Ephesians*, Downer's Grove, IL: InterVarsity Press, 1979, p. 167.
55   *The Measure of Your Faith*, p. 21.

whole vocabulary of church activity will change if we really begin to take seriously the New Testament pattern." And then he quotes Richard Halverson as saying:

> When we ask, "How many ministers does your church have?" the traditional answer is "One, or two, or five", depending on how large the paid staff is. The true answer is two hundred or two thousand depending on how large the membership is. Every believer is a minister. The church which bottlenecks its outreach by depending on its specialists, its pastors or evangelists, to do the witnessing, is living in violation of both the intention of the Head and the consistent pattern of early Christians."[56]

E. Stanley Jones, a Methodist minister in India years ago, said:

The church at Antioch was founded by laymen, carried on by laymen, and spread through that ancient world by laymen. This is important for the reconstruction of the church today. The next great spiritual awakening is going to come through the laity. Hitherto the center of gravity has been on the minister. Now the center of gravity has to be shifted to the laity. We ministers, missionaries, and evangelists are never going to win the world. We are too few to do it, and if we could do it, it wouldn't be good, for it would take away from the laity that spiritual growth and development which comes through sharing our faith. But we will never get the laity to take responsibility for the Christian movement and its spread by saying, "Come on and help the pastor." Their inner response and some times outer response is "Why should we? That's his job. We pay him for that."[57]

The very set-up of the ordinary church tends to produce the anonymous. The congregation is supposed to be silent and receptive, and the pastor is supposed to be outgoing and aggressive. That produces by its very makeup the spectator and the participant. By its very makeup it produces the recessive, the ingrown,

---

56   Ford, Leighton, The Christian peruader, NY: Harper and Row, 1966, p. 49.

57   Jones, E. Stanley, *The Reconstruction of the Church—On What Pattern?* Nashville, TN: Abingdon Press, 1970, pp. 42-43.

the non-contributive, and the parasite. Men and women who, during the week, are molders of opinion, directors of large concerns, directors of destinies, are expected to be putty on Sunday. And they are supposed to like it! They have little responsibility, hence make little response except perhaps to say, "I enjoyed your sermon." They have little to do because they do little.[58]

The laity, on the whole, have been in the stands as spectators, and the clergy have been on the field playing the game. If the clergyman kicks a goal or makes a touchdown, he is applauded: "Good pastor. Hope he will stay." That setup must be changed; the laity must come out of the stands as spectators, and take the field as players, and the clergyman must come off the field as players and take the sidelines as coaches of the team. The clergymen must be guides, stimulators, and spiritualizers of an essentially lay movement. Downgrading them? No, upgrading them. For it is better to be a coach than to be a player. It is better to get ten people to work than to do ten men's work.[59]

You'll notice that many of these men keep talking about clergy, laity, and ministers in the exclusive sense, not realizing that these are unscriptural terms. However, give them credit for sensing the weakness of the clerical system.

Bryan Green says, "The future of Christianity and the evangelization of the world rests in the hands of ordinary men and women, and not primarily in those of those professional Christian ministers."[60]

Harnack claimed that "When the church won its greatest victories in the early days of the Roman Empire, it did so not by preachers or teachers or apostles, but by informal missionaries, the people going everywhere and gossiping the gospel."[61]

In *New Paths in Muslim Evangelism*, Phil Parshall reminds us:

---

58   Ibid., pp. 109.
59   Ibid., p.46-47.
60   Quoted by E. Stanley Jones in Conversion, Abingdon Press, 1959, p. 219.
61   Ford, Leighton, The Christian Persuader, New York, NY: Harper & Row, 1966, p. 46.

In Christian circles the word *ministry* has come to refer to the professional clergy, but in the New Testament *diakonia* (ministry) is not the function of one class. It is a role to which all believers are called. In 1 Corinthians 12:4-30, Paul speaks of the different gifts bestowed by the Holy Spirit as "varieties of *diakonia*" (v. 5) and he includes all believers in his picture of the body.

The New Testament does not focus on one leader in the local church. The churches met in homes and were guided by groups of elders. Acts 20:17-38 speaks of Paul's interaction with the elders from Ephesus. There is no focus of attention on one leader in this passage.[62]

David Gooding agrees. He writes:

Whatever way a church organizes its meetings, one thing it must not do, and that is to arrange that one member and only one member shall continually do all the preaching, teaching, evangelism, and spiritual ministry...It is seriously detrimental to the growth of the body of Christ, as in this matter we depart from the pattern of the New Testament.[63]

And then, finally, I'd like to read what J. A. Stewart said. He reminds us that "Each member of the local assembly went out to win souls for Christ by personal contact, and then brought these newborn babes back into these local churches, where they were indoctrinated and strengthened in the faith of the Redeemer. They in turn went out to do likewise." In another place, Stewart says, "The world will never be evangelized as God intended as long as we have a clerical system."[64] That's powerful!

At a time when many evangelical Christians are moving away from the clerical system, many in the assemblies are moving toward clerisy. They want to hire one man to perform their religious functions for

62   Parshall, Phil, New Paths in Muslim Evangelism, Grand Rapids, MI: Baker Book House, 1980, p. 169.
63   Gooding, David, Freedom Under God, Bath, England: Echoes of Service, 1988, p. 18.
64   Stewart, James, Evangelism, Asheville, NC: Revival Literature, 1955, p. 14.

them. They're buying high and selling low. Their cry is, "Give us a minister like the other churches." "They're like those in the social sciences who adopt popular trends of thought at the time that secular professionals are beginning to subject the trends to serious criticism. It's just a matter of climbing on the bandwagon as its slowing down."[65] That's what's happening today.

What's the harm of the clerical system? It always has the danger of gathering people to a man instead of to the blessed Lord Jesus Christ. It stifles the gifts of the members of the congregation. There is always a danger, too, when one man does all the teaching. No one man has a monopoly on the truth, and the Spirit of God loves to take different people and speak through them. It's easier to introduce error when people look to one man as their teacher.

The clerical system ignores the purpose for which the gifts were given. They were given for the perfecting of the saints unto the work of the ministry. The saints are the ones who are to do the work of the ministry.

With the clerical system there is usually a salaried ministry. And this is a curse in the work of God. This has the terrible danger that when a man is judged by the size and growth of a church, he is tempted to lower the standards. Those who pay the piper call the tune.

THE CENTRALITY OF WORSHIP

Another great truth of the New Testament assembly is that worship is central. Many people who fellowship for years in an assembly and then leave and go elsewhere, say, "I *do* miss the breaking of bread." I feel like asking, "Why did you leave?" Worship is central. If you don't like to worship, you won't like heaven, because worship is going to be the central activity of heaven.

Every believer has some gift or gifts. We believe this, and there should be liberty in the assembly for the exercise of gifts. These gifts

---

65   Paul Vitz, quoted by Dave Hunt, The Seduction of Christianity, Eugene, OR: Harvest House Publishers, 1985, p. 205.

are given for the benefit of the body. Not for selfish display, but for the benefit of the body. Of course, some of the gifts like evangelism and hospitality are not limited to serving believers.

PRINCIPLES PLUS POWER

I would like to emphasize this: New Testament principles require New Testament power. There is no substitute for spirituality. There is nothing worse than to see people trying to go through the motions unspiritually. God wants a people who are in touch with Himself, people who are walking in the Spirit day by day, people who are walking in fellowship with the blessed Lord Jesus Christ. It's not enough just to have correct doctrine. We must be correct spiritually.

There's a reproach connected with maintaining the truth of the New Testament church today. If you're not willing to bear that reproach, you're going to really drift. If you stick to the truth of the New Testament, you'll always be a speckled bird in the evangelical community. I could give you instance after instance of that. But I think of this. On the day before her execution, Anaken Janz wrote to her infant son:

> Where you hear of a poor, simple, cast-off little flock that is despised and rejected by the world, join them. For where the cross is, there is Christ.

Years ago, Alfred Mace said to me, "Bill, when you get divine principles, stick to them." And that saying stayed with me. I've sought to follow it. When you get divine principles, stick to them. Don't compromise them and don't drift away from them. And he said something else to me, "No man's gift is too big for God's principles." I might think that my gift is too great for the little, despised assemblies. Never! No man's gift is too big for God's principles.

In closing, be committed to the assembly. Be enthusiastic about it. Don't be a church-hopper. Don't be a religious butterfly. Be one to whom Christ can say, *"You have continued with Me in My temptation and I appoint unto you a kingdom."*

Remember that the smallest, weakest assembly of God's people means more to God than the greatest empire in the world. When God talks about an empire, He compares it to a drop in a bucket. He never says that about the church. The church is the body and bride of Christ. Imagine!

Remember that a godly elder in an assembly means more to God than the ruler of a nation. More space is devoted in the New Testament to the work of an elder than to the work of a president or a king.

Get these convictions. Let them mold your life, and live in the light of them.

THIRTY-TWO
OBEY THE COURTESY CODE

SOME GENERAL SUGGESTIONS

Wear neat, clean clothes. Be an example to others. Remember Oswald Chambers' words: "Slovenliness is an insult to the Holy Spirit."

Be prompt for appointments. It is not smart to be late. It is saying that your time is important and the other person's is not. If you find you are going to be late, call and explain. When some people were late for a prayer meeting, Mrs. Wetherell Johnson warned them against letting that happen again. She said, "Don't insult the majesty of the Holy Spirit."

Avoid body odor and bad breath. Use a deodorant, and floss and brush your teeth regularly. Mints are helpful.

Don't be a compulsive talker. People who never come up for air are a bore. Be a good listener and you'll be surprised how much you can learn.

Be sensitive to the feelings of others. Never make joking or negative remarks about them—their clothing, haircut, appearance, ability, etc.

Be sensitive to local cultural and social customs, and try to fit in as much as possible. This applies especially to dress. When you are invited to speak at a meeting, find out how the leaders dress and follow their example.

Men shake hands with men, when introduced. When a man is

introduced to a women, he should wait until she extends her hand.

Be sure to see that strangers in a group are introduced.

A man always rises to speak to a woman who is standing. It's a good idea to stand for an older man also.

Never intrude in a conversation that is going on between others.

Never interrupt when a person is reading or is obviously busy.

Don't enter a room when prayer is in progress or when the Scriptures are being read. Wait.

When using someone else's car, always replace the gasoline you've used.

When you have a cold, don't sniffle. Try Kleenex.

Have a servant heart. Try to see ways in which you can serve others and do it without fanfare or trumpet blowing. See things to be done and do them.

If you ask someone to go to a restaurant with you, it is your responsibility to pay the bill. But whether you ask or not, don't always be on the receiving end. Share the responsibility of picking up the tab.

When you are in company, don't read and thus separate yourself from the conversation. It might give the impression that you don't consider their conversation worth listening to. Besides, it's rude.

If you are in a room with company and have to leave before the others, excuse yourself courteously and say good-bye. Don't slip out without explanation.

Acknowledge all gifts promptly. Use your letter as an opportunity to minister to people spiritually. That's what Paul did when he wrote the letter to the Philippians.

In answering a question, don't say "Of course." That's a put down. It's like saying, "Yes, you dummy."

Use your cell phone in private, not at the table or in company or in public. Shut it off when you are in a meeting. Don't ask a caller to hold so you can take another incoming call. It's not courteous.

AS A GUEST IN A HOME

If you are going to be in full time work for the Lord, you will be a guest in the homes of the Lord's people. It is important that you know how to behave. You don't want to have the reputation of being a boor. Notify your host and hostess of your expected time of arrival and mode of travel. If by air, name airport, airline, flight number, and time. Sometimes there are two airports in the area, so be sure to say which one.

Don't bring others with you except by prior arrangement. It is commonly accepted for your wife to accompany you, but if that is the case, be sure to notify in advance. When the eccentric Mr. Buchman shook hands with Mrs. Hibben, he said,

"The Lord told me to take these three other men to dinner too."

"Oh, I don't think so,"

"Why not?"

"Because," responded Mrs. Hibben, "God is a gentleman."

In the house, try to fit into the family schedule as much as possible. Cause a minimum of disruption. Don't hog the bathroom. Be prompt at meal times. Retire at a reasonable time.

Clean the bathtub and hand basin after each use. Someone else will be using it.

Don't help yourself to personal items in the home, such as cologne, tooth paste, etc.

Don't use the phone without permission. If you do use it with permission, leave payment before departing.

Make up your bed in the morning, and leave your room neat.

Offer to help with work in the home, such as washing and drying dishes. Don't worry if the host good-naturedly complains that you are setting a bad example for him.

Don't peer into your host's correspondence, files, closets, or drawers.

Thank the host and hostess before leaving, and always send a thank you note for overnight hospitality.

AT THE TABLE

Wait to be seated until a signal from the host or hostess. A man should help the lady to the right of him to be seated (unless her husband is on the other side. Then it's his duty.)

Don't start eating until the host or hostess does. This applies to the beginning of the meal and to every subsequent course.

Try to be thoughtful to see that others are served. Don't let all the serving dishes come to a dead stop in front of you.

When asked to pass something, don't help yourself first.

Avoid conversation that is not conducive to pleasant eating.

Keep elbows off the table. Avoid any inelegant behavior.

Curb your appetite. Take modest helpings, making sure there is enough for those who follow you. Second servings are acceptable. After that you might give the appearance of being gluttonous.

Don't be a picky eater. *"Eat whatever is set before you, asking no question for conscience' sake"* (1 Cor. 10:27). It's good missionary training.

Don't shop around for better accommodations. Didn't Jesus say to stay in the first house where you are welcomed and not go from house to house (Lk. 10:5-7)?

Ephesians 4:29 is a golden rule for the Christian's speech: *"Let no corrupt communication proceed out of your mouth, but what is good for necessary edification, that it may minister grace to the hearers."* *"Corrupt"* here goes beyond what is dirty, off-color, and profane to what is worthless. We should not indulge in small talk but constantly try to steer the conversation to what will build up the listeners.

When a servant of the Lord is with company, they like to hear him tell about triumphs of the gospel and incidents in his ministry. He should discipline himself to keep his conversation on a spiritual level.

Try to involve children and quiet adults in conversation so they won't feel "left out."

Avoid excessive levity. Don't be remembered as a jokester. The issues of the Christian faith are serious. Many preachers think that they can have rapport with young people by constantly cracking jokes. Most young people expect something more serious and worthwhile from them.

Never say anything to embarrass someone else. When a preacher was giving an illustration and saw a person in the audience on whom the story would reflect unfavorably, he stopped in the middle. After the meeting someone asked him why he had allowed the story to die in mid-air. He replied, "Better to spoil a good story than to hurt a good person."

YOUR WIFE

Love your wife as Christ loves the church (Eph. 5:25). No woman would mind being submissive to a man like that.

Treat your wife like a lady. Open the door of the car for her to enter or exit. Walk with her on the curb side of the sidewalk.

Never criticize her, contradict her, or put her down in public. On the contrary, a public word of praise and thanks is never out of order.

NOW TO SUMMARIZE

If you are ever in doubt in a particular situation, just treat others as you would have them treat you. Courtesy is esteeming others better than yourself. It is imitating the Lord Jesus in interpersonal matters. Courtesy is a lubricant that makes life run more smoothly, saves from embarrassment, and gives a pleasant glow to life.

THIRTY-THREE
DON'T BE GULLIBLE

Christians tend to be gullible. They think that because love believes all things, they should believe everything. Two bus drivers had stopped at a vista point so the tourists could get out and enjoy the view.

One driver said to the other, "I have a group of Christians."

"Really. What do they believe?

"They believe anything I tell them."

God does not want us to check our mind at the door when we become Christians. He wants us to be discerning. He wants us to distinguish between what is good and evil, true and false, and holy and unholy. The theme is found often in the Bible.

If you take out the precious from the vile, you shall be as My mouth (Jer. 15:19b).

And they shall teach My people the difference between the holy and the unholy, and cause them to discern between the unclean and the clean (Ezek. 44:23, referring to Lev. 10:10).

But the natural man does not receive the things of the Spirit of God, for they are foolishness to him, nor can he know them because they are spiritually discerned (1 Cor. 2:14).

But the manifestation of the Spirit is given to each one for the profit of all...to another discerning of spirits (1 Cor. 12:7, 10).

In malice be babes, but in understanding be mature (1 Cor. 14:20).

And this I pray, that your love may abound still more and more in knowledge and all discernment (Phil. 1:9).

Test all things; hold fast what is good (1 Thess. 5:21).

For everyone who partakes only of milk is unskilled in the word of righteousness, for he is a babe. But solid food belongs to those who are of full age, that is, those who by reason of use have their senses exercised to discern both good and evil (Heb. 5:13-14).

Beloved, do not believe every spirit, but test the spirits, whether they are of God, because many false prophets are gone out into the world (1 Jn. 4:1).

WE MUST LEARN TO DISCERN

The Bible is the basis of all discernment.

To the law and to the testimony! If they do not speak according to this word, it is because there is no light in them (Isa. 8:20).

How do you detect a crooked line? It is one that is not straight. How do you detect that a cloth is dirty? Just compare it with one that is clean.

Here is a sampling of areas in which we need to exercise discernment.

We used to be able to judge which Christian publishers are dependable. Some of the most dependable have slipped from their moorings.

We used to be able to judge various Bible colleges and seminaries, whether they had remained true to the faith. Now it must be said of many of them, *"The glory has departed."*

For years Christian parents raised their children according to Dr. Spock's book *Baby and Child Care.* Instead of obeying the Bible, and especially the book of Proverbs concerning discipline of children, they followed Dr. Spock in his promotion of a lax approach to disciplinary matters.

Years later, Dr. Spock said, "Inability to be firm is, to my mind, the commonest problem of parents today." He placed the blame for brattiness at least in part on the experts, the child psychiatrists, psychologists, teachers, social workers, and pediatricians, like himself. He concluded that parental submissiveness only encourages children to be more pesky and demanding, which, in turn, makes the parent increasingly resentful...until this finally explodes in a display of anger—great or small—that convinces the child to give in.

Said Dr. Spock, "In other words, parental submissiveness doesn't avoid unpleasantness; it makes it inevitable."

As Berean Christians (see Acts 17:10-11), we should learn to evaluate the following:

• The contemporary wisdom is that bigness is success. Church growth statistics emphasize large congregations. Is size the criterion or is the holiness of the members?

• Proponents of the ecumenical movement say, "Doctrine divides, service unites." How would you answer it?

• In many Pentecostal and Charismatic meetings, the speaker touches a person and he is "slain in the Spirit," falling to the floor. Here again we need discernment. Where do you find that in the Bible?

• Add to this the healing campaigns, where the TV evangelist professes to lengthen legs, deliver from cancer, and solve many other physical problems. Don't we believe in divine healing? Yes, we do, but we also know that many faith healers indulge in crafty methods that simulate healings.

• The prosperity doctrine takes promises of material prosperity in the Old Testament and applies them to the church today. Is it correct to do this?

• We need discernment in appraising the signs and wonders

movement. Does it square with what the Bible teaches?

• A perennial problem facing many believers is judging whether the tongues movement is according to the Word. What do you say?

• Is it right for women to preach or occupy positions of leadership in the church?

• To what extent should we trust our feelings in spiritual matters?

• A popular teaching is that you can't love God if you don't love yourself. Is this true?

• Another doctrine being floated is that a Christian never confesses his sins; he just thanks God that he has been forgiven.

• A Christian girl has just been murdered and her attacker is now in jail. The girl's mother goes to the jail and assures the murderer that she forgives him. Is this righteous?

• Some teachers say that when we pray, we should never say, "If it be Thy will." That betrays a lack of faith. Do you agree?

• "Praise God for everything" was the theme of a book that sold thousands of copies. After all, doesn't the Bible say, *"In everything give thanks?"*

• Those who object to male leadership in the home teach the mutual submission of husbands and wives. They quote Ephesians 5:21, *"...submitting to one another in the fear of God."* We should be able to answer this.

• The cults come to the door with a Bible and with religious literature, so people think they must be all right. We must be able to test their teaching by the Scriptures.

• We should not be in a hurry to believe undocumented stories that please gullible Christians. They want to believe them.

• There is a tract that says that Darwin confessed Christ on his deathbed. The story is a hoax. Another says that says that Nikita Khrushchev was converted to God and that's why he was removed from power in the Soviet Union. When I was a boy, I read a tract that said that the stones for the temple, made of Indiana limestone, were stored in a New York warehouse, ready to ship to Israel.

One Christian leader told Jim Elliot: "Young man, we are within forty years of the millennial reign of Christ, and that's a conservative estimate." That was on January 2, 1956![66]

A report circulated that a computer in Belgium accounts for the long day in Joshua 10 (when the sun stood still). Maybe it is the same computer that is said to be known as 666.

A hitchhiker is said to have told the host driver and his wife that Jesus was coming almost immediately. A few minutes later the driver glanced back in the car. The hitchhiker had vanished, even though the car was going 65 mph.

We should be discerning when we hear financial appeals by radio and TV evangelists. They offer to send prayer cloths, blessings, holy water from the Jordan, sacred crosses, etc. Some offer to pray daily for the donor. Christians have been bilked out of millions by religious charlatans. Ponzi schemes, pyramid schemes, and lotteries appeal to the greed in human nature. Christians beware! There are no free lunches.

THE TRUE GOSPEL

It is of first importance that we be men and women of the Book. We should read the Bible, study the Bible, memorize the Bible, meditate on the Bible, obey the Bible, and test all things by the Bible.

People today are increasingly illiterate as far as the Bible is concerned. That is why it is so easy for false teaching to spread.

We must be clear on the true gospel of the grace of God. Here is a summary:

There are only two religions in the entire world—salvation by works and salvation by grace through faith. Only the true Christian

66   Elisabeth Elliot, Shadow of the Almighty, New York: Harper Collins, 1989, p. 115.

faith teaches the latter. It is a very exclusive gospel.

- Only sinners can be saved.
- Only Christ can save.
- Only He died as a Substitute for sinners.
- Only His blood can wash away sins.
- Only trusting Him as Lord and Savior saves us.
- The only ones who will be in heaven will be sinners redeemed by the blood of Christ.

In summary, don't be like the Christians on the tour bus who believed everything the driver told them.

THIRTY-FOUR
NEVER GIVE UP

Therefore we also, since we are surrounded by so great a cloud of witnesses, let us lay aside every weight, and the sin which so easily ensnares us, and let us run with endurance the race that is set before us, looking unto Jesus, the author and finisher of our faith, who for the joy that was set before Him endured the cross, despising the shame, and has sat down at the right hand of the throne of God.

For consider Him who endured such hostility from sinners against Himself, lest you become weary and discouraged in your souls. You have not yet resisted to blood, striving against sin, and you have forgotten the exhortation that speaks to you as to sons:

My son, do not despise the chastening of the Lord, nor be discouraged when you are rebuked by Him; for whom the Lord loves He chastens, and scourges every son whom He receives (Heb. 12:1-6).

DEFINITION

Endurance is not the mere acceptance of trial and suffering but triumphing in it. It is not the patience of fatalism, but the patience that masters things. Endurance halts neither for discouragement from within nor from opposition from without. It is the steadfastness that carries on until, in the end, it gets there. Endurance is not the

269

fatalistic acceptance of circumstances but the steadfastness that carries on until the end.

Endurance is not the way of salvation, despite one or two verses that seem to say so. *"But he who endures to the end shall be saved"* (Mt. 24:13). Here the subject is the Tribulation Period. Believers should not think that safety lies in yielding to the enemy. It is those who endure who will be saved to enter the Millennium. *"No one, having put his hand to the plow, and looking back, is fit for the kingdom of God"* (Lk. 9:62). The subject here is service, not salvation. Quitters are not fit servants.

AREAS IN WHICH WE NEED ENDURANCE

We need it in family life and in raising children. We need it in getting an education.

We need it in the local church where "the normal condition…is difficulty" (J. Alexander Clarke). We need it on the mission field with its constant inter-personal conflicts. And we need it in days of illness and disability when the spirit is willing but the flesh is weak: "The Christian life must not be an initial spasm followed by chronic inertia."

THINGS THAT CAUSE PEOPLE TO GIVE UP OR TURN BACK

• A wrong love affair or a marriage not made in heaven.

• Sin in one's life: *"The foolishness of a man twists his way, and his heart frets against the Lord"* (Prov. 19:3). Or as Today's English Version puts it: *"Some people ruin themselves by their own stupid actions and then blame the Lord."*

• False profession as seen in the four soils of Matthew 13. The seed that fell on the wayside, the seed that fell on stony places, and the seed that fell among thorns are all false professors. Only the seed that bore fruit was genuine. Today people turn aside because of materialism, covetousness, false expectations, disappointment in people, discouragement, and persecution. The cost is too great.

BIBLICAL EXAMPLES OF ENDURANCE

Job suffered more material loss in one day than any other person in the Bible. He was not always patient but he did endure.

When we read of Paul's afflictions, dangers, persecutions, and sufferings for Christ's sake (2 Cor. 11:23-28), it is easy to wonder if we ourselves are Christians.

Jesus, of course, is the prime example of endurance (Heb. 12:1-4). The worst testings that demons and men could heap upon Him did not deter Him from going on to the cross.

EXAMPLES OF PHYSICAL ENDURANCE

Robert Bruce had suffered six military defeats in his efforts to make Scotland independent. Hiding in a cave, he saw a spider trying to connect the web from one point to another. Six times it failed, but the seventh time it succeeded. This spoke to Bruce and encouraged him to try again. This time he succeeded.

Five fishermen from Costa Rica were caught in a storm. Their boat was badly damaged. It took on water so that constant bailing was necessary. The radio went out. After days they ran out of food and water. At one time a tanker drew near and gave them water, then pulled away. When they were finally picked up, they had set a world's record for drifting at sea. They survived 142 days living on water, fish, and an estimated 200 turtles. They had traveled over 3600 miles and crossed four times zones.

Although he is a paraplegic, Mark Wellman climbed El Capitan, the world's largest monolith. It took him seven days and four hours to climb the 3000 feet, six inches at a time. Sometimes strong winds blew him out 10 feet from the face of the cliff. Then he climbed up the face of Half Dome, also in Yosemite National Park. It took almost two weeks to climb the 2200 feet.

These men were like Timex watches—they took a licking but kept on ticking. The Christian life is a marathon, not a hundred-yard dash. Remember the words of Winston Churchill. "Never give in. Never give in. Never, never, never, never—in nothing, great or small, large or petty—never give in, except to convictions of honor and good sense."

Coleman Cox said, "Even the woodpecker owes his success to the fact that he uses his head and keeps pecking away until he finishes the job he starts."

And a prominent leader said, "Most people give up just when they're about to achieve success. They quit on the one-yard line. They give up at the last minute of the game, one foot from a winning touchdown."

> *When things go wrong, as they sometimes will,*
> *When the road you're trudging seems all uphill,*
> *When care is pressing you down a bit,*
> *Rest, if you must—but don't ever quit.*
> *Often the goal is nearer than*
> *It seems to a faint and faltering man;*
> *Often the struggler has given up*
> *When he might have captured the victor's cup.*
> *Press on.* (Author unknown)

There was a man who failed in business. He ran for a seat in the Legislature and lost. Then there was another business fiasco. After finally getting elected to the Legislature, he suffered a nervous breakdown. During the next ten years, he failed in elections for Speaker, Land Officer, Elector, and Congressman. He was finally elected to Congress, but was defeated for re-election. He tried for the U.S. Senate but lost. A year later he was defeated in a bid for the Vice Presidency. And once again he failed to reach the U.S Senate. Finally, after all these reverses, he was elected President of the

United States. His name was Abraham Lincoln.

The Lord Jesus endured untold contradiction of sinners against Himself (Heb. 12:3). He endured the cross, despising the shame (Heb. 12:2). He finished the work which His Father had given Him to do (Jn. 17:4). There was never the slightest thought of turning back. It was like nourishment for Jesus to finish the work the Father gave Him to do (Jn. 4:34).

If we would be like Jesus, we must have endurance. We must have the spirit of Amy Carmichael when she wrote:

> *My hand is on the plow, my falt'ring hand;*
> *But all in front of me is untilled land.*
> *The wilderness and solitary place,*
> *The lonely desert with its interspace.*
>
> *The handles of my plow with tears are wet;*
> *The shares with rust are spoiled, and yet, and yet,*
> *Out in the field, ne'er let the reins be slack;*
> *My God! my God! keep me from turning back.*

THIRTY-FIVE
HAVE A CONSCIENCE
LIVE AND KEEN

Everyone is tempted to violate his conscience at one time or another. No matter what your occupation may be, there are built-in ethical problems. Used car salesmen feel pressured to extol a car even if they know it is a heap of junk. Doctors are asked to sign insurance claims for injuries or illnesses that do not exist or to make out prescriptions for drug addicts. Lawyers plead the innocence of people they know are crooked as a ram's horn and guilty as sin. Real estate agents can become experts at withholding the truth or even perverting it. Police officers accept favors from people who hope it will help if they are ever in trouble with the law. Contractors can increase their profit by failing to get the required permits or by using shoddy materials. Writers plagiarize the works of others. Aircraft mechanics sign that work has been done when it has not been done; it helps his record of keeping planes in the air. People who sell goods or services ask to be paid in cash so the transaction would not leave a paper trail; they won't have to pay income taxes on it. Employees call in sick or because they must to go to their grandmother's funeral; you'll find them at the baseball game.

Christians constantly face the temptation to lie. When income tax time rolls around, there is the fleshly desire to understate income and bloat expenses. Missionaries could get on with their work faster if they would bribe the customs agent or grease the policeman's palm with silver. The housewife gets too much change in the supermarket but decides to keep it anyway. Evangelists find it helpful to exaggerate the number attending their crusade or making a decision for Christ. Students face the ever-present temptation to cheat on exams. Zealous Christians witness for Christ on company time; that is not what they're being paid to do. Why do we slow down on the freeway when we've been speeding and now see a car coming after us with a ski rack on the roof? It looks uncomfortably like a police car. A beggar asks for money and we say, "Sorry, I haven't any." Or the office phone rings and the secretary says, "He isn't in." But he really is. Do you use a postage stamp when it has escaped cancellation? We could add the unlawful duplication of copyrighted audio and videocassettes and the use of pirated computer software.

Children face problems all the time. They steal from mother's purse, then to escape punishment they lie, blaming a sibling or denying any involvement.

Some of these things may seem petty but they are the little foxes that spoil the vines. The same arguments used to justify violation of ethics could be used to justify taking the mark of the beast.

A conscience that is live and keen speaks for God in an age of corruption. One believer had the reputation of building his Christianity into his houses. A businessman said of a Christian competitor, "You don't need a contract from him. His word is enough." A soccer referee said, "When I'm refereeing a game in which Tommy Walker is playing, I know I have only twenty-one players to watch, not twenty-two, because Tommy would never do a dirty thing." Tommy's Christianity affected his soccer.

When a blue-collar worker told his tax consultant about a large bloc of income that no one would have known about, the latter said, "Forget it. The government would never know." The worker replied, "I can't forget it. I'm a Christian."

These are examples of practical righteousness. Compare them with the professing Christian who, when confronted with his shady practice, said, "Listen! That's for Sunday. This is Wednesday."

Persistence in ethical failures has an atrophying effect on the conscience. Like a rubber band, the more it is stretched, the more it loses its elasticity.

The easy way is to salve the conscience with the glib idea that no one will know. But Someone will know. All things are open to the eyes of Him with whom we have to do. He reads not only our actions but the thoughts and intents of our hearts.

The results of a violated conscience are the same as the results of any sin:

- Fellowship with God is broken (1 Jn. 1:6).
- The joy of salvation is lost (Ps. 51:12).
- There is a loss of effective testimony (Gen. 19:14) and a leakage of spiritual power. We can't sin and get away with it. It takes its toll on us. We may think we are as effective as ever, but God's blessing is not on our service. The chariot wheels drag heavily.
- It brings shame on the name of the Lord (2 Sam. 12:14a).
- It stumbles other people (Jn. 17:21).
- The person loses access to God in prayer (Ps. 66:18).
- It is among the sins that crucified the Savior.
- It breaks the heart of God.
- It opens a person to temptation and bad decisions.
- It brings the chastening hand of God (Heb. 12:6).
- Unless confessed and forsaken, it results in loss of reward at the judgment seat of Christ (1 Cor. 3:11-15).

Where there is failure, there is always the way of recovery. It is found in 1 John 1:9. We drag the wretched evil out into the open and confess it as sin. When we do that, God is faithful and just to forgive us our sin and cleanse us from all unrighteousness.

We all have to establish our priorities. In what order would you arrange these: Profit, Products, People, Principles?

Sometimes it's costly for Christians whose conscience is educated by the Word of God and who are sensitive to obey. A young believer was ordered to make misleading statements to his customers about materials and costs. He prayed with his wife and asked the Lord what he should do. The next day he told his supervisor that he would not lie to the customers. That Friday he was laid off. He knew why.

It should be our ambition and joy to be able to say with the apostle Paul, *"I have lived in all good conscience before God until this day"* (Acts 23:1). If our conscience is guided by the Word of God, it will not only deliver us from sin, but will also free us from being unnecessarily scrupulous.

In one of his hymns that deserves to be better known, Charles Wesley wrote:

> *I want a principle within, of jealousy, of godly fear;*
> *A sensibility of sin, a pain to feel it near:*
> *I want the first approach to feel, of pride, or fond desire;*
> *To catch the wandering of my will, and quench the kindling fire.*
> *From Thee that I may no more part,*
> *No more Thy goodness grieve,*
> *The filial awe, the fleshly heart, the tender conscience give.*
> *Quick as the apple of an eye, O God, my conscience make!*
> *Awake my soul when sin is nigh, and keep it still awake.*
> *If to the right or left I stray, that moment, Lord, reprove;*
> *And let me weep my life away for having grieved Thy love.*
> *O may the least omission pain my well-instructed soul,*
> *And drive me to the blood again which makes the wounded whole.*

THIRTY-SIX
LIVE PEACEABLY WITH ALL— WHENEVER POSSIBLE

The title of this chapter is just a fancy way of saying "Getting Along With Others." That happens to be one of the biggest problems in the Christian life. It looms large in the home and in the church, on the home field and on the foreign field. It is a problem with people of all races, nationalities, and cultures. It's what Will Rogers meant when he said, "The trouble with the world is people."

Needless to say, we cannot cover all the bases in a chapter like this. It would take a volume the size of a telephone directory to even come close to that. So we will confine ourselves to some positive actions we can take, and then acts and attitudes we should avoid.

In dealing with others, try to think about their good qualities rather than their flaws. If they are believers, try to see Jesus in them. Said Bishop Whipple of Minnesota, the apostle to the Indians, "For thirty years I have tried to see the face of Christ in those who have differed from me."

Don't look for the flaws as you go through life;
And even when you find them,
It is wise and kind to be somewhat blind
And look for the virtue behind them,
For the cloudiest night has a hint of light
Somewhere in its shadows hiding,
It is better by far to hunt for a star
Than the spots on the sun abiding. (Ella Wheeler Wilcox)

Instead of majoring on people's quirks, we should concentrate on their potential. What they can become is greater than what they are now. We must remember that we all have faults and failures. We mustn't expect perfection in others as long as we can't produce it ourselves. Jesus accepted the disciples where they were, then built from there. He didn't demand that they would be spiritual giants before He would work with them. We can accept people as people without necessarily approving their actions. Said Dale E. Galloway:

> Many of us never learn to distinguish between approval of behavior and accep-
> tance of the person. When I talk about accepting a person unconditionally, I am
> not meaning that you have to approve of the other person's attitudes or actions.
> What you do is to love the person as he is, despite his flaws.

It is wise to make allowance for people's backgrounds, their vary-ing abilities and experiences, their differing levels of spiritual matu-rity. We make allowance for them by moderating any criticism we might have of them or holding back criticism altogether. Sometime when people rub us the wrong way, it is because of some difficult time they are going through. It pays to be patient and sympathetic.

We should appreciate the differences that God has made in His people. There is only one body—the body of Christ, but there are many members and no two members are alike. Try to visualize what a dull world it would be if each member were like yourself. This will cure you from trying to pour everyone into your own mold.

We tend to judge people by outward appearance. If they are good-looking, we automatically assume that they are good. James Dobson says that beauty is the golden coin of human worth. He goes on to explain that that's not the way it should be but very often it's the way it is.

A young lady who planned to marry Mozart became disenchanted with him because he was short, and she found a better looking man, one who was tall and attractive. After Mozart became famous, she regretted her decision. She said, "I knew nothing of the greatness of his genius. I only saw him as a little man."[67]

We should get to know people before making a judgment. Haste is dangerous. If we have to make a mistake, it is best to make it on the side of grace.

And we should never make a judgment without knowing all the facts. John Wesley had a bad attitude toward a man because he thought he was stingy. One day when Wesley noticed that the man had put a small amount in the offering, he openly criticized the poor man.

Later the man told Wesley that he had been living on parsnips and water. It seems that before he was saved, he had run up some huge bills. Now he was scrimping and saving to pay off his creditors. "Christ has made me an honest man," he said, "and so with all these debts to pay, I can only give a few shillings above my tithe. I must settle up with my worldly neighbors and show them what the grace of God can do in the heart of a man who was once dishonest." What could Wesley do but apologize to the man whom he had criticized so unfairly.[68]

It is a good idea to treat people with their good in view rather than our own advantage. We shouldn't "use" people, that is, exploit them,

67   Bosch, H. G., *Our Daily Bread*, Grand Rapids, MI: Radio Bible Class, August 17, 1992.
68   Bosch, H. G., *Our Daily Bread*, Grand Rapids, MI: Radio Bible Class, Sunday, August 17.

manipulate them, or use them to further our own ends. "God created us to *love* people and *use* things; our problem comes in *loving* things and *using* people" (Anonymous).

Ask the Lord for special patience to deal with people with difficult characters. Also realize realistically that there are probably some with whom you cannot work smoothly. Even Paul and Barnabas separated from one another in their service for the Lord.

Paul says that we should esteem others better than ourselves. This doesn't mean that everyone has a better character than our own. But it does mean that we should live for others rather than ourselves. We should put their interests above our own, and we should treat them the way the Lord Jesus has treated us.

When we meet people, we should make them feel that it is a meaningful experience for us. I have a friend who greets people, even strangers, with such warmth and enthusiasm that it practically makes their day.

We should go out of our way to meet strangers. If we find it difficult, we might have to force ourselves. We should be quick to introduce ourselves, then ask questions that evidence a genuine interest. Jesus introduced Himself to the Samaritan woman by asking a favor (Jn. 4:7).

The sure way we can prove our interest in others is by remembering their name. Elisabeth Elliot wrote,

It is said that the sweetest sound in any language is the sound of one's own name. People who engage in public relations know the importance of using a person's name. Whether we call people by name at all, and what name we use, are deeply significant, and are often a dead giveaway of our attitude toward a person.

Too often we excuse ourselves by complaining, "I just can't remember names." That is a cop-out and it is not true. We remember what we consider important. The simple device of writing down names is all that is often necessary to remember them.

We should remember the advice of Oliver Cromwell: "I beseech you by the tender mercies of Christ that you conceive it possible that you might be wrong." Too often there is that horrible possibility. When it is there, we should never be too proud to say, "I was wrong. I am sorry. Please forgive me." People shun the wiseacre or know-it-all. They feel more comfortable with those who admit that their knowledge is finite and that they are capable of being wrong.

If someone apologizes to us, we should tell him that he is forgiven. We shouldn't shrug it off as if no apology is necessary. It was probably a long, difficult struggle for him to come to the place of repentance. Now he wants to hear that he is forgiven.

We should maintain eye contact without staring. If our gaze wanders when we are talking to someone, it looks as if our mind is doing the same. And yet a fixed stare is disconcerting to the person to whom we are speaking.

A lot of current books are emphasizing the warmth and friendship that are conveyed by a touch, whether a firm handshake, an embrace, or a kiss. This is true, of course. Paul asked the Corinthians, *"Greet one another with a holy kiss"* (1 Cor. 16:20). But it must be balanced by the fact that if the touch is not holy, it can lead to strong temptation and sexual sin. Also it should take into account the fact that some legitimate touches may have the appearance of evil in our society and should therefore be avoided (1 Thess. 5:22, KJV).

In our encounters with others we should not be super-sensitive. Some people register hurt and resentment at the slightest provocation. They can't take a joke. They fly off the handle at remarks that are not intended as a put-down. A Christian should learn to have the hide of a rhinoceros.

> *I've asked the Lord to take from me*
> *The super-sensitivity*
> *That robs the soul of joy and peace*
> *And causes fellowship to cease.* (Author unknown)

The way in which we take criticism is an index of our character and spiritual maturity. We should realize that we have mannerisms, idiosyncrasies, and habits that annoy other people. We have numberless faults and failures. So we should take criticism humbly and benefit from it. We should say, "Well, Brother, I'm glad you don't know me better because, if you did, you'd have a lot more to criticize."

Sometimes the criticism is unjustified. At such times we should listen patiently and leave it with the Lord to vindicate us. We should ask Him to keep us from becoming cold, bitter, or cynical in spite of any criticism that is leveled against us; He always will.

People like friends who are upbeat, positive, and optimistic. Don't be a gloomy Gus. I've known people who were so radiant that when they entered a room, it seemed as if the lights went on. A good example to follow.

One of the greatest offenders in dealing with others is the tongue. This is dealt with at length in the chapter on the Christian's speech, so there is no need of repeating it here.

Special attention is needed to deal with inter-personal relations when serving as an elder, deacon, board director, trustee, or member of a committee. On matters of fundamental importance, there must be complete unanimity. The great doctrines of the Christian faith are not negotiable. Neither are matters of right and wrong. On lesser matters there has to be a certain amount of give and take. In such matters, compromise is not a bad word. There must be a willingness to discuss, negotiate, and eventually abide by the consensus of the group.

Anyone who has to have his own way all the time or who thinks that his judgment is infallible should never agree to serve with a policy-making group. He can wreck a work of God by being fiercely opinionated and stubbornly unyielding. Paul warns that God will wreck anyone who wrecks a local church (1 Cor. 3:16-17).

The Lord Jesus was congenial, compatible, and courteous. He is our example. The more we are like Him, the more we will learn the fine art of getting along with others.

Let me close with three guidelines that help to preserve peace in the valley:

- We should resign as general manager of the universe. Let the Lord run it.
- We can't live other people's lives for them. Don't try.
- No advice is as unwelcome as unasked advice. Wait until you are asked.

THIRTY-SEVEN
LIVE SACRIFICIALLY

It is a privilege to give. The question is not: How much must I give? But how much may I sacrifice. In thinking of our financial steward-ship, we must start with the determination to give God His portion (Prov. 3:9-10; Mal. 3:10). We should give:

- Regularly (on the first day of the week, 1 Cor. 16:2).
- Individually (each one of you, 1 Cor. 16:2).
- Determinedly (lay something aside, 1 Cor. 16:2).
- Proportionately (as he may prosper, 1 Cor. 16:2).
- Liberally (the riches of their liberality, 2 Cor. 8:2; 9:13)
- Sacrificially (more than could have been expected, 2 Cor. 8:3).
- Accompanied by a consecrated life (they first gave themselves to the Lord, 2 Cor. 8:5).
- Voluntarily (a willing mind, 2 Cor. 8:12, not by commandment, 2 Cor. 8:8).
- Sincerely (testing the sincerity of your love, 2 Cor. 8:8).
- Purposefully (as he purposes in his heart, 2 Cor. 9:7).
- Ungrudgingly (2 Cor. 9:7).
- Cheerfully (God loves a cheerful giver, 2 Cor. 9:7).
- Inconspicuously (do not sound a trumpet before you, Mt 6:2; do

not let your left hand know what your right hand is doing, Mt. 6:3).

Another basic rule is: Work hard for your current needs and the needs of your family (2 Thess. 2:10; 1 Tim. 5:8); put everything above that in the work of the Lord (Mt. 6:19); and trust God for the future (Mt. 6:33; 2 Cor. 5:7). A Christian couple should decide before God on a standard of living with which they would be satisfied so that everything above that could go into the Lord's work.

Current needs require a modest bank account so that bills can be paid promptly and a person's credit record be a good testimony. That is not what is meant by laying up treasures on earth.

In general we should avoid buying on credit; the borrower is slave to the lender (Prov. 22:7). We should avoid borrowing if it means paying an exorbitant rate of interest or if there is any doubt as to your ability to repay. In that sense we should owe no man (Rom. 13:8). Sometimes it is better discipleship to buy a house than to rent. A mortgage is legitimate since the house secures it in case of default. If you cannot pay, the lender takes possession of the house.

Don't buy until you've prayed and given God a chance to provide. He can give you something better than you would have bought.

Avoid impulse buying. Make a list of what you need, then confine your purchases to it.

Avoid luxury buying or purchasing non-essentials. A Rolex watch does not keep better time than a $15.00 Casio. Enjoy the luxury of sales resistance to items without which you can live a normal life.

Buy house brands rather than nationally advertised brands. Guess who pays for the national advertising? You save that when you buy items with the store's own name.

Compare weights to avoid being deceived by a lower price.

Weigh price against quality. It would be better to buy quality shoes than to buy cheap ones if you have to pay money to the foot doctor.

Avoid eating in expensive restaurants. Think of how many steaks and roasts you could buy at the grocery store with that money.

Use it up, wear it out, make it do, do without. That's a timeless formula for those who want to maximize the usefulness of their money for the Lord.

Avoid waste. When Jesus fed the 5,000, He ordered them to gather up the uneaten loaves and fishes.

Sometimes it's better to buy used items like a car, especially if the dealer is a Christian. Otherwise you might be buying someone else's troubles. Don't be too proud to patronize thrift shops. There are bargains galore if you shop carefully.

Don't sign guarantees for others, even for relatives, unless you are willing to part with your money forever (Prov. 6:1-5; 11:15; 17:18; 20:16; 22:26; 27:13). In Bible language, it's becoming surety for someone else. When money comes in the door, love often goes out the window.

Don't lend to another Christian unless you can do so without being disturbed if you never get it back.

Don't go to law for financial repayment. If you go to law, the law will get you.

Although some insurance is obligatory, such as auto coverage, don't be insurance poor. Trust the Lord to care for you and your family.

Go through your possessions periodically and sell or give away what you don't need. One woman said she spent the first twenty-five years of her marriage accumulating things, the next twenty-five years getting rid of them.

In general, live modestly so that you can maximize your investment in never-dying souls.

THE SIMPLE LIFESTYLE IS THE BEST

1. It is taught in the Word (2 Cor. 8:9). See also Matthew 6:19 and 1 Timothy 6:8. *"Give us this day our daily bread."*

2. It is the proper way to represent our penniless Friend from Nazareth.

Soren Kierkegaard once said:

I went into church. I sat on the velvet pew. I watched sun shining through the stained glass windows. And the minister, dressed in a velvet robe, opened the golden, gilded Bible, marked it with the silk marker, and said, *"If any man would be My disciple, let him deny himself, sell whatsoever he hath, give to the poor, take up the cross and follow Me."* And I looked around and no one was laughing.[69]

3. It deepens our spiritual life, casting us on the Lord more and more and making our prayers more fervent.

4. It is the happiest, most carefree life.

5. The need of the world calls for it. Untold millions are still untold. Speaking of William Burns, Hudson Taylor said:

Simplicity in living was his great delight. He enjoyed quietness and the luxury of having few things to care for. He thought the happiest state on earth for a Christian was that he should have few wants. 'If a man have Christ in his heart,' he used to say, 'heaven before his eyes, and only as much of temporal blessing as is needful to carry him safely through life, then pain and sorrow have little to shoot at.' To be in union with Him who is both sun and shield comprehends all a poor sinner requires to make him happy between this and heaven."[70]

---

69   Quoted by Tony Campolo in tape, It's Friday. Sunday's a Coming.

70   Taylor, Mrs. Howard, Hudson Taylor in Early Years. The Growth of a Soul, London: China Inland Mission, 1921, p. 347.

THIRTY-EIGHT
GUARD YOUR TONGUE

No one will be surprised to learn that a Christian's speech is a barometer of his character. *"Out of the abundance of the heart, the mouth speaks"* (Mt. 12:34). By simply listening to a person's talk, you can tell where he is spiritually.

James reminds us of what we have already learned by experience—that though the tongue is small, it is capable of great good and great evil. Although man can tame all creatures in wildlife, no man can tame the tongue. *"It is an unruly evil, full of deadly poison."* Unlike other things in nature, the tongue can produce opposites, such as sweet and bitter, blessing and cursing (Jas. 3:1-12).

Even if we can't tame the tongue, we can be everlastingly grateful that God can. By the power of the Spirit, He can make the sharp tongue gracious and the gossiping tongue edifying.

Here are some of the qualities that should characterize our speech:

It should be truthful. Our Lord was transparently honest. He never lied or even shaded the truth. Never once did He resort to exaggeration or to flattery. *"Therefore, putting away lying, each one speak truth with his neighbor, for we are members of one another"*

(Eph. 4:26). Since God cannot lie, He cannot grant that permission to anyone else. This rules out fibs, white lies, exaggerations, flattery, and broken promises. Reports of results in Christian service must not be overdrawn. The secretary must not say the boss is not in when he is. Children must not be prompted to lie to an unwelcome visitor.

If a person is honest he doesn't have to have a good memory. Said E. Stanley Jones, "If you tell a lie, you have to have a good memory to cover up the lies; but if you tell the truth every time, you do not have to have a good memory—you just tell the truth. That is simple."

It should be worthwhile. *"Let no corrupt communication proceed out of your mouth..."* (Eph. 4:29a). Here the word corrupt means of poor quality, unfit for use, worthless. When tape recorders first came out, it was a fun game to hide one and record the conversation at the table. When the tape was replayed, the speakers were often embarrassed by the sheer emptiness of their talk. Jesus warned that *"for every idle word men may speak, they will give account of it in the day of judgment"* (Mt. 12:36). Therefore, empty chatter should be confessed as sin and put away from our lives.

Admiral Hyman Rickover of the U.S. Navy said, "Great minds discuss ideas. Average minds discuss events. Small minds discuss people." He could have added that the greatest minds discuss eternal truths.

It should be edifying. *"...but what is good for necessary edification"* (Eph. 4:29b). In other words, we should constantly seek to build up others by what we say. H. A. Ironside always directed a conversation to edifying subjects, He would often ask, "What do you think this verse means?" and then quote a problem text. If the other person didn't know, Ironside would graciously suggest, "Do you think it might mean this?" His explanations were unforgettable.

A friend of mine started to say something negative about another person. It sounded as if it was going to be a juicy bit of gossip. But he stopped in the middle of the sentence and said, "No! That wouldn't be edifying." I've been dying of curiosity ever since, but I learned a valuable lesson that day on how to discipline the tongue.

Our speech should be appropriate. *"Let no unwholesome word proceed from your mouth, but only such a word as is good for edification according to the need of the moment..."* (Eph. 4:29c, NASB). Our Lord answered Satan's temptations in the wilderness with three fitting portions from Deuteronomy. It is a great gift to be able to say the right thing at the right moment. Like the godly elder who leaned over the bed of a dying saint and quoted Song of Solomon 8:6, *"Who is this coming up from the wilderness, leaning upon her beloved?"* Or the Christian woman who wrote Isaiah 49:4 at the end of a letter to a discouraged preacher, *"Then I said, 'I have labored in vain, I have spent my strength for nothing and in vain; yet surely my just reward is with the Lord, and my work with my God.'"*

When Dr. Alexander Whyte walked into a lawyer's office, he was staggered by the question, "Have you any message for an old sinner?" He repeated the text on which he had been meditating, *"He delights in mercy"* (Mic. 7:18). The lawyer thanked him for the only word that would have given him comfort. These words were according to the need of the moment. So *"a word fitly spoken is like apples of gold in settings of silver"* (Prov. 26:11). And *"a word spoken in due season, how good it is"* (Prov. 16:23).

It should be gracious. Not only should our speech be appropriate, it should be gracious. *"Let your speech always be with grace..."* (Col. 4:5a). Our Lord was gracious, so much so that men *"marvelled at the gracious words which proceeded out of His mouth"* (Lk. 4:22). Was it not grace for Him, a Jew, to ask for a drink of water from a despised Samaritan woman (Jn. 4:7)? And what was it but grace when He said to the cowering woman caught in adultery, *"Neither do I condemn you"* (Jn. 8:11b)? Graciousness requires that we refrain from sharp, cutting remarks; from unkind innuendos;

from barbed sarcasm. Said Lady Astor, "Sir Winston, if I were your wife, I'd put poison in your coffee." To which Mr. Churchill replied, "Lady Astor, if I were your husband, I'd drink it." Terribly funny but not terribly gracious!

But our speech should also be seasoned with salt. *"Let your speech always be with grace, seasoned with salt"* (Col. 4:6). The same Lord who said, *"Give me a drink"* also said *"Go, call your husband"* (Jn. 4:16). After saying, *"Neither do I condemn you"* He added *"Go and sin no more."* The words have a sharpness to them; they are spicy. Salt is also a preservative; it hinders corruption. And salt creates thirst. So by our speech we should preserve standards of moral integrity, and stimulate a thirst for the living waters that Christ offers.

Of course, the believer's speech should be pure. *"But fornication and all uncleanness or covetousness, let it not even be named among you, as is fitting for saints; neither filthiness, nor foolish talking, nor coarse jesting, which are not fitting, but rather giving of thanks"* (Eph. 5:3-4). The more freely we talk about sin and immorality the less serious they seem to us and to those who hear us. They acquire a deadly familiarity, and we cease to be horrified by them. It is true that the Bible sometimes discusses heinous sins, but always in a way to create loathing of them, never in such a way as to condone, make light of them, or create a desire to commit them.

No one is opposed to some clean humor, but the truth is that excessive levity leads to a leakage of spiritual power. The Holy Spirit has often been quenched in meetings through a barrage of funny stories. Entertaining anecdotes have dispelled the solemnity of a gospel appeal. We are not called to be stand-up comedians.

Our conversation should be unconfirmed by oaths. *"...Do not swear at all: neither by heaven...nor by the earth...nor shall you swear by your head...But let your 'Yes' be 'Yes,' and your 'No,' 'No.'*

For whatever is more than these is from the evil one" (Mt. 5:34-37). *"But above all, my brethren, do not swear, either by heaven or by earth or with any other oath. But let your 'Yea' be 'Yea,' and your 'No,' 'No,' lest you fall into judgment"* (Jas. 5:12). A Christian's speech should be so consistently honest that he never needs to confirm it with an oath. As someone has said, "Oaths are of no use. A good man does not need one and a bad man would not heed one."

Well, what about taking an oath in a court of law? When our Lord was on trial, the high priest said, *"I adjure You by the Living God that You tell us if You are the Christ, the Son of God."* To adjure means to command under oath. As a Jew under the law, Jesus was required to testify under oath (Lev. 5:1), and He did so. This settles the matter for many Christians. But if they still have a conscience against taking a legal oath, in the United States they are allowed to testify by affirmation. This means answering questions or giving evidence without swearing to God.

We all know that it is wrong to take the name of the Lord in vain and to use offensive four-letter words. But what about minced oaths, that is, euphemisms for forbidden words? For example, gosh and golly for God; gee or geez for Jesus; jeepers creepers for Jesus Christ; darn for damn; heck for hell. These violate the Scriptures just as surely as their more obvious counterparts.

Our speech should be reverent. We should not talk lightly or disrespectfully about sacred things. We should not make puns on Scripture, that is, quote Bible verses in a humorous, out-of-context matter. We should be serious about divine matters.

Servants of Christ should avoid making quips and smart aleck remarks. The lust to intrude into every conversation with wisecracks, or to go one better in telling jokes earns for one the deserved reputation of a spiritual featherweight.

Our speech should be free from complaining. Complaints are an insult to the providence of God. It means that He doesn't know what He is doing. It accuses Him of error or faulty judgment. It says He doesn't care. We should remember that when we are tempted to complain. Better to dismiss the thought or swallow the words and say instead, *"As for God, His way is perfect"* (Ps. 18:30).

Our speech should be brief and to the point. *"In the multitude of words, sin is not lacking, but he who restrains his lips is wise"* (Prov. 10:19). In other words, the more we talk, the more apt we are to sin. We can avoid this danger by resisting the urge to be always saying something. *"Do not be rash with your mouth, and let not your heart utter anything hastily before God. For God is in heaven and you on earth; therefore let your words be few"* (Eccl. 6:2). While this refers especially to vows made to God, the advice is good for general use.

Actually, a compulsive talker is a bore. He never comes up for air. No one else has a chance to get a word in edgewise. He monopolizes every conversation and every unfortunate listener's time and attention.

The tongue should follow thought, not lead it. More have repented speech than silence. He who speaks sows, but he who listens reaps.

We should not indulge in gossip. Some years ago the following appeared in the *Atlanta Journal*:

> I am more deadly than the screaming shell of a howitzer. I win without killing. I tear down homes, break hearts, and wreck lives. I travel on the wings of the wind. No innocence is strong enough to intimidate me, no purity pure enough to daunt me. I have no regard for truth, no respect for justice, no mercy for the defenseless. My victims are as numerous as the sands of the sea, and often as innocent. I never forget and seldom forgive. My name is Gossip! (*Choice Gleanings*)

Perhaps James was thinking particularly of the sin of gossip when he wrote, *"...we all stumble in many things. If anyone does not stumble in word, he is a perfect man, able also to bridle the whole body"* (Jas. 3:2).

It is so easy and natural to gossip, so difficult to kick the habit.

What is gossip? Wm. R. Marshall says that it is the art of saying nothing in a way that leaves nothing unsaid. Bill Gothard says it is sharing information with someone who is neither part of the problem or of its solution. We can expand the definition to say that it is talking in a derogatory manner about someone who is absent. Gossip puts its victim in an unfavorable light; it says things that are not kind, edifying, or necessary. It is badmouthing a person behind his back rather than confronting him face to face. It is a form of character assassination.

The writer of the Proverbs said it well: *"Death and life are in the power of the tongue, and those who love it will eat its fruit"* (Prov. 18:21). The Bible comes down hard on the practice. *"You shall not go about as a talebearer among your people"* (Lev. 19:16a). *"A talebearer reveals secrets, but he who is of a faithful spirit conceals the matter"* (Prov. 11:13. See also 20:19). *"A perverse man sows strife, and a whisperer separates the best of friends"* (Prov. 16:28). *"The words of a talebearer are like tasty trifles, and they go down into the inmost body"* (Prov. 18:8). *"Where there is no wood, the fire goes out; and where there is no talebearer, strife ceases"* (Prov. 26:20).

In Romans 1:29 Paul lists gossips (whisperers) along with murderers and immoral persons.

Sometimes we try to camouflage gossip by pretending that we are sharing information as a matter for prayer. "I mention this only so that you can pray about it, but did you know that…" Or we think we are avoiding offense by telling it in confidence. The following is often the result.

Two women were talking in Brooklyn.

"Tillie told me you told her that secret I told you not to tell her."

"She's a mean thing. I told Tillie not to tell you I told her."

"Well, I told Tillie I wouldn't tell you she told me—so don't tell her I did."

In his book, *Seasons of Life,* Charles Swindoll deals with rumor-mongers, another name for gossips. Here is what he says:

Those who feed on rumors are small, suspicious souls. They find satisfaction in trafficking in poorly lit alleys, dropping subtle bombs that explode in others' minds by lighting the fuse of suggestion. They find comfort in being only an "innocent" channel of the unsure information...never the source. The ubiquitous "They say" or "Have you heard?" or "I understand from others" provides safety for the rumor-spreader.

"Have you heard that the Hysterical Concrete Memorial Church is about to split?"

"I understand that Ferdinand and Flo are divorcing...they say she was unfaithful."

"They say his parents have a lot of money."

"Did you hear that Pastor Elphinstonsky was asked to leave his former church?"

"I was told their son is taking dope...got picked up for shoplifting."

"Someone said they had to get married."

"Somebody mentioned he is a heavy drinker."

"I heard she's a flirt...watch out for her."

"The word is out...he finally cheated his way to the top."

"It's a concern to several people that he can't be trusted."[71]

We all know how gossip and rumors grow as they travel from one to another. Each person adds a negative touch until the final story has little resemblance to the original.

Someone may object that Paul spoke critically about Hymenaeus and Alexander (1 Tim. 1:19, 20); about Phygellus and Hermogenes (2 Tim. 1:15); and Alexander the coppersmith (2 Tim. 4:14). And John did not spare Diotrephes (3 John 9-10). This testimony is true. But the purpose was to warn believers about these men, not to scurrilously attack them.

It is often necessary for leaders to discuss individuals when discipline or correction is necessary. But this is intended to help the persons involved, not to tear them down. This is not the same as gossip.

---

71   Swindoll, Charles, Growing Strong in the Seasons of Life, Portland, OR: Multnomah Press, 1983, pp. 105-106.

There are certain positive steps we can take in dealing with gossips. First, we can ask the person to identify the source. Paul set an example for us in 1 Corinthians 1:11, *"For it has been declared to me concerning you, my brethren, by those of Chloe's household, that there are contentions among you."*

Second, we can ask permission to quote the gossiper to the person being discussed. "Would you mind if I were to tell him what you just said about him?"

"Oh, horrors, don't do that. That would be the end of our friendship!"

Or we can refuse to listen to gossip. We can do this by saying courteously that we'd rather not hear it, or we can redirect the conversation into more edifying channels. "If nobody ever listened to gossip, nobody would ever tell it. Make the audience deaf, and you make the gossiper dumb" (Wm. R. Marshall). A Turkish proverb reminds us, "Who gossips to you will gossip of you."

In conclusion, let me quote a pithy summary. I don't know who wrote it, but I wish I had been the one.

What should a Christian do with his tongue? He should control it, never seeking to dominate in conversation. He should train it to say less than it might. He should never use it for falsehood, half-truth, malice, innuendoes, sarcasm, unclean talk, or empty chatter. He should always use it where circumstances call for testimony, confession, or the word of encouragement. If he is one of those strange people who find it difficult to say "thank you," he should train the tongue to utter the words, and deal with the vicious pride that inhibits them.

THIRTY-NINE
MARRIAGE

Some of the following material has been touched on in previous chapters. It is worth repeating. We call it repetition for emphasis.

God instituted marriage in the Garden of Eden before sin entered the world (Gen. 2:21-24). Therefore the writer to the Hebrews reminds us that *"Marriage is honorable among all, and the bed undefiled"* (Heb. 13:4a). Jokes that demean marriage are not appropriate. It is an honorable and pure relationship.

In marriage, two persons, male and female, become one (Gen. 2:24; Mt. 19:5; Eph. 5:31b, 33). God intends this union to last for life (Mt. 19:6b; 1 Cor 7:39). A spouse without his or her mate is incomplete and alone.

God intends marriage to be monogamous, that is, only one mate at a time (1 Cor. 7:2). This rules out bigamy and polygamy. While God records instances of these two irregularities, He never approved them.

There are five purposes for marriage. It satisfies the need for companionship. *"It is not good that man should be alone"* (Gen. 2:18). It is the means of procreation. *"Be fruitful and multiply, fill the earth and subdue it"* (Gen. 1:28). It is designed to promote moral purity. *"Nevertheless, because of sexual immorality, let each man have his own wife, and let each woman have her own husband"* (1 Cor. 7:2). It is intended to be helpful. God said, *"I will provide him (Adam) a helper comparable to him"* (Gen. 2:18). When lived in obedience to the Word of God, it is a source of joy and pleasure (Prov. 5:18-19).

In the marriage relationship, headship is the man's role (Eph. 5:23). This chain of command was instituted by the order of creation (1 Tim. 2:13), the manner of creation (1 Cor. 7:8), and the purpose of creation (Eph. 5:22). The woman is to be submissive to the man. Eve usurped headship (Gen. 3:1-6), and brought the horrific consequences of sin on the world. But the sin is attributed to Adam because he is the head of the human race. *"Therefore, just as through one man sin entered the world..."* (Rom. 5:12).

The wife's submission to her husband is fitting because the Lord said so (Col. 3:18), and because it is pleasing to Him. Even if she is more capable and spiritual than he, she should encourage him to take the place of headship in the home rather than assuming it herself.

The husband should love his wife as Christ loves the church. (Eph. 5:24). He should treat her like a lady. Even more, he should love her as he loves himself (Eph. 5:28, 33a). Someone has said, "No woman would mind being submissive to a man who loves her as Christ loves the church."

The first requirement in choosing a partner is that he or she must be *"in the Lord"* that is, a believer (1 Cor. 7:39; 2 Cor 6:14). But that is not enough. The two should have unity in biblical convictions. They should have similar life goals. *"Can two walk together unless they are agreed?"* (Amos 3:3).

Marriage is God's general rule for the human race. An exception is found in Matthew 19:12—there are some who are eunuchs for the kingdom's sake. These people are willing to forego marriage in order to give themselves without distraction to the work of the Lord.

In his zeal for God a young disciple may vow that he will never marry. He wants to give himself without distraction to the service of the Lord. His motive is good, but it might be better not to vow. How does he know? It is best to live a day at a time and let the Lord lead. Perhaps it will be God's will for him to marry at some future date.

The apostle Paul stipulates that "even those who have wives should be as though they had none" (1 Cor 7:29). This means that Christ must come first in our priorities. Wives must play second fiddle. Does this mean that wives are neglected? No, but it does mean that any woman whose husband puts Christ first has the right kind of husband.

When a man marries, he is to leave his father and mother and cling to his wife (Eph. 5:31). This means that she now takes precedence over his parents. But someone must have first place in his or her life. That One is the Lord Jesus. Husband and wife must play second fiddle to Him.

Many marriages could be saved if the instructions in 1 Corinthians 7:4-7 were obeyed. What these verses say is that the marriage act should be repeated whenever one partner so desires. The husband has a rightful claim on the wife's body, and so does the wife with respect to her husband. That is the general rule. An exception is when one wishes to devote himself or herself to fasting and prayer. Of course a spouse will want to be sensitive to the physical and emotional differences of the partner. Neither spouse should use the body as a weapon by withholding it.

A husband should never be bitter against his wife (Col. 3:19) but dwell with her with understanding, giving honor to her as an heir of the grace of life (1 Pet. 3:7). This will guarantee liberty as they pray together.

One of the principal requirements for a happy marriage is brokenness. When either person has wronged the other, he or she must apologize and ask for forgiveness. It hurts to do this but it's better than having to endure the cold treatment interminably. It will be hard on your pride, but confess before the sun sets.

There are questions that have to be decided by a couple as they wait on the Lord. Should they use birth control? How large should their family be? There is no one right answer to these questions. It is up to every couple to get their guidance from the Lord. Other Christians should refrain from judging them or from forcing their own dogmatic views as the right ones.

The ideal for marriage is "till death do us part." However, provision is made for divorce when one partner has been unfaithful (Matt. 19:9). Divorce is not commanded but is permitted. In that case, the innocent spouse is free to remarry. When we read in Malachi 2:16 that God hates divorce, it can only mean unscriptural divorce, because God divorced Israel (Jer. 3:8), and it was for the same reason—unfaithfulness.

When asked to give 10 pithy points on marriage, missionary Carl Knott suggested the following:

Get your priorities straight! Put God first in everything. Right from the beginning dedicate your marriage to the Lord and recognize His lordship in your home.

Don't navigate without a compass. Read the Scriptures daily, consult them, talk about them, and obey them (Deut. 6:6-9; James 1:22).

Husband, you're the man. Be godly, not worldly. Take full responsibility for the leadership of the family in a Christian way (Gen. 3:16; 18:19; Col. 3:18). Set an example for your wife and children.

Wife, you're the woman. Your God-given career and place of ministry is the home (Titus 2:3-5). Be oriented to your husband and support him. Serve the Lord in and through your home (Prov. 31).

If possible, never disagree with your spouse in front of others, and never criticize your spouse to others, or listen to criticism. Whatever needs settling should be taken up in private and in a godly manner.

Let the Lord control your family finances. Don't accumulate treasures on earth (Matt. 6:19) and be generous with what you have. The Lord is a generous giver.

Have an open door policy, that is, be hospitable. Care about others and use your home to prove it. Don't worry about what you don't have (2 Cor. 8:12).

Work together in support of the local assembly, reaching out and ministering to others for Christ's sake and the Gospel's (Mark 1:28-34; Luke 18:28:30; Acts 18:24-26).

Be a praying family. Pray as you go and go as you pray. Pray before making decisions. Pray when problems arise. Pray when everything is going well.

Cultivate your marriage relationship. Marriage is a relationship, a friendship, and a partnership. Some people are more occupied with their business than they are with their spouse. Become closer friends as time goes by. Enjoy time alone together. Go out to eat, go for a walk, spend a day in the country, and talk about the things on your heart.

There is always the problem of Christians who earnestly desire to be married but for one reason or another are not able to do so. They can practice sublimation that is, redirect a primitive drive into a life of service for the Lord Jesus and for His people. Examples of fruitful lives of singleness are Amy Carmichal, John Nelson Darby, Gladys Aylward, Corrie ten Boon, and Fanny Crosby. No one needs to feel to be left out of God's program. Any believer can find true fulfillment in a life poured out for Jesus.

FORTY
PARENTING

Our golden text for this chapter is Exodus 2:9: *"Take this child away and nurse him for me, and I will give you your wages."* For believing parents, the key words are for me. We are commissioned to raise our children for Christ. Not for the world but for the Lord. Not for hell but for heaven.

A vital step in this process is to give God's Word an overshadowing place in the home.

And these words which I command you this day shall be in your heart; you shall teach them diligently to your children, and shall talk of them when you are in your house, when you walk by the way, when you lie down, and when you rise up. You shall bind them as a sign on your hand, and they shall be as frontlets between your eyes. You shall write them on the doorposts of your house and on your gates (Deut. 6:6-9).

There is no better heritage that parents can give to their children than a solid foundation in the Bible.

Prayer should have a dominant place in a child's education. He will probably learn more about it by example than by all the books he reads. One of life's most precious memories is of a mother wearing out her knees in prayer for her offspring.

A big part of parenting is education. Every child should learn respect for mother and father, obedience to authority, choosing good companions, resisting sinful temptations, diligence in work, and simple courtesies.

Obedience to parents is a must. Have it understood that you give an order only once. Repeat it and you weaken it. Tolerate no back talk or sassiness.

Obedience to authority applies to school, employment, government, and church. In every ordered society, there must be headship and there must be submission to it (except when this submission would violate loyalty to Christ). Without it, there is anarchy. Children should learn this early.

Fathers should be careful not to provoke a child to wrath (Eph. 6:4). That is the natural tendency. A father can provoke the child to wrath by neglect, by making undue demands, by speaking negatively of the child or using his superior knowledge to make the child feel inferior.

A mother's inclination is to spoil the child. Which is worse?

Children must learn how to choose good companions. Too often parents have to confess with tears, "He (or she) got in with the wrong crowd."

Parents are responsible to talk with their children about sinful temptations, especially in the realm of sex. Otherwise they will learn it in the gutter. Young people today live in a world of sex obsession, pornography, and passion. They must be adept in using the remote control on the TV. They must learn to say No to the world's allurements and the evil appetites of the flesh.

It is a kindness to train young people to work around the home. They can be especially encouraged in those areas in which they seem to have a natural aptitude. Fathers and mothers who do everything for their offspring are short-changing them.

Parents determine whether their children will be courteous or not. Boys and girls who think of others, share with others, put others before self have good manners. This will help them in all of life.

It is heart-warming at the end of a meal to hear a youngster say, "That was a great dinner, Mom." But gratitude is not inborn. It has to be learned.

People like to be with kids who have learned these lessons. They don't appreciate brats, that is, kids who are out of control.

Eventually every child will need correction. Doesn't the Bible say, *"Foolishness is bound up in the heart of a child, but the rod of correction will drive it far from him?"* (Prov. 22:15). The reason for the discipline should be explained. It should not be carried out in anger. It should be suited to the disobedience. After it is finished, the parent should reconfirm his love for the child. This shows that the father or mother is not rejecting the child but is rejecting his behavior. The purpose of discipline is to teach obedience. It is love to discipline a child; it is hatred not to do so (Prov. 13:24).

Parents must be united in taking discipline. Children are skillful in detecting any weakening on the part of mother or father, and they play one against the other.

Children should be encouraged to come to their parents at any time with the assurance that they will find a listening ear.

Let them know that you really do love them. It's not unspiritual to hug them. Too often we hear young people say, "My father never told me that he loved me." Tell them before it is too late.

It is good for a child to engage in team sports. It teaches teamwork and good sportsmanship. If a youngster learns to play a musical instrument, he develops coordination of mind and muscle and an appreciation of good music.

Parents should avoid putting a son or daughter under pressure to accept Christ. There is a danger of their making a false profession.

It is better to pray them into the kingdom.

Even in their early years, children can be molded to stand for Christ and for truth. They can learn to separate the precious from the vile (Jer. 15:19). They can develop convictions and stick to them in the face of ridicule and opposition. Stories of the Christian martyrs are excellent.

Incidentally, parents should keep the house well stocked with good Christian literature. Hudson Taylor's mother left a tract on a living room table, then left on an errand. Hudson read the tract and trusted Christ. God used him to reach Inland China with the gospel.

We have only scratched the surface. Volumes could be written on the subject. But perhaps the above tips will suffice until these are successfully incorporated into your Christian family.

FORTY-ONE
GOD'S WAYS, NOT OUR WAYS

In Romans 12:1-2 the Apostle Paul reminds us that we should not only present our bodies as a living sacrifice to God but we should also *"be transformed by the renewing of our minds."* This means that we should abandon the world's way of thinking and learn to think as our Lord does. The Bible tells us how God thinks.

The Lord Himself has made it clear that as the heavens are higher than the earth, so are His thoughts and ways are higher than man's (Isa. 55:8-9). The difference is radical.

Take the gospel, for example. Man in general believes that you get to heaven by good character and good works. You have to deserve it or earn it. "Not so," says God, in effect: "The only people who get to heaven are those who don't deserve it but who receive the Lord Jesus as their Lord and Savior. It's a matter of believing, not working."

The gospel is foolishness to man. It's too easy. Receiving it as a gift by faith just doesn't make sense. But the foolishness of God is wiser than man. Anyone can be saved by God's method. No one can be saved by man's.

Here are some other ways we have to adjust our thinking.

God does not judge by appearance. He knows that all is not gold that glistens. Man looks on the outward appearance, but the Lord looks on the heart (1 Sam. 16:7).

He is not impressed with physical beauty. *"Charm is deceitful and beauty is vain, but a woman who pleases the Lord, she shall be praised"* (Prov. 31:30). Neither is He captivated by athletic prowess. *"He takes no pleasure in the legs of a man"* (Ps. 147:10). *"He takes pleasure in them that fear Him, in those who hope in His mercy"* (Ps. 147:11).

Natural man likes to hobnob with the rich and famous and drops the names of the high and mighty. How unlike our Lord. He doesn't call many from the highly educated, from the powerful, or from the upper classes. Instead He uses foolish, weak, and base nobodies to accomplish great things (1 Cor. 1:26-27).

The Lord has a different concept of leadership. Man equates leadership with lordship. But from the divine viewpoint, the true leader is a servant. The one who is great in His kingdom is the one who stoops to serve (Mt. 20:25-27)

He is not impressed by material wealth (Lk. 18:24-27). Man measures worth of others by their wealth. How much are they worth? Spiritual riches are the true ones. A hoard of money can keep a person out of heaven.

God does not judge by numbers (Jud. 7:2). Contrary to what Voltaire said, God is not on the side of the big battalions. Gideon had too many soldiers. The Lord reduced his army from 32,000 to 300 and he won the battle. Little is much if God is in it.

Not to the strong is the battle, not to the swift is the race. Eric Liddell set a new world's record in the 1924 Olympics although his running style was atrocious. He had honored God by refusing to run on the Lord's Day, and God honored him in return.

Our Lord has a special love for the poor (Jas. 2:3). We will choose them too when we come to think as He does.

He goes by need, not by greed. This is shown in the parable of the workers in the vineyard (Mt. 20:1-16). The landowner paid the employees he hired first exactly what they had bargained for. They got justice. All the other trusted the boss to do what was right. They got grace. He knew they needed money to support their family so he gave them what he felt they needed. The first-hired complained because they went by greed and not by need.

He goes by faithfulness, not by success (Mt. 25:21, 23). We all can be faithful, but success comes from Him.

He goes by desire as well as by achievement. David got credit for building the Temple because the desire was in his heart (1 Ki. 8:18). It was Solomon who eventually built it.

The ones blessed in God's sight are despised by the world (Mt. 5:3-10). Jesus' family thought he was deranged (Mk. 3:21). Paul's critics said he was beside himself (2 Cor. 5:13). If we are Christlike, the world will consider us mad.

Murder and adultery begin in the heart (Mt. 5:21-22; 27-30). Murder begins with hatred and adultery with a lustful look. Defilement comes from within (Mt. 15:11).

Men redefine sin as sickness. Who are they kidding? God doesn't send men to hell for any illness.

The world says with Shakespeare, "To thine own self be true." Paul says by divine inspiration, "Let each esteem others better than himself" (Phil. 2:3).

God desires mercy and not sacrifice (Mt. 9:13). Tithing is not enough if we neglect justice, mercy and faith (Mt. 23:23).

Greatness in the kingdom is to be like a little child (Mt. 18:4).

Men like honorific titles. Only God should get them (Mt. 23:9-10). Men also like special clothing, supposedly indicating some superlative degree of holiness or religious position (Mt. 23:5). Christ made Himself of no reputation.

It's not the gold that sanctifies the temple; it's the temple that sanctifies the gold (Mt. 23:18-22). It isn't the gold that gave the temple its value. It was a special privilege for the gold to be used in God's house. It's the temple that set the gold apart in a place of special honor. Likewise it is the altar that sanctifies the gift that is on it.

The way up is down. He who abases himself will be exalted (Mt. 23:12).

God's definition of love goes out to enemies (Lk. 6:27). Men of the world love those who love them.

God makes His sun rise on the just and the unjust, and sends rain on the just and the unjust (Mt. 5:45). We should imitate His impartiality, although it goes across the grain of nature.

Well, these are just a sampler of how God's thoughts and ways differ from man's. They should serve as a starter for us in seeking to think as He does. The Bible is a full revelation of the divine thought processes.

For a fuller treatment of this subject, see Appendix F, page 417.

SECTION IV
CHRISTIAN SERVICE

FORTY-TWO
KNOW YOUR GIFT(S)

One of the ministries of the Holy Spirit, which occurs at the time of conversion, is the granting of special spiritual talents, generally known as gifts. These are not the same as natural talents. A non-believer may inherit ability as an inventor, an artist, or a mathematician. These can be passed down through the genes.

Gifts of the Spirit are different. They are special powers which only the Spirit can bestow and which He bestows only on those who are born again. Often they enable a person to do things that he would not ordinarily be able to do. They are so contrary to his natural ability that people conclude it must be the Lord who is working through him. I have read that C. H. Spurgeon was so fearful to preach in public that he often vomited blood before entering the pulpit. Others had serious speech impediments, yet when they spoke, they had perfect verbal control. When we exercise our gifts, people should conclude that it is the power of God at work and not that of the Christian.

Gifts are listed in Romans 12:3-8; 1 Corinthians 12:7-11, 28; and Ephesians 4:11. There may be others that are not named in these passages. Those in Ephesians seem to be special service gifts, concerned primarily with the inauguration of the New Testament church

317

and with the planting of New Testament assemblies. Apostles and prophets were men who received the New Testament by inspiration and gave us *"the faith once for all delivered to the saints."* They are no longer with us in the primary sense of the words. We no longer need them because we have their ministry preserved in the pages of the New Testament.

In a secondary, lesser sense, an apostle is one who is sent forth by the Lord to preach the good news and establish local churches. Also, in a secondary sense, a prophet is one who expounds the Word of God and applies it to his hearers.

Some of the gifts are known as sign gifts. Tongues are an example. Because of abuses in the use of this gift, the Holy Spirit laid down seven controls on the use of tongues in the church. These are:

1. Forbid not to speak in tongues (1 Cor. 14:39).

2. If anyone speaks in tongues, there must be an interpreter (1 Cor. 14:13, 27-28).

3. Not more than three may speak in tongues in any one meeting (1 Cor. 14:27).

4. They must speak one at a time (1 Cor. 14:27).

5. What they say must be edifying (1 Cor. 14:26).

6. The women must keep silent in meetings of the assembly which are led by the men (1 Cor. 14:34).

7. All must be done decently and in order (1 Cor. 14:40).

Everyone has at least one gift. Some believers have more. As mentioned, the gifts are given automatically when a person receives Christ. There is no use praying for any particular gift.

When Paul said, *"Earnestly desire the best gifts,"* he was not speaking to an individual but to the church in Corinth. The you (implied) is plural, not singular. This is not obvious in the English. A church may feel that it lacks someone with a certain gift. In that case, the saints should pray that the Lord will send someone to fill that need.

The gifts are given for the benefit of all (1 Cor. 12:7), and not for personal edification or exaltation. They are distributed to each one individually as the Holy Spirit pleases, that is, sovereignly (1 Cor. 12:11). There should be no feelings of superiority or inferiority (1 Cor. 12:27). The Lord did not intend that everyone should have the same gift—there is unity in diversity, just as in the members of the body (1 Cor. 12:29-30).

The gifts should be exercised in love (1 Cor. 13). Love thinks of others, not of self. To speak in a foreign language in a meeting without a translation is not thinking of others. Prophesying is better than tongues without interpretation because the people know what is being said.

How can a person know what his gift is? First, he should make it a matter of earnest prayer. He should study the gifts. Then he should engage in a variety of ministries in the area of these gifts. Some will seem burdensome to him. Others will yield "maximum effectiveness with minimum fatigue" (Bill Gothard). Discerning Christians may confirm your guidance by telling you where your gift lies.

We should exercise our gift(s) with all the strength that God gives us, at the same time thanking the Lord for those with different gifts.

"No man's gift is too big for God's principles" (Alfred Mace). A preacher may think that he is too gifted to remain with small fellowships that seek to walk in obedience to the Word of God. He feels called to a mega-church that compromises doctrine for large numbers. He would be wise to stick to divine principles and let the Lord decide on how large his audience will be.

FORTY-THREE
BE A SERVANT OF ALL

As we have already seen, Jesus was the true bondslave who put His ear to the door and said, *"I love My Master. I will not go out free."*

He is still saying as He said that fateful night in the upper room, *"I have given you an example, that you should do as I have done unto you"* (Jn. 13:15).

Borden of Yale followed that example. Though a son of wealth, he was sometimes found doing dishes at a skid row mission.

A Bible school professor was not above getting down on his knees to wipe up the washroom floor after the male students had left it at flood stage and rushed off to class.

Steve Farrar gives us a humorous description of how we respond to servanthood. He was writing a book and came to this paragraph:

> Let me ask you a question. Do you want to change? Are you willing to change? Are you willing to become a servant? Unless I miss my guess, that serving stuff may not come naturally for you. It may not be your knee-jerk reaction to situations in your life. It's certainly not in mine. But do you know what? I really don't have an option. I'm *called* to do it...

Farrar continues:

> Now do you believe that God has a sense of humor? I can guarantee that He does. In

fact, let me prove it to you. Do you see the last sentence of the previous paragraph? The sentence says, "I'm *called* to do it." Just as I was finishing this last sentence, I heard the faint words, "Daaaaad...Daaaaad..." I walked out of my office to see my son vomiting in the hallway between his bedroom and the bathroom. And since I am here alone with my son, the job of serving fell to me. In the last ninety minutes—when I should have been completing this chapter—I have cleaned up my son, put him to bed, cleaned up the vomit off the carpet, gone to the grocery store, rented a carpet shampooer, shampooed the carpet...well, you get the idea.

It is now 9:48 PM. This completed chapter needs to be at FedEx by 10:30 PM. So, FedEx closes in forty-two minutes.

When my son threw up, my first question was, "Where is Mary? Actually that's not quite right. My first question was, "WHERE IS MARY? She promised on our wedding day to be faithful in sickness and in health—and this is sickness," Now I didn't say that out loud. But I was thinking it.

After I cleaned Joshua up and got him into bed, I looked at my watch and noticed that the time was quickly coming when "no man shall work."

I began to think, "Where is that woman and what is she doing? I didn't have time to clean this crud up! I have to get this chapter done and get it to FedEx! I have to finish this section on servanthood so that these guys can be the men that God wants them to be! Where is she? I'm about ready to throw up myself after getting this stuff off the carpet! I'm supposed to be doing something important for the kingdom of God instead of getting recycled hot dogs and chili off this rug!"

When I finally sat down to figure out where I left off, I noticed the last paragraph that I had written:

Let me ask you a question: Do you want to change? Are you willing to change? Are you willing to become a servant? Unless I miss my guess, the serving stuff may not come naturally for you. It may not be your knee-jerk reaction to situations in your life. It's certainly not in mine, But do you know what? I really don't have an option. I'm *called* to do it.[72]

It is an authentic mark of Christlikeness when we stoop to serve.

72   Farrar, Steve, Finishing Strong, Sisters, OR: Multnomah Books, 1995, pp. 158-163.

FORTY-FOUR
THE CHALLENGE OF PERSONAL EVANGELISM
by David Dunlap

Witnessing for Christ is a way of life. By virtue of the fact that one is a Christian, one is a witness for Christ. I may or not be a good witness, but nevertheless I am one. Jesus said, *"...you will be witnesses unto me..."* (Acts 1:8). Our witnessing is important. We can have a considerable impact on those who do not know Christ. The question is not when to witness or where to witness. If we are Christians we are witnesses. But how can we become more effective communicators of the gospel? Knowing the truth is essential for an effective witness. *"Ye shall know the truth and the truth shall make you free"* (Jn. 8:32). We live in a day of methods. By and large our evangelism has become method centered. Many have attended seminars on better methods of evangelism. Yet at the same time the church has become weaker in its understanding of the content of the message, and in her ability to communicate it.. We have forgotten that the New Testament defines "to evangelize" as "to tell/declare/announce good news." News, by the very meaning of the word, means content. Any presentation to the unsaved must have Bible-based content.

GOD—THE HOLY AND LOVING CREATOR

We can't assume that people today have a proper concept of God. We must make them see that He has an absolute claim on their lives. The concept that we want to drive home is God's ownership of each one of us. We should speak of a sovereign Creator who brought all things into being out of nothing, creating and sustaining us of His own will so that we are dependent on Him for everything (Gen. 1–2; Acts 17:25; Isa. 40:28; Ps. 100:3). From this foundation come the two great pillars of His Being—light and love. Light speaks of God's majesty, truth and holiness (1 Jn. 1:5; 1 Tim. 6:15-16). But our God is also a God of love. Out of His love He created us in His image so that we could have fellowship with Him. Worship, therefore, can be the only appropriate response (Deut. 6:4-5).

MAN—THE SINFUL CREATURE

Man disobeyed God and willfully rebelled. The Bible calls this sin. We must both define sin and state its consequences to a lost world. Sin is comprised of two parts: first, it is the attitude that I am my own god and therefore I live as if God did not exist. Romans 1:21 portrays this attitude when it defines sin as not worshipping God. We thereby deny all that God has revealed to us about Himself. Second, sin is rebelling against God—breaking His law. Listing the Ten Commandments in evangelism helps people feel the guilt of sin, and creates a desire for the forgiveness found in Christ alone (Rom. 3:12; Jas. 2:10; Jer. 17:9).

The consequence of sin is death. The Bible speaks of death as spiritual and physical separation. These two elements, when joined together, comprise the essence of life. Physical death is separation from the body. The symptoms of disease and physical suffering indicate that physical death is near. Spiritual death is separation from God for eternity. Symptoms of this type of death are hatred, war, alienation, purposelessness, guilt, and despair (Isa. 59:2; Eph. 2:1).

CHRIST—THE MERCIFUL REDEEMER

When you read the Old Testament, you see clearly that Jesus Christ came to fulfill three roles: prophet, priest, and king. Evangelism over the last hundred years has tended to speak merely of His role as Savior. This has led many people to make superficial "decisions for Christ." We must present Christ in all three roles—His perfect life, sacrificial death, and His victorious resurrection.

As Prophet, He revealed God through His teaching and life (Deut. 18:15-19; Jn. 1:14-18; 7:16-24). His perfect life qualified Him to be our substitutionary sacrifice (Acts 2:36).

The Priest represented the people to God. We must present the cross not merely as a vague demonstration of God's love, but as the place in history where, in the death of His Son, God dealt with the sins of the whole world. God is still just and holy, yet loves us through Christ, who bore our sins (1 Pet. 2:24; Heb. 7:27; 10:10).

We must speak of His office as King. The New Testament refers to Jesus Christ as "Savior" twenty-four times, but calls Him Lord 694 times—more than twenty-eight times for every reference as "Savior." All who will have Jesus as Savior should also have Jesus as their King. Jesus now lives to rule His people in love and truth (Mt. 25:24; Acts 2:3-36; Rev. 5).

OUR NECESSARY RESPONSE FOR SALVATION

Since man's only hope is to be saved through the finished work of Christ, how can man come to know Christ as Savior? We must urge the unsaved to acknowledge with their mind and heart that they stand guilty before God and deserve His judgment. They must acknowledge their rebellion against Him, and turn from it, trusting in Christ's redemptive work. They must realize that they can do nothing. They must realize that they can do nothing to make themselves acceptable to God. We then invite them to trust in Christ and rest in Him as Savior (Jn. 1:12; 3:16; Eph. 2:8-9).

SOME KEY POINTS TO REMEMBER

Use your Bible: Have the person read the text himself, and have him explain to you his understanding of the meaning. Many times this is the turning point in the presentation of the gospel. It prevents tangents, and confronts them with God's final authority.

Memorize Scripture: Memorize verses and their references so you can give the appropriate portion of God's Word to that person.

Pray: Our message may seem foolish to the non-Christian, but if we really believe that only the Holy Spirit can make them respond, we will pray—before, during, and after our presentation of Christ to the sinner.

Communicate: Communicate absolute biblical concepts clearly so that a person does not read his or her ideas into them. Be careful to explain that you are speaking about absolute truth, not just your opinion. Your message should be faithful to the Word of God in content and emphasis. But be encouraged: God did not commission tape recorders to evangelize so He could have the "perfect message." You will make mistakes, as all do. But if you seek to be faithful to God and His message, He will teach you on the job.

WORK HARD AND KEEP AT IT

"Let us not be weary in well doing for in due season we shall reap if we faint not" (Gal. 6:9). Many Christians give up too quickly at gospel work. They go out a few times and knock on doors during a weekend. When a few contacts are made, they tell themselves, "This isn't for me. I'm just not cut out for it." No one is cut out for it; it's hard work! Satan will fight it at every turn. Keep at it, keep praying, scattering seed, and God will give you the increase.

BE AUTHORITATIVE

They said of Jesus, *"He taught them as One that had authority, and not as the scribes"* (Mk. 1:22). A witness must be authoritative, but not arrogant. Some Christians witness with almost an apologetic manner. Generally this approach does not see many results. The unsaved will not have confidence in a message that is given in an unsure, indecisive manner. They need a *"Thus saith the Lord."*

LEAVE THE DOOR OPEN

If the person being witnessed to is not receptive, don't push. If the person makes smart remarks, never give an unkind remark in return. This can damage all the progress you have had thus far, or bar opportunities others may have in the future. Never argue. *"The servant of the Lord must not strive"* (2 Tim. 2:24). You may win an argument, but lose a soul for Christ. If a witnessing situation is beginning to heat up, stop! Apologize. Let the person know you don't want to argue, and are sorry for anything you have said or done to be offensive. If the gospel is offensive, so be it. But if I'm offensive, that must be corrected.

DON'T USE DIFFICULT THEOLOGICAL TERMS

A witness must learn to think as the unsaved think. Put yourself in their shoes. Many have heard the term "born again" but don't know what it means. To talk about "propitiation" and "justification" may only confuse the issue. They will understand terms like "sin," "forgiveness," "heaven," "hell," and "judgment." Keep it simple.

LEARN TO GIVE INVITATIONS

Truth not only informs but transforms. Many people will take up the offer when it is given. Learn to give people the opportunity to respond. Don't manipulate or force decisions, but do give the unsaved a chance to say yes to God. You never know the heart. An individual may be bursting inside with conviction without any indication or outward emotion. After you have explained the gospel and answered objections and questions, you might want to simply say,

"Would you like to receive Christ tonight?" The biblical pattern is to call men and women to response after presenting the gospel. Paul said, *"We...preach unto you that ye should turn from these vanities unto the living God"* (Acts 14:15). Peter said, *"Repent ye, therefore, and be converted, that your sins may be blotted out"* (Acts 3:19).

AVOID DETOURS

Don't get off on a tangent. If Satan can't defeat you, he'll try a detour. If a person asks a question that may be a detour, suggest that you first finish presenting the plan of salvation and then you will answer the question. Don't get into a discussion about the doctrine of other churches, or the errors of prominent television preachers, Bible translations, etc. The main thing is that the main thing remains the main thing in presenting the gospel.

PRESENT THE ISSUE OF SIN

We must clearly and boldly press the issue of sin in their lives (Rom. 6:23). We should present the love, grace, and mercy of God, but we must press the judgment and consequences of sin. This is the biblical method. Note Peter preaching, *"Ye denied the Holy One and the Just, and desired a murderer to be granted unto you, and killed the Prince of life"* (Acts 3:14-15).

GIVE PERSONAL TESTIMONY

Learn how to give a brief and clear account of how you were saved. Emphasize your need of salvation because of sin, and the change in your life afterward. You may want to open the conversation by saying, "May I tell you the most amazing thing that ever happened to me?" After a brief account, you can say, "I found it so wonderful to know that all my sins were forgiven and that I'm going to heaven. I had to tell others about it." Afterwards you can add, "Do you know for sure that you are going to heaven?"

USE THE WORD OF GOD

In answering the temptations of Satan in the wilderness, Christ used the Scriptures. In the preaching of the apostles in the book of Acts, the Old Testament was used. Jeremiah said, *"Is not My Word like a fire? saith the Lord, and like a hammer that breaks the rock in pieces"* (Jer. 23:29).

Many have used established methods of presenting God's salvation with great success. One of the best known is called "The Roman Road"—3:10; 3:23; 5:8; 6:23; 10:9. Many use this outline but add variations. It's good to have an outline to keep you on track; then other verses can be added to suit the individual's need.

One fatal mistake is to be accusative: "You need to know that you are a sinner." They will usually become defensive rather than receptive. Instead, have them read, *"There is none righteous, no, not one"* (Rom. 3:10); *"For all have sinned and come short of the glory of God"* (Rom. 3:23). Then say, "We've all sinned, haven't we?"

FORTY-FIVE
PREACH THE WORD—
THE GLORY OF THE MINISTRY

The apostle Paul never got over the fact that God had entrusted him, formerly a persecutor of the church, with the gospel of the glory of Christ. Neither should we. I am indebted to J. H. Jowett for his writing on the tremendous privilege and dignity of preaching the Word of God. Let me share a few choice paragraphs:

> Now a man who enters through the door of divine vocation into the ministry will surely apprehend "the glory" of his calling. He will be constantly wondering, and his wonder will be a moral antiseptic, that he has been appointed a servant in the treasuries of grace, to make known *"the unsearchable riches of Christ."* You cannot get away from that wonder in the life of the apostle Paul. Next to the infinite love of his Savior, and the amazing glory of his own salvation, his wonder is arrested and nourished by the surpassing glory of his own vocation. His "calling" is never lost in the medley of professions. The light of privilege is always shining on the way of duty. His work never loses its halo, and his road never becomes entirely commonplace and gray. He seems to catch his breath every time he thinks of his mission, and in the midst of abounding adversity, glory still more abounds. And, therefore, this is the sort of music and song that we find unceasing, from the hour of his conversion and calling to the hour of his death. *"Unto me who am less than the least of all saints, is this*

grace given, that I should preach among the Gentiles the unsearchable riches of Christ." Do you not feel a sacred, burning wonder in these exclamations, a holy, exulting pride in his vocation, leagued with a marveling humility that the mystic hand of ordination had rested upon him? That abiding wonder was part of his apostolic equipment, and his sense of the glory of his calling enriched his proclamation of the glories of redeeming grace. If we lose the sense of the wonder of our commission, we shall become like common traders in a common market, babbling about common wares.

This sense of great personal surprise in the glory of our vocation, while it will keep us humble, will also make us great. It will save us from becoming small officials in transient enterprises. It will make us truly big, and will, therefore, save us from spending our days in trifling...Preachers of the gospel, whose work is done beneath the lofty dome of some glorious and wonderful conception of their ministry, will acquire a certain largeness of demeanor in which flippancy and trivialities cannot breathe.

I have been in the Christian ministry for over twenty years. I love my calling. I have a glowing delight in its services. I am conscious of no distractions in the shape of any competitors for my strength and allegiance. I have had one passion, and I have lived for it—the absorbingly arduous yet glorious work of proclaiming the grace and love of our Lord and Savior Jesus Christ."[73]

Ian Macpherson shared Jowett's sentiments. He said, "Preaching is something august, sublime, awe-begetting—a supernatural act, the transmission of a Person through a person to a company of persons, the Person so conveyed being the everlasting Jesus."[74]

PERSONAL PREPARATION FOR THE MINISTRY

In preparation for the ministry, there must be the constant confession and forsaking of all known sin. *"Be clean, you who bear the*

---

73   J. H. Jowett, The Preacher: His Life and Work, New York, NY: Hodder and Stoughton, 1912, pp. 21-22.
74   Macpherson, Ian, The Burden of the Lord, Nashville, TN: Abingdon Press, 1955, p. 14.

vessels of the Lord" (Isa. 52:11).

You might tell me that you know of a man who was living in sin, yet when he preached, souls were saved. Yes, that's possible. The message is always greater than the messenger.

God honors His Word. But if you want fruit that remains (Jn. 15:16), you must be abiding in Christ.

A CONSECUTIVE, VERSE-BY-VERSE EXPOSITORY MESSAGE

The best method is, without a doubt, verse-by-verse exposition of the Scriptures. That is the best way to present all the truth, and in the balance in which the Lord gave it. It forces us to face some of the hard sayings of Jesus. We are called to teach the whole counsel of God (Acts 20:27).

When asked how a servant of the Lord prepared for preaching, he replied, "Well, I come to the Bible, and I think myself empty, and I read myself full, and I write myself clear, and I pray myself hot."

Begin with prayer.

Immerse yourself in the passage. The best preaching relies heavily on the Scriptures. It is the Word that God has promised to bless.

Preach Christ. Present Him as the object of faith and the answer to problems. A Spirit-filled message is full of the Savior.

Face the problems and difficulties. If you don't know the answers, admit it. Don't try to bluff your audience.

If there are two or more valid interpretations, give them. Then tell which one you prefer and why.

Get help wherever you can. Use different version of the Bible, Bible dictionaries, reputable commentaries, and Bible teachers.

Make applications of the passage (Eph. 2:14-18). For example, Christ broke down the wall between believing Jews and Gentiles. We should not erect walls between various racial and ethnic groups.

PREPARING A TOPICAL MESSAGE

Pray about the needs of the people. Ask the Holy Spirit to empower the message.

We are called to preach Christ. Every message should point inevitably and irresistibly to Him. "God may have other words for other planets, but His word for this planet is Jesus."

Paint on a large canvas. You are to be in the pulpit to do tremendous work. Wherefore focus all your forces on the central task. Concentrate massively on the main thing. Preach Christ.[75]

We are called to preach the gospel, the good news of salvation through faith in Him. We have the best of all messages. We don't have to be like the unfortunate man in 2 Samuel 18:22 who wanted to run but didn't have news to announce.

Every message should have unity, coherence, and emphasis. Unity requires that the message have a single theme that is apparent throughout. Each paragraph should also have a discernable unity. Coherence means that the paragraphs should be linked so that the flow of thought is smooth and not jerky. Emphasis is achieved by building toward a climax that leaves no doubt as to what you want your listener to know and do.

OPENING THE MESSAGE

Paul O'Neil, a writer for *Life* magazine said, "Always grab the reader by the throat in the first paragraph, sink your thumbs into his windpipe in the second, and hold him against the wall until the tag line." This is now known as O'Neil's Law.

DELIVERY OF THE MESSAGE

We should preach enthusiastically. It is a sin to present our glorious message in a matter of fact manner. I think it was Spurgeon who

---

75   Source unknown.

said, "Get on fire for God and the world will turn out to see you burn." In his *Lectures to My Students,* he also said, "When you speak of heaven, let your face light up, let your eyes shine with reflected glory; when you speak of hell, your ordinary face will do."

We should keep ourselves in the background. James Denney said, "In preaching you cannot produce at the same time the impression that you are clever and that Christ is wonderful."[76]

When telling Thy salvation free,

Let all absorbing thoughts of Thee

My heart and mind engross;

And when all hearts are bowed and stirred

Beneath the influence of Thy Word,

Hide me behind the cross. (Author Unknown)

You never help by advertising yourself. Self-advertisement is deadly in the ministry of the Lord Jesus. Puff, showy paragraphs concerning ourselves and our work: egotistical recitals of our powers and attainments—all forms of self-obtrusion and self-aggression—all these are absolutely fatal to the really deepest work committed to our hands. Our fellow-laborers know when our work is marred by self-conceit. The devil is delighted when he can lure us into self-display. Our own highest powers shrink and wither when we expose them to the glare of self-seeking publicity. They cannot bear a light like that, and they speedily lose their strength and beauty. I urge you to avoid it. Never tell people what a clever fellow you are…Of one thing we can be perfectly sure: when we display ourselves we hide our Lord: when we blow our own trumpet men will not hear "the still, small voice of God."[77]

CLOSING THE MESSAGE

Don't go on talking endlessly when you are no longer saying anything important. I've read of a Puritan who started his exposition of

---

76   Stewart, James A., Evangelism, p. 14.

77   Jowett, J. H., The Preacher: His Life and Work, pp. 236-237.

Job with 800 hearers, and ended with only 8. "The patience of his audience was not equal to that of the patriarch on whose experience he descanted so long. Everything reminded him of something else" (Wm. R. Marshall). Another preacher is said to have had a ponderous way of saying nothing in infinite sentences.

After the war, a little girl was attending a church service with her mother. The long-winded preacher was droning on for an hour and a half. The girl quit listening and looked around the church building. She saw a row of flags with a brass plaque under each one. What are those flags for, Mother?" The mother was sympathetic to her little daughter's restlessness. She said, "They commemorate those who died in the Service." The little girl, asked, "Which one, the 9:00 o'clock service or the 11:00 o'clock one?"

GENERAL SUGGESTIONS

We are limited in what we preach and teach by the extent to which we ourselves have obeyed the Scriptures. We can't lead others beyond what we ourselves have attained. If we try, they are apt to say, *"Physician, heal yourself."*

We need to be on fire for the Lord. The danger is that the zeal will dwindle away with the time. *"Maintain the spiritual glow"* (Rom. 12:11c, Moffatt's Trans.). It is good to see our heart as an altar, where the fire must be kept burning. "And the fire on the altar shall be kept burning on it; it shall not be put out" (Lev. 6:12).

A good sermon is one that stretches the mind, warms the heart, tans the hide, and provokes the will. It is not the kind that causes the hearers to say, "That was a great message." Instead they go away saying, "I must do something."

Preach at your own heart and you'll be surprised at how many hearts you'll hit.

Don't make puns on the Scriptures.

Be guarded in your use of humor. People will remember your

jokes far longer than the message itself. Vance Havner said, "The men of God in the Scriptures do not suggest the present-day back-slapping, uproarious variety of sanctified morons cracking jokes sometimes doubtful, and making puns on sacred Scriptures.[78]

Fight against "deadening familiarity with the sublime."

Let me close with another quotable quote from J. H. Jowett:

> I do not know how any Christian service is to be fruitful if the servant is not primarily baptized in the spirit of a suffering compassion. We can never heal need that we do not feel. Tearless hearts can never be the heralds of the Passion. We must bleed if we would be the ministers of the saving blood.

It is true. Winners of souls must first be weepers for souls. Lord, deliver us from the curse of a dry-eyed Christianity.

---

78   Hearts Afire, Westwood, NJ: Fleming H. Revell Co., 1952, pp. 59-60.

FORTY-SIX
ENTERTAIN ANGELS UNAWARES

One of the marks of a true disciple is that he is hospitable. His house is open to the household of faith and to non-Christians as well. It is one of the ways by which he can show Christian love.

Lazarus, Mary, and Martha were good at hospitality. Theirs was a home in which Jesus loved to be. Every Christian home can be like that. When we entertain anyone in His name, it's the same as if we were entertaining Him.

An English lady once bought a house on the Mount of Olives so she could serve Jesus a cup of tea when He returned. She could have done that any day by serving tea to one of His followers. But now she has gone, and Jesus hasn't come yet.

Our hospitality should not be confined to our relatives and friends. Jesus exposed our all too human tendency when He said,

When you give a dinner or a supper, do not ask your friends, your brothers, your relatives, nor your rich neighbors, lest they invite you back and you be repaid. But when you give a feast, invite the poor, the maimed, the lame, the blind; and you will be blessed, because they cannot repay you; for you shall be repaid at the resurrection of the just (Lk. 14:12-14).

We should treat every guest as we would treat Him. That is a high standard.

According to Middle Eastern tradition, a person is responsible for the safety of his guest, even if he doesn't particularly like him. That explains the expression in Psalm 23: *"You prepare a table before me in the presence of my enemies."* The enemies are standing at a distance, glaring at the guest, but he is safe in the care of the shepherd.

It is a common courtesy not to speak ill of a guest after he has departed, no matter how he may have behaved.

Men who itinerate in the work of the Lord are commonly shown the kindness of God for Jesus' sake. It becomes comfortable to be always on the receiving end. But these men should also be models of hospitality. Their home should be open to the Lord's people too.

What is true of individual saints should be true of assemblies also. I often think what a wonderful opportunity an assembly has to welcome first-time visitors and see that they are invited out to dinner at someone's home or at a restaurant. It is so uncommon a practice that visitors never forget it. Even if they have some other plans, it gives them a warm feeling to be shown such love. Many are in the assemblies today, not because of the teaching concerning prophecy or the church, but because they were entertained at a meal the first time they showed up.

Let me run two scenarios past you:

Scenario #1: Tom and Fran moved into the neighborhood recently. Sunday morning comes and they decide to look for a good church. So 10:45 A.M. finds them walking into the chapel, a bit intimidated. People are busy visiting in clutches. One man intercepts them, shakes hands and comments on the fine weather. They dodge between knots of people to find their way to seats—toward the rear of the chapel. The service proceeds on schedule—good singing, good message. Twelve o'clock. The closing prayer. The people rise to leave. Here and there some saints lean toward each other and whisper, "Who are those strangers?"—almost as if they were intruders. Others visit with their friends animatedly, catching up on the news of the week. Tom and Fran are almost at the door when an elder greets them, "Glad to have you with us today. Hope you'll come back." They leave and go to the local McDonald's for a hamburger.

Scenario #2: Euphoric over the birth of their first child, Ron and Ruth decide they should start going to church. They don't want their son to grow up as a heathen. They approach the door of the chapel apprehensively. An usher greets them warmly, explains about the nursery, and tells them that they will be invited out for dinner. They don't know it but there is a standing rule in the assembly that all strangers will be invited out. Sure enough before the service even starts a pleasant couple introduce themselves and invite the new-comers home for a meal. Ron and Ruth are relaxed and feel a warmth about this church. This has never happened to them before.

At dinner the host gives thanks for the food. The conversation is low-key—just a time to get acquainted. It turns out that both Ron and Ruth are from Christian backgrounds, but neither is a believer. The visit is profitable as an icebreaker. The newcomers feel that they have found some caring people.

Question: Which couple is more likely to return?

Answer: Tom and Fran never came back. Ron and Ruth are saved now and in happy fellowship. The results speak for themselves.

Why are we so hesitant to entertain strangers when it has proved so rewarding in the past? Fear is probably one of the main reasons—fear of the unknown, fear of a new situation, fear of new people, fear of not knowing what to do or how to do it. And of course there is the fear of not knowing what to talk about, of not being "spiritual" enough, of not being able to witness effectively.

A second reason is that we have other plans for Sunday afternoon, and taking strangers home would interfere with those arrangements.

Then we think of the added work involved, getting the house

immaculate, preparing a meal, then cleaning up afterward. And trying to entertain people at the same time.

Hospitality can be expensive, depending on the menu, and this may discourage those who have to operate on a limited budget.

A final reason for not showing hospitality. A chosen few in the assembly get saddled with the responsibility all the time. They are the only ones who do it, and it gets old hat after a while.

In answer to the first objection, there is no real need to fear. We should just determine to be ourselves, to let people see us as we are. It is not necessary to force the gospel on them. The mere giving of thanks, a testimony shared, or verses read after the meal are enough.

It is true that if we are to be hospitable, it may interfere with our Sunday plans. We have to determine in advance that this is going to be one of our priority ministries.

Hospitality does involve work and inconvenience, but we should not offer to the Lord that which costs us nothing. And we should remember that what is done in His Name is reckoned as being done for Himself. Imagine having Jesus home for Sunday dinner!

Hospitality need not be expensive. We don't have to cook up a fancy meal. A simple fare in pleasant company is all that matters.

But the ministry of hospitality should not be left to one or two in the assembly. If enough families take up the ministry, many strangers can be accommodated without burdening anyone.

Here are some practical pointers as to how some assemblies have grown through hospitality.

In one, the elders and their wives consistently invite visitors to their home. If there aren't enough visitors, then they invite some of the saints to whom they can minister in one way or another. Needless to say, the example of the elders speaks to the other believers.

Another assembly has an Angels' Committee. Each Sunday two couples are assigned to bring a casserole, salad, rolls and dessert. Ushers direct visitors to them for a meal in the chapel dining area after the morning service. The saints thus entertain angels unawares, giving rise to the name of their committee. Once again, if there aren't enough visitors, the hosts are free to invite guests from the chapel.

Many assemblies have a hostess who assigns visitors on particular Sundays. The emphasis is on reaching out to those who attend for the first time.

Most fellowships are careful to see that the visiting speaker is invited to someone's home for a meal. What they don't realize is that often the preacher would prefer to relinquish this privilege if he could know that strangers were being taken care of.

If a family holds back for fear of not being able to carry on a profitable conversation, let them consider inviting the speaker along with strangers to handle this part of the ministry.

If Christians are afraid to invite strangers, they should know that very often visitors are equally afraid of entering a new situation. And visitors frequently cannot accept because they already have other plans. But the fact that they have been invited gives them a sense of warmth and acceptance.

Scores of people in assemblies today will testify that they were drawn, not by New Testament church order, or by the preaching, or by the teaching, but by the kind hospitality that was shown to them on their first visit.

Is it possible that in our frenetic attempts to promote church growth, we are overlooking one of the most obvious and successful methods?

FORTY-SEVEN
THE LIFE OF FAITH

Christians are called to live by faith. The prayer, *"Give us this day our daily bread"* (Mt. 6:11) assumes that we are living in constant dependence on the Lord's provision.

Those who have a secular occupation receive a regular income. To them the question is not where their money is going to come from but what they will do with it when they receive it. For them the life of faith is to work hard for the supply of their current needs and the needs of their family, put everything above that in the work of the Lord, and trust God for the future.

However, to one who is engaged in full-time work for the Lord, the life of faith is depending on the Lord to meet all his needs. He believes that God has called him and that God pays for what he orders. He knows that God's work done in God's way will never lack God's provision. He does not have to beg for money. God will provide.

Sadly, this New Testament pattern is largely rejected in Christian circles today. Highly organized solicitation is the rule, not the exception. It has reached such bizarre proportion that the world looks on and says, "All the church wants is your money."

The first and foremost argument against this practice is that it does not have any scriptural precedent or support. The apostles never made their needs known to others. They did make known the needs of others. Paul, for instance, publicized the needs of the needy believers in Jerusalem (2 Cor. 8:10-15). But for themselves they looked to the Lord alone for the supply of their needs.

Then too, the whole subject is linked with the life of faith. God wants us to look to Him alone. The more we are cast on Him, the more glory He receives. The more we manipulate our own destinies, the less glory for Him and the more for ourselves. G. H. Lang offers some valuable insight about the life of faith:

"Because faith is the proper, morally indispensable quality in man to enable God to grant His approval, those methods that develop actual faith in us, and in the converts, are the only right and blessed methods. To hinder faith becomes, therefore, a most necessary aim of the devil, and among other of his snares, this is one of the most effective—that he induces us to adopt methods which falsely promise good results though they do not demand vital faith, such as counting on God only in all things at all times.

There is a real power in organizations: in magazines which make workers and their needs known to benevolent hearts; in lists of workers which give information about them; in large funds announcing their incomes and distribution. No one questions that such methods have power to serve certain ends; but they do not demand a persistent, energetic, direct faith in a living God. Men of the world can and do employ them for their own ends. Their tendency necessarily is to draw away the heart from God to themselves; at first with an attention divided between Him and them, and then at last to interpose between the soul and Him...Here is the basic reason why some oppose all such methods; here is reason enough why the Lord never adopted them. From these methods, men like Groves and Müller deliberately turned, so as to give to the disbelieving world and an unbelieving church a fresh proof of the reality and faithfulness of God and the power and sufficiency of faith and prayer."[79]

---

79   Lang, G. H., Anthony Norris Groves, London: The Paternoster Press, 1949, p. 275.

If I am really dependent on the Lord alone, then He will provide as long as the work is of Himself. When He wants a work to stop He will cut off the supply. This saves the worker from the misery of carrying on after the Spirit has departed. But by using appeals and solicitations, we can perpetuate a work long after the Lord has written Ichabod on it, long after the glory has departed.

As soon as you start soliciting, you introduce a new measure of success into Christian work. The one who is most clever in public relations is the one who gets the most money. And it may be that worthy works suffer because the high-pressure fund campaigns are siphoning off the money. This gives rise to jealousy, competition, and disunity.

WHAT HAPPENS WHEN YOU DEPEND ON PRAYER ALONE?

"God is all-powerful in every realm. He can do things in a variety of ways, but one way in which He works is to "move" in the realm of men's minds. God can place an idea in a person's mind. He can cause someone to feel a strong "urge" or "conviction" to do something. So when we pray for a certain amount of money, God can cause one person to reach for a check-book and send that amount, or He can cause a dozen people to send odd fractions of that amount, causing the total to be exact. You may not believe that He does this, but I am simply saying that when I talk about praying for money, this is what I mean."[80]

Only those who have experienced the deep thrill of seeing God provide exact amounts in answer to prayer at the exact right time without the need being made known, can appreciate the deliciousness of the experience.

When the work of God depends on human appeals, it often happens that the appeals lose their effectiveness. The people build up immunity to them, and the appeals must become louder and more

---

80   Schaefer, Edith, L'Abri, Westchester, IL: Crossway Books, 1992, p. 126.

sensational to produce the required result. That is where we are today. The modern version of Philippians 4:6-7 is: *"In everything by advertisement and begging letters, with exaggeration, let your requests be made known to men.* And the uncertainty of finances, which passes all endurance, shall keep your hearts and minds in continual suspense."

I make a distinction between information and solicitation. I feel it is legitimate to inform people as to what God is doing, but our motives must be pure. We must not be secretly or indirectly looking to men rather than to God.

The language of faith is, *"My soul, wait thou only upon God; for my expectation is from Him."* To make known my wants, directly or indirectly, to a human being, is departure from the life of faith, and a positive dishonor to God. It is actually betraying Him. It is tantamount to saying that God has failed me, and I must look to my fellow for help. It is forsaking the living fountain and turning to a broken cistern. It is placing the creature between my soul and God, thus robbing my soul of rich blessing, and God of the glory due to Him.[81]

There is no doubt that God is using many groups that solicit funds. But I think they are missing a great deal. And there is a better way. "The true life of faith is a grand reality. God delights in it, and He is glorified by it. There is nothing in this entire world that so gratifies and glorifies Him as the life of faith."[82]

Hudson Taylor's words are worth remembering:

Money wrongly placed and money given from wrong motives are both to be greatly dreaded. We can afford to have as little as the Lord chooses to give, but we cannot afford to have unconsecrated money...Let us see that we keep God before our eyes; that we walk in His ways and seek to please and glorify Him

---

81   Mackintosh, C. H., Living by Faith, p. 260.
82   Mackintosh, C. H., Miscellaneous Writings, further documentation unavailable.

in everything, great and small. Depend upon it, God's work done in God's way will never lack God's supplies.

Corrie Ten Boom said, "I would much rather be the trusting child of a rich Father, than a beggar at the door of worldly men."

Someone else put it this way: "Sons of the King do not conduct themselves like the devil's beggars."

FORTY-EIGHT
BE ZEALOUS FOR JESUS

A zealous person is one who is passionately devoted to another person or a cause. He talks about his obsession to anyone who will listen. Life revolves around this center.

Zealots are different. They don't fit the ordinary mold. They march to the beat of a different drummer. People think that they are mentally unhinged, but that does not deter them. They are indifferent to the praise or blame of others.

What is it that makes a Christian a person of zeal? In a moment unannounced, two great truths dawn upon his soul. He is overwhelmed by the realization that the One who died on the Cross of Calvary was the eternal God, the Maker of heaven and earth. The second astounding revelation that grips him is that the God the Son died for him, the sinner. Life can never be the same. He says, in effect:

> *I have seen a vision, and for self I cannot live.*
> *Life is worse than worthless unless all I give.*

The Lord Jesus was a zealous Person. As we have seen in a previous chapter, He was consumed with zeal for God when He saw the money changers desecrating the Temple courts.

W. Mackintosh Mackay elaborates on the Savior's zeal:

So zealous was He in His work that often He had no time even to eat, and His mother and brethren once wanted to take Him home because they thought He was "going off His head." They said, *"He is beside Himself."*

But it was Jesus who was then the sane man, not His brethren. For enthusiasm is the one thing in propaganda without which you can make no progress. History is written by enthusiasts. The mountain-peaks of time are all volcanoes. They were all raised by a hidden fire once burning within them.[83]

The apostle Paul was a man of zeal. People accused him of becoming mentally unhinged. His *mea culpa* was this: *"For if we are beside ourselves, it is for God"* (2 Cor. 5:13). His life as a believer was one of tireless travels, enduring hunger, persecutions, muggings, shipwrecks, imprisonments, and trials that would have caused others to turn back.

John Wesley was a man of zeal.

He traveled 250,000 miles on horseback, averaging twenty miles a day for forty years; he preached 40,000 sermons, produced hundreds of books; knew ten languages. At eighty-three he was annoyed that he could not write more than fifteen hours a day without hurting his eyes, and at eighty-six was ashamed he could not preach more than twice a day. He complained in his journal that there was an increasing tendency to lie in bed until 5:30 in the morning.

C. T. Studd was a zealot. He wrote: "Some want to live within the sound of church or chapel bell. I want to run a rescue shop within a yard of hell."

Jim Elliot's zeal was memorable. Listen to his heartbeat as he meditates on the verse, *"He makes His ministers a flame of fire"*:

Am I ignitable? God deliver me from the dread asbestos of "other things." Saturate me with the oil of the Spirit that I may be aflame. But flame is transient, often short-lived. Canst thou bear this, my soul—short life? In me there

---

83   Mackay, W. Mackintosh, The Men Whom Jesus Made, London: Hodder and Stoughton, 1924, p. 187.

dwells the Spirit of the Great Short-Lived, whose zeal for God consumed Him. "Make me Thy fuel, flame of God."[84]

We should be men and women of zeal. How can we be complacent when we realize that Christ is our Lord, that He died for us, and that there is a world out there that is dying without hope?

The world has incredible zeal at athletic events and political rallies. They will pay exorbitant prices to fill enormous stadia to endure the discomfort of heat or cold to watch teams of men contend over a ball of cowhide. Or if it is a political rally, they will yell themselves hoarse when their candidate regales them with promises, empty promises. If they can be so excited over moments of irrelevant and transient glory, how much more should we be over eternal issues?

I like what Bishop John Taylor said at a Keswick Conference some years ago:

> Young people, be as nutty as you like for Jesus Christ, because if you are not enthusiastic when you are in your teens and twenties—boy! will you be stuffy when you are forty! You will! Frankly, I would prefer the risk of over-enthusiasm that can possibly lead astray, to that steady caution that goes to the grave before you die.[85]

I believe that if the Bible is true, and if our redemption is so mind-boggling, then those who are fanatics of Jesus are the ones who are right.

---

84   Elisabeth Elliot, *Shadow of the Almighty*, New York: Harper and Bros., 1958, pp..58-59.
85   Taylor, Bishop John, The People and the King (Living in Hope), Bromley, Kent, England: STL Books, n.d., p. 98.

FORTY-NINE
AVOID PUBLICITY

Publicity is usually a bad thing in the work of the Lord. *"Do you seek great things for yourself? Do not seek them"* (Jer. 45:5). Christ didn't do it.

Why did the Son of God spend all those years in a woodworker's shop? Why did He not visit Rome and Athens and Alexandria and lecture in the great world centers? And why did He spend by far the greater portion of His earthly life as a carpenter? It does not add up on our little computers in this publicity-mad era of the mass media when people will do anything under the sun to land on the front page and show up on television...We would have had our Lord come to earth full-grown, a world traveler, university lecturer. Think what the news media could have done for Him! Instead, when He performed a miracle, He said, "Don't tell it." His brothers urged Him to get out of the backwoods and up on the boulevards. He needed a good press agent! He did miracles and never advertised them. Today we advertise them but cannot do them (Vance Havner).

When power is seen as a 'big deal,' we want to draw attention to what we have done. We put up our signs and carry on our advertising campaigns in a frantic effort to show that we are important. The one thing we cannot abide is for this great work of God (and ourselves) to go unnoticed (Richard Foster).

In his book *Christ and the Media,* Malcolm Muggeridge suggests that if Christ were going through the wilderness temptation today, Satan would add a fourth temptation, namely, to appear on national television. In *Jesus, the Man who Lives,* he writes:

> Suppose Jesus were to hurl Himself from one of the temple's high pinnacles in the sure knowledge that God would send His angels to ensure that no ill befell Him. What a sensation that would make! Headlines in all the papers, stories on all the television networks, everyone making for Jerusalem to interview the Man Who Jumped off the Top of the Temple without Hurting Himself. Jesus in great demand everywhere; a ready-made international audience hanging on His words; Herod interested, Pilate, too and maybe the Emperor Tiberias himself. All this not to boost Jesus—not at all, but to be sure that His words resounded through the great Roman Empire rather than just reaching a rag-tag and bob-tail following in Galilee.[86]

C. A. Coates warns against the dangers of publicity in the work of the Lord:

> The moment we want to put ourselves in evidence we are wrong and out of accord with the present character of service. The Lord shrank from publicity; it is most touching for it is so opposite to what we are naturally. We naturally like publicity, but the Lord on five or six occasions in Mark's Gospel clearly enjoins on those healed that they should not speak of it. We should go on content to take the little opportunities for service that may be allotted, and not desire any little bit of public-ity. Publicity is a most damaging thing; it needs much grace if the Lord gives it, as He does to some. The greater the measure of the publicity, the greater the necessity for the servant to maintain the desire for obscurity—for the little ship to be out of sight—to do his work and not talk about it, or be talked about. The true servant does his work and does not want it talked about; he wants to go on with it.[87]

---

86   Quoted in Money, Sex, and Power, Ronald Sider, San Francisco: Harper & Row, 1985, p. 180

87   Coates, C. A., An Outline of Mark's Gospel and Other Ministry, Sussex, England: Kingston Bible Trust, 1964, p. 30.

It is interesting to note that on Darby's gravestone are the words *"As unknown, yet well known."* He is the same one who said, "It is God's work. Man should be hidden and God glorified. Publicity in the Lord's things is not good."

John the Baptist didn't seek publicity. He disclaimed any greatness. He was not worthy to tie the Messiah's shoelaces. He was only a voice, crying in the wilderness.

The apostles didn't do it. In the presence of their Lord, they saw themselves as a ragtag bunch of fumbling, bumbling learners. Paul said, *"But God forbid that I should glory save in the cross of our Lord Jesus Christ, by whom the world has been crucified to me, and I to the world"* (Gal. 6:14).

Publicity shines the light on the wrong person. God's decree is that the Savior should have the preeminence in all things. He alone is worthy of the spotlight. Only to Him shall every knee bow as every tongue confesses Him Lord.

Publicity causes jealousy among other workers. It starts a contest of one-upmanship, workers trying to outdo one another in souls saved, auditoriums filled, and money reaped.

God will not share His glory with another (Is. 42:8). Rather He will stain the pride of human glory (Is. 23:9). Any disciple who covets the headlines puts himself in the way of shame and humiliation. Publicity exposes a person to satanic attack.

> There is always the utmost danger when a man or his work becomes remarkable. He may be sure Satan is gaining His objective when attention is drawn to aught or anyone but the Lord Jesus Himself. A work may be commenced in the greatest possible simplicity, but through lack of holy watchfulness and spirituality on the part of the workman, he himself or the results of his work may attract general attention, and he may fall into the snare of the devil. Satan's grand and ceaseless object is to dishonor the Lord Jesus. And if he can do this by what seems to be Christian service, he has achieved all the greater victory for the time (C. H. Macintosh).

It tempts people to stretch the truth, to make exaggerated claims.

> *Give me to serve in humble sphere;*
> *I ask not aught beside,*
> *Content to fill a little place*
> *If God be glorified.* (Anonymous)

Charles Wesley's prayer should be ours.

> *Never let the world break in;*
> *Fix a mighty gulf between.*
> *Keep me little and unknown,*
> *Prized and loved by God alone.*

FIFTY
PRIVILEGES & RESPONSIBILITIES OF THE LOCAL ASSEMBLY

PRIVILEGES

One of the outstanding features of the Christian life is the privilege of fellowship in a local assembly. There is nothing like it. No lodge or fraternity can compete. The communion of saints is one of the closest, most precious bonds known to mankind. Purchased for us at enormous cost, it is one of the four main purposes that bring believers together—the apostles' doctrine, fellowship, the breaking of bread, and prayer (Acts 2:42).

When God's people gather for these purposes, they are assured of the promised presence of the Lord Jesus Christ (Mt. 18:20). While it is true that He is always with His own, it is also true that there is a special sense in which He comes very near when believers gather in His Name. We accept this reality by faith.

In meetings of a local church, we fulfill one of the main reasons for our existence—the worship of God. Who can describe how "sweet the moments which, in blessing, musing o'er the cross we spend, life and health and peace possessing from the sinners' dying Friend?" Or who can fully know the thrill of singing a song that will resound throughout eternity, "Worthy is the Lamb that was slain?"

It is in the local assembly that we are grounded in the Word, called the apostles' doctrine in Acts 2:42. How I thank the Lord for men of God who stood firm on the verbal inspiration of the Bible, who expounded the Word to us, and who taught us to test everything by the Scriptures. The assembly was my Bible school and seminary. Some say, "The church was my mother." I know what they mean.

Just as the early believers continued steadfastly in prayer, so we come to value the practice of collective prayer. In the prayer meeting, we learn how to pray. We expand the scope of our prayers. And we rejoice together when the answers come.

The local church affords us the special benefit of serving, whether in a Sunday School class, in tract distribution, in gospel outreach, or in visitation. Friendships are deepened in cooperative labor. The Lord uses it to polish the rough places in our character and to conform us more and more to His image.

Giving is too often taught as a duty. Why not think of it as a privilege? When we give, we give to the Lord. What we give is multiplied in blessing to others and in reward to ourselves. The gifts of a local church can reach out in influence to the far corners of the earth. They are an investment for eternity.

The local assembly forms us into a family that serves us well in times of need, sorrow, trial, or tragedy. I know of nothing in the world that is comparable to it.

RESPONSIBILITIES

Wherever there are privileges, we should also be cognizant of responsibilities. The French have a phrase, *Noblesse oblige.* It means that nobility has obligations. That is true of our place in the local church. As God's aristocracy on earth we are obligated to live as His children and do as He has commanded.

Let me give a list of our responsibilities in the local assembly. The list is suggestive but not exhaustive.

We should love all the saints and pray for them. Some believers take the assembly directory and pray for each person every day. It is a worthy habit, worth imitating.

We should be faithful in attendance at all the meetings. The Lord misses us when we are not there, and we miss the superlative privilege of being with Him. Irregular attendance sets a poor example for weaker believers who are eager to find an excuse for their lack of dependability.

We should submit to the elders as those who must give account. *"Let them do so with joy and not with grief, for that would be unprofitable for you"* (Heb. 13:17).

We are responsible to exercise our spiritual gift(s). Just as the health of the human body depends on the proper functioning of the individual members, so the health of a local fellowship depends in part on the members carrying out their functions.

Personal holiness is a great responsibility. What affects one part of the body affects the whole body. When sin is unconfessed and not forsaken, this holds back the flow of blessing in the church.

We must endeavor to keep the unity of the Spirit in the bond of peace. Whenever we are tempted to exercise our gift of criticism, we should bury that gift. Instead we should be positive and enthusiastic about a fellowship that seeks to present a model of Christ's body to the world.

Sharing in the financial needs of the assembly and in financial fellowship with full time workers is both a privilege and a responsibility. It is still true that giving is more blessed than receiving.

Mutual help, exhortation, and edification are ways that we can minister to one another. These are ways in which we can wash the feet of our fellow-believers, as taught by our Lord.

Sharing in the ministry of hospitality is a sign of a healthy, growing assembly. This practical demonstration of Christian love is often more effective than a sermon.

Sharing in the practical work of maintaining the chapel may seem mundane and not an especially spiritual work, but if done for the Lord, it is as spiritual as preaching the gospel or teaching the Word.

There is no doubt about it. We are the most privileged people on the earth. To be a true disciple of the Lord Jesus requires that we assume the responsibilities that go with our fellowship in a local assembly.

FIFTY-ONE
ASSEMBLY PLANTING

In the courtyard of a hotel in Honolulu, I saw my first banyan tree. As the branches of this tree grow out, they send down shoots that reach to the ground, take root, and form secondary trunks. I have always felt that this tree is a parable of ideal church growth. It pictures the way assemblies should multiply. As a local fellowship grows, it should send forth human "shoots" to take root in adjoining areas and form new assemblies.

This is the ideal, but unfortunately we don't live in an ideal world. While leaders generally pay lip service to church planting, they display a natural resistance to it whenever it becomes a live possibility. They parade their sixty well-rehearsed reasons why, in their particular case, it is not a desirable option, or why the time is not yet ripe. They do not want to see the status quo disturbed when everything is going along so smoothly. They need all the help they can get. There is not sufficient qualified leadership for a new work. A hive-off would make it harder for the home church to meet its financial obligations. The children and young people in a new work would not have the same opportunities for fellowship with their own age groups as they would in a larger work. The leaders agree that they will encourage a new work some day—but not yet.

Other evangelical churches are not deterred by these consider-ations, and they experience steady growth. Certainly the cults refuse to be held back by this conventional wisdom, and they charge ahead like gangbusters.

If we are to escape the indictment, "faithfulness without fruitful-ness" or "truth without growth," we must not listen to our hesita-tions, but must abandon our natural reluctance and determine before God to give ourselves to the ministry of assembly planting, what-ever the cost may be.

How is a new assembly born? It should start with a heaven-sent vision placed on the heart of one or more believer(s). There should be a burden that will not go away, a persistent consciousness that God is leading. The Holy Spirit plants the idea, and creates an answering desire in the hearts of His people.

The vision must be bathed in prayer. In this way we acknowledge our inability to make correct judgments and our absolute depen-dence on His wisdom. Christ, after all, is the Head of the assembly, and only the Head has the right to decide. As we pray, the vision comes more and more into focus. What was a general burden at first gradually becomes specific as to location, agenda, and leadership.

There must be strong, spiritual leadership. Without it, the work is liable to fall apart at an early stage. It is desirable to have what could be called a church planting team—at least two or three couples. Efforts by one man, working alone, have not had a good track record. The Lord Jesus worked with twelve disciples. Paul traveled with a team of men, planting assemblies. It seems to be a divine pattern.

If the new work is to be a hive-off from an existing assembly or assemblies, it is important to proceed with tact, love, and unity. Very often there is that natural hesitation and reluctance in existing assemblies to see valued members leave. Elders often fear what seems to be a threat to their numbers. It takes prayerful waiting on the Lord to see Him incline the hearts of the leaders to extend the right hand of fellowship to the new work.

The church planting team will want to agree on certain basic issues and to adopt certain ground rules. For example, they will draw up a statement of faith. In addition, they might consider the following ground rules which one team agreed on:

1. There must be absolute unity on the fundamentals of the Christian faith. No deviation from these basic truths would be tolerated.

2. On secondary matters, the assembly would submit to the consensus of the fellowship.

3. The church planting team would not necessarily constitute the permanent leadership. They would serve for at least one year. At the end of that time, the assembly would meet to ascertain which men the Lord had raised up to be elders. There would then be a public recognition of this leadership and the church planting team would be dissolved.

4. When the assembly would grow in numbers to between 100 and 150, positive steps would then be taken toward the formation of another work.

5. No efforts would be made to grow by transfers from other assemblies or churches. Rather the goal would be to reach unsaved people, see them converted, baptized, discipled and brought into the fellowship.

A decision must be made with regard to location. New residential neighborhoods are ideal, but it is preferable not to locate in the front yard of an already-established evangelical church. At first, the assembly can meet in a home. Then when it outgrows the home, it can move to rented facilities or it can purchase or build a modest building. Sometimes zoning laws and parking regulations preclude home meetings. The leadership must weigh all the pros and cons.

The nature and order of meetings are generally fairly easy to decide. The team will take into account the centrality of worship, the importance of collective prayer, and the spiritual diet needed for the flock.

Just as there is joy when a baby is born, so there is a deep-seated ecstasy in connection with the planting of a new assembly. Believers experience a new warmth of fellowship, an enthusiasm in striving together to see the assembly grow, and a satisfaction in exercising gifts that are stifled in a larger church.

Just as human families rejoice when sons and daughters marry and start families of their own, so assemblies should rejoice when they are privileged to "parent" new works and to see them functioning as autonomous churches.

Assembly planting is the will of God. Blessed are those who work with Him in accomplishing His will!

FIFTY-TWO
CHURCH GROWTH
THROUGH EVANGELISM

Any assembly that desires to grow must face this fact: between 80% and 90% of new converts are originally contacted by individual believers within the context of their daily lives, whether at work, at school, or in the neighborhood. This does not belittle other methods of evangelism, but it shows that personal, lifestyle evangelism towers above all others.

We should not be surprised. This was how the faith spread in the early days of the church. The Christians took the risen Savior's words seriously, *"...you shall be witnesses to Me"* (Acts 1:8b). They *"went everywhere preaching the Word"* (Acts 8:4). The world will never be evangelized in any other way.

We must abandon the common misconception that the believer's sole responsibility is to get the unsaved to attend the meetings so that the preacher can present the gospel and then lead them to Christ. Every believer should be doing the work of an evangelist. He should be able to present the way of salvation to his contacts. Then when he senses that the Holy Spirit has thoroughly convicted them of sin, he should be able to lead them to Christ as their only hope for heaven.

This does not mean that our evangelism should be unrelated to the local assembly. While our main goal is to see people come to Christ, we also want to see them added to the fellowship. We bring the unsaved to the meetings to confirm the testimony we have already given to them. Or, if we have already pointed them to Christ, we bring them to the assembly in order to see them discipled in accordance with the Great Commission.

An evangelistic assembly is a praying assembly. The place to start is in prayer. This is where the work is done. The saints must be desperate before God in fervent intercession for lost relatives, friends, and neighbors. No amount of programs and gimmicks will ever take the place of prayer. We are in a spiritual battle, and it must be fought with spiritual weapons.

An evangelistic assembly is a holy assembly. Effective witness cannot be divorced from sanctified lives. The fruit that a tree bears is a reflection of the condition of the tree itself. A healthy tree brings forth good fruit. Those who bear the vessels of the Lord must be clean.

An evangelistic assembly is a loving assembly. It has a warm, accepting atmosphere. It reaches out to strangers, to those who hurt, to those who have needs. It is people-oriented. It manifests its love by being hospitable. It is outgoing, not ingrown. It cares.

An evangelistic assembly is a united assembly. The saints are united in an enthusiasm to see souls saved. They are united in a common, prayerful expectancy. And they are united in a shared joy when people are converted.

We mentioned that the most effective way of making new contacts is through the daily witness of the believers. But there are other methods that should be mentioned. For instance, there is door to door visitation. This certainly makes the presence of the assembly known in any community. There are home Bible studies, which have been greatly used in laying a doctrinal foundation for those who later trust the Lord. There is campus evangelism, a good way to reach young people for the Lord and for the assembly. There is the ministry of literature; its possibilities are tremendous (see Appendix G, p. 421). There are special evangelistic crusades, with an anointed gospel preacher. These have been wonderfully used in some places, and sadly ineffective in others. An assembly can advertise its meetings in the local paper. God has used this method to lead isolated individuals to the meetings. Then, of course, there are special programs, films, and musical events.

To break down the natural resistance toward attending an assembly for the first time, some fellowships have used less formal methods successfully: picnics, baseball or volleyball games, and hospitality in homes. By attending these, people get to know the local Christians and can more easily be induced to attend the meetings.

In order for believers to be enthusiastic about bringing their contacts to the meetings of the assembly, they must be assured that the ministry will be of a high spiritual quality. This fact should cause the elders to be much before the Lord concerning those whom they schedule to minister the Word. Christians will not bring their friends to hear a stumbling, rambling sermon. They want to be sure that there will be a *bona fide* presentation of the gospel and that there will be solid teaching for those who are already believers.

Does this mean that the speakers must be seminary-trained men or those with advanced educational credentials? Not at all! Mere scholarship without deep spirituality can be a boring, deadening thing. Knowledge puffs up, but love edifies. A scholarly message might reach the head without ever getting down to the heart. What is needed is ministry empowered by the Holy Spirit, ministry with unction, ministry that produces conviction, contrition, conversion, and consecration. God very often uses homespun and untrained men for this work, so that the glory will be His, not man's.

There are few things as good for an assembly as to see souls saved on a regular basis. This produces ecstasy like that of a maternity ward. And it can be the experience of any assembly that is willing to devote itself to New Testament evangelism. But we must have a holy horror of going year after year without seeing any conversions. And we must be willing to use new methods where the old ones are proving singularly ineffective. We get what we go after in life. Let us go after souls.

FIFTY-THREE
ONE-ON-ONE DISCIPLESHIP

In the previous chapter, we talked about church growth through Spirit-led evangelism. Now the question is, "What are we going to do with the new converts? What is the best way to assure their growth to spiritual maturity?"

A common approach is to encourage the new believer to faithfully attend all the meetings of the assembly and receive his instruction in this way. But this method has drawbacks. It is extremely slow; it usually has to extend over many years. It is incomplete; there is no guarantee that all important subjects will be covered. It does not teach the convert how to engage in practical Christian work; it is all academic. Jesus not only taught doctrine; He took the disciples out and showed them how to do the work.

As soon as someone is saved, a spiritually mature believer should undertake the responsibility of discipling him. If the convert is a woman or girl, then an older sister should become the teacher (see Titus 2:3-5).

Rather than following the same stereotyped program for each person, the one doing the discipling should look to the Holy Spirit for individual guidance. Then he must ask himself, "What are the

371

subjects that we should cover so that this convert will be a well-grounded and well-rounded believer?" The following might be a representative list: assurance of salvation; eternal security; baptism; worship and the Lord's Supper; daily quiet time; personal holiness; Bible study; prayer; guidance; Scripture memory; stewardship of time, talents, and money; personal evangelism. And all this should be supplemented by the consecutive, systematic study of the Scriptures themselves.

It is important to have a regular weekly appointment with the convert, lasting no less than an hour. Here the teacher not only covers the truth of believer's baptism but encourages the disciple to take this step of obedience. Here the teacher explains about the Breaking of Bread service and urges compliance with the Savior's request, *"This do in remembrance of Me."* He teaches the baby Christian how to pray by praying with him. He shows him how to study the Bible, using available helps (concordances, Bible dictionaries, commentaries, etc.). He guides him in the selection of books for his library. He answers questions that may arise. He gives help on personal problems. He commends every evidence of progress, and counsels concerning areas of Christian character that need attention.

When the teacher goes out witnessing, he takes the disciple with him. When he visits the sick, he takes the disciple with him. He opens his home, giving practical training in Christian marriage, the Christian home, and proper child training. As much as possible, he shares his life with the one he is seeking to train.

On-fire assemblies today know that it is important to give each new believer individual attention in addition to the training he receives in the meetings. It is costly, but it is effective. It is the method which the Lord used, and therefore it must be the best.

FIFTY-FOUR
LEADERSHIP TRAINING
By Rick Belles

As important as gospel preaching is in the mission of the church, if we incline our vision no higher than seeing souls saved, of having as our ultimate goal the conversion of unbelievers to become faithful meeting-attenders, then we are guilty of short-sightedness and will eventually be faced with the prospect of a spiritually weak and impotent assembly.

We must set our sights on nothing less than the transformation of immature believers who have potential into leaders of the church if we are to share the vision of the One who declared, *"I will build My church."* In fact, the key factor that insures the continuance of His living edifice is the raising up of spiritual leaders from generation to generation, a strategy that the Master Himself was busily engaged in when He uttered the preceding statement.

But if we are to share the vision of the Lord Jesus for church leadership, then we must also adopt His method if we hope to succeed. And His method was personal discipleship—the choice of certain men to be with Him. If the Savior Himself trained His men through three years of constant, personal attention, how can we expect to see effective leaders raised up by relying solely on Bible classes and pulpit ministry?

An illustration of the Lord's method is seen in His work with Peter. Study the occurrences of statements and questions that He directed to Peter, and you will begin to catch glimpses into the personal relationship between Peter and his Lord. And you will see the Savior at work in the life of His disciple—confronting, challenging, encouraging—transforming a rough, untaught fisherman into a faithful shepherd of the flock of God. We can assume that the Savior's method was no different with the eleven other disciples. When the training was complete, He had raised up men who, when filled with the Holy Spirit, actually turned the world upside down.

Of course, we can think of objections to following this strategy in our own lives. It seems to us that greater numbers in the training relationship would produce greater dividends in the end. So we prefer to teach large classes and preach to hundreds, hoping to affect more lives at one time. But the result too often is hundreds of shallow Christians. You cannot disciple crowds. Yet when considering the option of spending our time with one or two key men on a regular basis, we think within ourselves, "Why this waste?" and prefer to scatter our efforts across the masses. But this was not the Lord's approach to leaving a legacy of strong leaders.

Another difficulty to overcome in adopting our Lord's approach is the cost of transparency. We run the risk of being known by our disciple in a way that would never be true in a class or from a pulpit. The Lord did not shrink from that intimacy, but allowed Himself to be seen, heard, and handled by twelve men every day for three years. When the time had ended, all except one had acquired the same selfless love for others that they had seen and experienced in Him.

This is not to imply that specially gifted and charismatic men cannot have a strong influence on the lives of others solely through ministry to the multitudes. But such men represent a small percentage of the body of Christ, and to expect this method to be the chief source of church leadership is both unrealistic and unscriptural. The result of this method will be a church that flourishes during the active ministry of one man and then dies away with his passing—for want of faithful men to carry on in his place. Contrast this situation with the Lord's parting words to Peter (Jn. 21:15) and those of Paul to Timothy (2 Tim. 2:2).

Man-to-man discipleship does not require specially gifted or charismatic leaders to be effective. Its success depends on a Spirit-filled man who loves God, His Word and His people, and is willing to open his life to another. Given this as the strategy, the tactics are simple.

• Meet together often for Bible study and prayer.

• Teach by example. Let the disciple see your godly life and your burden for people up close. Jesus did.

• Teach through practical experience. Take your disciple with you when visiting the saints and witnessing to the unsaved, and afterwards explain what you did and why you did it. Jesus did.

• Work on character. Think of the Lord constantly reminding Peter of his impulsiveness and self-confidence. What is it about your disciple that prevents the adjectives "holy and blameless" from being applied practically?

* Exhort and encourage him in the Word, and pray for him. That's what Jesus did.

If anyone had a vision for the growth of the church, it was the Lord Jesus Christ, who gave Himself for it. If we are to share that vision with Him in its fullest sense, that is, beyond seeing souls saved to the raising up of leaders of the flock who will be able to teach others also, then we must adopt His methods as our own. If the Son of God Himself found it necessary to concentrate on a few faithful men, how much more should we.

FIFTY-FIVE
PARACHURCH ORGANIZATIONS

A parachurch organization is a ministry that works alongside the churches. It is usually organized as a business corporation, and does not engage in such functions as baptism and the Lord's Supper.

Considerable controversy has swirled over these organizations. Is there a place for them in the Christian community or is the church God's exclusive agency for carrying on His work? Perhaps the fairest approach is to consider the arguments in favor of and opposed to these companies.

PRO

1. Parachurch organizations carry on ministries that the church cannot do, or should be doing but isn't, *e.g.*, translation, publishing, radio, TV, prison work, evangelism, discipling, counseling, etc. It is difficult to see how a local fellowship could do the work now being handled by the Bible societies.

2. They reach vast segments of the population that are untouched by the churches. We cannot deny that millions have heard the gospel through them.

3. Parachurch ministries can effectively reach many people who

are turned off by the church. They seem to avoid the oft-heard barb, "all the church wants is your money."

4. In missions, social services, evangelism, and church planting, parachurch organizations have taken the lead. They serve as a gadfly to the churches, motivating them to greater zeal in the work of the Lord.

5. Whereas the organized church often requires formalized training for its fulltime workers, the parachurch organizations train lay persons and put them to work.

6. They provide ministry outlets that Christians do not find in local churches. Christians that the churches have allowed to atrophy in lives of idleness find a place for their ambitions and talents.

7. They provide honorable, salaried employment for some. In many cases, this is a family's primary income.

8. They are effectively bearing fruit. God is blessing them. The Gideons, for instance, can document the conversion of thousands who have been saved through Bibles left in hotels.

9. Churches tend to emphasize buildings more than missions. The money spent in bricks and concrete might be better used in the distribution of gospel literature.

10. Churches are inflexible, resistant to change. Parachurch organizations are an answer to this lack of flexibility.

That is one side of the picture. Now let us consider some of the problems connected with these parachurch ministries.

CON

1. Parachurch organizations are unbiblical. They are nowhere found in the Acts or elsewhere in the New Testament. The church is God's unit on earth for propagating the faith. Everywhere the apostles went they planted churches. Everywhere we go we establish parachurch organizations.

2. The time and talents of men and women are diverted from the

local church. Preachers, teachers, and leaders are taken away from their primary ministry and seated behind a desk as administrators.

3. Money is diverted from the local church, yet these organizations depend on the churches for their support.

4. People serving with a parachurch organization cannot carry out the Great Commission, *"teaching...to observe all things."* Because they depend on a wide spectrum of churches for support, they cannot declare the full counsels of God. In trying to relate to many different churches, they tend to weaken their doctrinal position.

5. There are many overlapping and competing ministries, with factions, jealousies and rivalries. This is inevitable when organizations publicize their accomplishments and boast of their successes.

6. They are not accountable to anyone but themselves. It is often true that many of their leaders are loose cannons, and this can lead to moral, business, and doctrinal problems.

7. Some parachurch people tend to be antichurch. They look on their own work and the work of their organization as superior.

8. Others who have a parachurch mentality often find it difficult to adapt to the fellowship of a local church, and to function with the broad mix of people found in most congregations. They consider themselves (and often are) a select group of committed people.

9. They usurp functions and responsibilities that belong to the churches.

10. Instead of feeding converts into local churches, the organization tends to take the place of the church in the lives of the people. They are given assignments that take them away from meetings of the church.

11. They promote professionalism, climbing up the corporate ladder, etc.

There are some arguments against parachurch organizations that may be equally true of churches:

1. They do not die easily, but are often perpetuated after they have

outlived their usefulness.

2. There is a danger of focusing on a charismatic leader, and of thus establishing a personality cult.

3. They do not meet the total needs of the people.

4. They are sometimes the result of a person's inability to work with others. In frustration he starts a work where he can be independent.

Now what is the conclusion of the matter? Perhaps we find it in Luke 9:49-50. One day the disciples said to Jesus. *"We saw one casting out demons in Your name, and we forbade him because he does not follow with us."* The Lord answered, *"Do not forbid him, for he who is not against us is for us."*

Evangelical parachurch organizations are engaged in the same spiritual war as we are. We should not forbid them. They are for us.

FIFTY-SIX
SMALLER MAY BE BETTER

The emphasis on bigness in our society is so strong and so pervasive that it is almost inconceivable to think that smaller could possibly be better. The world's success syndrome, measured by numbers, has thoroughly engulfed the church. But what are the facts concerning numbers? The philosophy that big is beautiful and is the divine goal is not only missing from the Bible but is contrary to Scripture.

1. The big congregation perished in the flood; only eight people were saved.

2. Gideon's army was reduced from 32,000 to 300 so that the victory could be attributed only to divine power.

3. Jesus chose twelve disciples, not twelve thousand.

4. Voltaire's sarcastic idea that God is on the side of the big battalions represents worldly wisdom, in this case, the wisdom of an infidel.

5. The emphasis in the Scriptures is on quality rather than numbers.

6. Down through the ages God has characteristically worked through a remnant testimony.

The majority of Christian churches through the centuries have been small, and that is still true worldwide.

The bigger the church, the more difficult it is for the leadership to carry on an effective, personal pastoral ministry with the entire congregation.

The larger the church, the more difficult it is for the believers to know one another, to share joys and sorrows, to enjoy body life. It has been well said that a church which is a collection of strangers, or best, of acquaintances, is not a true church in the deepest sense of the term.

The larger the church, the greater the percentage of saints who do not have an opportunity to exercise their gifts.

If size becomes the goal, the greater is the pressure to soft-pedal the message of the gospel, the stern demands of Christian discipleship, high standards of holiness, and other hard sayings of Jesus.

If size becomes the goal, the temptation to neglect discipline is great. There is a tendency to look the other way so as not to lose members. But the real success of a church is not found in the number of its members but in their holiness.

It is conceivable that big churches cater to man's vanity and that they exist more for the leadership than for the congregation.

It is easier for small churches to go underground in times of persecution and oppression.

United prayer is often one of the first casualties in large churches.

Having said all that, there is no virtue in a small church if its smallness is a result of lack of evangelism, apathy, or any other failure. Small churches should be growing churches. But instead of becoming mega-churches, they should parent new churches. When a church reaches a certain size, the leadership should think in terms of hiving off.

What are the arguments that are commonly advanced for large churches?

- It is possible to have better facilities.
- There can be a wider variety of ministry.
- More people mean more money for the work of the Lord.

- There is better cultural acceptance.
- There is more opportunity for children and young people to be with those of their own age.
- A big church means better opportunity to have a large missionary outreach.
- It provides a better quality of teaching.

Some of these arguments may have a measure of truth; some are not necessarily true at all; and none can be supported from the Word.

Let me call to the witness stand a group of respected Christian leaders who have spoken out on the subject.

First is Vance Havner, a perceptive and articulate Southern preacher. He writes:

> The church has moved from the catacombs to the Coliseum in its emphasis on size. We stage mammoth demonstrations and gigantic convocations. We put celebrities on the platform and borrow from Caesar to enhance the banner of Christ. We have gone crazy over bigness...
>
> Actually, we need a thinning instead of a thickening. I learned long ago that growing corn and cotton must be thinned. We reduced the quantity to improve the quality. Gideon had to thin his troops, and a similar procedure might help God's army today. Jesus thinned His crowd, as recorded in the sixth chapter of John, and doubtless there was many another occasion. Today the persecuted minority has become the popular majority.
>
> This is the Age of Goofus, of trickery, hocus-pocus, freaks, sleight-of-hand, "now-you-see-it-and-now-you-don't." Everything is done with mirrors. Everything is measured by "how big?" and "how loud?" Everything must be huge, gigantic, colossal, super-duper. Ever the new drugs are "wonder drugs"— you take them and wonder what will happen next. In such a time it is hard to interest people in plain old obedience and faithfulness. Even Christians must be entertained at church. The Light of Truth is looked at but not walked in, and, being hearers but not doers, men are blinded by excess of light. Too much light will blind as surely as not enough light.

In his book *From Now On,* Ralph Shallis advises:

Choose a church which is faithful to the Scriptures and also full of the Holy Spirit; that is to say, a group where Jesus is really present. It doesn't matter if it is small or poor. If Christ is there, you are richer than all the banks in the world combined. Besides, in a small church you will find a purpose in being alive; you will be a valuable and important member of the family; you will have a real contribution to make. If, on the other hand, you are in a very large church you will probably be submerged in an anonymous mass—which is very bad for your spiritual health. You become lazy and useless, or just frustrated.[88]

Francis Schaeffer adds his testimony with these incisive words:

As there are no little people in God's sight, so there are no little places... Nowhere more than in America are Christians caught in the twentieth-century syndrome of size. Size will show success. If I am consecrated, there will necessarily be large quantities of people, dollars, etc. This is not so. Not only does God not say that size and spiritual power go together, but He even reverses this (especially in the teaching of Jesus) and tells us to be deliberately careful not to choose a place too big for us. We all tend to emphasize big works and big places, but all such emphasis is of the flesh. To think in such terms is simply to hearken back to the old, unconverted, egoist, self-centered Me. This attitude, taken from the world, is more dangerous to the Christian than fleshly amusement or practice. It is the flesh.[89]

James S. Stewart agrees. He writes:

God's strategy does not depend on numbers. We count heads. God does not. God counts hearts. We talk about extending the kingdom, producing more disciples: God aims at intensifying the kingdom and producing better disciples. We talk about High Church, Low Church, Broad Church, but what God wants

---

88   Ralph Shallis, *From Now On,* Bromley, Kent, England: STL Books, 1973, P. 43.
89   Francis A Schaeffer, *No Little People* (in the complete works of Francis A Schaeffer), Westchester, IL.: Crossway Books, 1982, Vol. 3, page 9).

to see is the Deep Church. "Do not give me the big ecclesiastical battalions," cried John Wesley, "give me a hundred men who fear nothing but sin and love nothing but God, and I will shake the gates of hell!" Where did Wesley learn that attitude? Surely from his royal master Jesus...who made clear once for all the divine strategy of His world campaign. What that strategy means is this, that Christ would rather any day have a poor five percent minority of resolute souls to work with, than a great 95 percent majority unconvinced and pliable in their allegiance.[90]

In his commentary on the book of Judges, Samuel Ridout says:

There is a subtle desire for numbers with us all. Why the desire for statistics, numbers of conversions, numbers of "members" if man has not the thought that the power is in the numbers? On the contrary, does not Scripture abound with illustrations just to the contrary? Numbers have too often been the occasion for the pride that goes before destruction. When the numbers of the disciples increased, the murmuring began. Far be the thought that we are to refuse numbers for their own sake. We should surely rejoice for the many who receive blessing, but our eye is not to be on the many, but on the Lord.

Particularly is this true in a day of decline, when God has raised up a remnant testimony to His truth. Numbers...will but make the testimony unwieldy. Better far the little company, tried and tested by God Himself, than the large and respectable body which commands respect in the eyes of the world by its numbers.[91]

E. Stanley Jones said, "I loathe this scramble for numbers, leading to collective egotism."

Finally Charles Bing makes this cryptic comment: "Masses in classes produce flashes and ashes."

When one of the largest Protestant denominations was having a drive for members, it adopted the slogan, "A million more in '84." One minister leaned over to another when the catchy title was

---

90   James S. Stewart, *King For Ever*, Nashville: Abingdon, 1975, P.91.
91   Samuel Ridout, *Lectures on Judges and Ruth*, N. Y., Loizeaux Bros., 1958, p. 25.

announced and whispered, "If we get a million more like we have now, we're sunk."

It is fine to desire numbers for the glory of God. But it is wrong to depend on them for strength. It is wrong to glory in them. It is wrong to lower standards in order to get them. As Vance Havner suggested, it is wrong to win banners and raise quotas rather than to know God. Better to have small, growing, spiritual assemblies than large, unwieldy, unprincipled ones.

SECTION V
CONCLUSION

FIFTY-SEVEN
CLOSING TIPS

You have now studied some of the major elements of Christian discipleship. Notice that I said "some." There are more. The only complete book on the subject is the New Testament.

It is not enough to have a head knowledge of the contents of this book. They must be fleshed out in the disciple's life. He must walk the talk. He must prove himself to be a devoted follower of the Lord Jesus. Others must see Jesus in him.

Something else is important. A mentor must expose his disciple to various forms of Christian service. The disciple, in turn, must be willing to go with his teacher and see how he witnesses to the unsaved, how he teaches Christians, how he preaches the gospel, how he counsels those who need direction, how he conducts a wedding and a funeral, and how he visits the sick. Ideally the disciple will learn how to do everything that an elder in a local church might be called on to do.

The apostle Paul said,

So, naturally, we proclaim Christ! We warn everyone we meet, and we teach everyone we can, all that we know about him, so that we might bring every man up to his full maturity in Christ. This is what I am working and struggling at, with all the strength that God puts into me (Col. 1:28, Phillips).

In saying this he left for us a splendid picture of a disciple in action.

We close with a few pithy suggestions that any disciple would do well to weave into the pattern of his life.

- Practice a random act of kindness and a improbable act of beauty each day. It might open wonderful opportunities for witness.

- Speak a word of encouragement each day. Someone needs it.

- Don't complain. If you read 1 Corinthians 10, you'll see that God doesn't like complaining.

- Pray that, like Andrew Bonar, you will "wear well to the end." Don't explode onto the Christian scene like a Roman candle, then peter out in falling ashes.

- Be cheerful. The Lord will forgive you for this. Franz Joseph Haydn said, "God gave me a cheerful heart. He will surely for give me if I serve Him cheerfully." Didn't the psalmist say, *"Serve the Lord with gladness"*?

- If you make a promise, keep it. If you don't mean it, don't say it.

- Never refuse an inward prompting to do something good. Do it quickly.

- Be thankful. Count your blessings. It will surprise you what the Lord has done.

- Don't waste time. Keep busy for the Lord.

- Visit the ill, the aged, and those in mourning. Just being there says that you care.

- Live each day in the light of the judgment seat of Christ. We'll be there tomorrow; we just don't know which tomorrow.

- Set a watch before your lips. Be a good listener. You might be astonished how much you learn.

- Don't try to run other people's lives. Resign as general manager of the universe.

- Don't publicize your aches and your pains. Everyone has enough of his own.

- Try to see Christ in other believers. It helps you shape a good attitude toward them.

- Show a godly interest in boys and girls. Jesus loves them.

- Go out of your way to befriend the mentally and physically challenged. Every one of them is special and precious to the Lord.

"And the things you have heard from me among many witnesses, commit these to faithful men who will be able to teach others also" (2 Tim. 2:2).

Additional material on subjects discussed in this manual may be found in the following books by the author:

> *True Discipleship*
> *The Forgotten Command; Be Holy*
> *Christ Loved the Church*
> *My Heart, My Life, My All*
> *Once in Christ, In Christ Forever*

> Booklets:
> *Think of Your Future*
> *Lord, Break Me*
> *The Day Jesus Came to My House*
> *Grasping for Shadows*
> *Does it Pay to Pray?*
> *Singleness—A Male Perspective*

APPENDIXES

APPENDIX A
SHOW IT, DON'T BLOW IT
The story of a young man who found Christ but lost his parents

The enthusiasm of youth often clashes with the caution of older people. When the young person is a brand new Christian, and on fire for Christ, and when the older people feel their own religion is threatened, the testimony can be rendered ineffective.

When the older people are the parents of the young person, the results can be disastrous. Greg's experience is a case in point. But the disaster can be turned to victory if Greg learns to moderate his zeal with love and wisdom.

First, let's have Greg tell his own story:

Man, did I ever blow it!

After I was saved, I went home and tried to ram the gospel down the throats of my family. They opposed me fiercely and I responded with hostility. That why I say I blew it.

Let me give you a little background. I was brought up in a fairly religious home. We kids learned the catechism, went to confessions, attended church regularly. In time, I became and altar boy. As far as I can tell now, our religion consisted of going through ceremonies, but none of us was really born again.

In high school, I started to steal in order to support my drug habit. My father had to bail me out of the can three times. But even after that it was easier to get the money by stealing than by working.

But this time, of course, I was deeply into sex. There was no trouble finding girls. I looked on myself as Mr. Macho.

For some time I rode the crest of the wave. I enjoyed the acceptance of my friends, and my wild life gave me a real high.

The first thing that sobered me was when my closest friend was killed in a crash. Shortly after that I was jailed on a drug charge. When I got out on bail, I landed in the hospital with what was suspected to be leukemia.

In the hospital, for the first time I can remember, I prayed. "O God, if there is a God, show Yourself to me."

An hour later, a friend from high school days came to visit the guy in the next bed. After he recovered from surprise at seeing me, he told me that he was a Christian now, that he had turned his life over to Jesus Christ. Then he carefully explained how I too could start a new life in Christ.

I was ready. We prayed. The best way I knew how, I trusted Christ as my Substitute, my Lord and my Savior.

My life changed radically. God gave me a new tongue, no longer spilling out filth and profanity. I turned away from drugs and booze and the immoral lifestyle I had known. My old friends began to desert me. One of them said, "Man, you're dead!"

Well, I expected my parents to be ecstatic over the change in my life. I thought that when I shared the gospel with them, they would all want to be saved right now. Sure, they hadn't been as bad as I, but they still needed to be saved. So I started witnessing to them rather vigorously.

Did I get a shock? They didn't admit any enthusiasm for the change in my life. Rather they seemed to say that they would rather have a dope-head in the family than a religious fanatic.

My mother wept that I had deserted her religion, calling me a traitor and a renegade. They resented my suggestion that they needed to be "born again." They wanted me to know that they were "born again" when they were baptized as infants. Now I had gone and broken the family unity.

The more I pressed the gospel on them, the more hostile they became. There were incidents of shouting, threats and insults. I felt a widening chasm between my family and myself. I was increasingly resentful of their attitudes and behavior, and became more and more withdrawn. Finally after one particularly loud shouting brawl, I moved out of the house in a rage.

That's why I say I blew it. Instead of winning them to Christ, I only succeeded in driving them away. I really love them, and that is why I wanted them to be saved. That's why I kept hammering away with the gospel. But I guess it was zeal without knowledge. Now I'm alienated from them and depressed in my spirit. Is there anything I can do to make right the wrongs of the past?

Greg's experience is a familiar scenario. Many a young convert has tried to be faithful to Christ and to his relatives, yet has acted in such a way as to negate his testimony. What shall we tell him?

Jesus stated quite frankly that His coming would mean alienation and division within families. For instance, He said, *"I came to set a man against his father, and a daughter against her mother, and a daughter-in-law against her mother-in-law; and a man's enemies will be the members of his household"* (Mt. 10:35-36, NASB).

The Lord did not mean that the direct purpose of His coming was to produce hostility in families, but rather that this would sometimes be the inevitable result. Whenever people follow Him, they can expect bitter opposition from relatives and friends. In that sense, He *"did not come to bring peace but a sword"* (v. 34).

But none of that justifies Greg's anger and resentment toward his family. It is pleasing to God if we are ridiculed, persecuted and abused because of our connection with Christ. There is no merit when we suffer because of our own stupidity, carnality, and acts of unlove.

Greg need not feel that all is lost. What he needs to do now is demonstrate to his relatives that Christ makes a difference in the life. The first way he can do that is by going back and apologizing to them for his anger and bitterness. It is hard to eat humble pie, but he must do it. And he must not try to soften the impact on himself by saying, "If I have done anything wrong, I am sorry." Instead, he must bite the bullet by stating frankly, "I was wrong. I am sorry. Please forgive me."

This will speak loudly to his parents and his brothers and sisters. They will think, "Greg never apologized like this before, and we never do it either when we're wrong."

Then instead of ramming the gospel down their throats, Greg should adopt a low-key stance, waiting for them to bring up the subject. They will, almost invariably. This will give him a chance to answer them graciously and without pressure.

If invited, it might be good for Greg to move back into the house. Once there he should help with the work, see things to be done, and do them without being asked. He should keep his room neat and clean instead of the bombed-out disaster area it used to be.

Greg should show acts of kindness that are completely out of character with what he has been in the past. This would include remembering birthdays, anniversaries and other special days, and gift giving with no other purpose than to express his love. He should pray for ways to be original and innovative in being kind.

Greg should respect his parents' authority, obeying them up to the point where their advice would mean disobeying the Lord. Then he must quietly refuse, without provoking a scene.

It is always in order to express appreciation to parents, because they never do get thanked adequately for what they have done. Instead of giving a box of chocolates on his mother's birthday, or on Mother's Day, Greg will find that a handwritten letter like this will be much more appreciated.

To my Mother:

On this day set aside to honor you in a special way, I should like to express something of the thanks I feel for all you have meant in my life.

It was you who brought me into the world—and I understand today that it meant pain and suffering to you. But you quickly and unselfishly forgot about all that for joy that a son had been born to you.

As I have grown older, I realize better the days, and months, and years you devoted to my upbringing. I often think of the times when I was sick or in accidents, and all it cost you by way of sleepless night and anxious waiting. I don't think I could ever thank you enough for your lonely vigil when it seemed that death would snatch away one of us kids.

Thanks, Mother, for all the cooking, washing, sewing, mending, house-cleaning. Thanks too for disciplining us when we deserved it; we knew you were doing it in love.

Well, there's a lot more I could say, but I think this will let you know how much I appreciate all you have done for me.

I want you to know I thank the Lord for you, and pray that we as a family will be united not only in this life, but in eternity as well.

Your son,

Greg

A letter like this will mean more to Mother than a Dior original. And Greg should try a similar letter to Dad on Father's Day. Dad will try hard to keep his eyes from bubbling, but the letter will affect him deeply.

Parents like to be consulted for advice, even when their children are grown up. It is just another way in which Greg can honor and respect them.

Hopefully these radical changes in Greg's life will not cause his parents to have cardiac arrest. But if they produce another kind of heart attack, they will be worth it—namely, a heart overcome by the love of Jesus.

One final word, Greg. When your parents ask questions or express appreciation for the change that has come in your life, use it as an opportunity to give credit to the Savior. Make them realize that it is not you, but Jesus in you.

God loves to save families, Greg. You can cooperate with Him by demonstrating the life of Christ before them day by day. You can win them by prayer and good works, without nagging or pressuring them. God bless!

APPENDIX B
LIFESTYLE EVANGELISM
by Andreas Lindner

Evangelism is often seen as an outreach, or as an event, when the gospel is presented to someone in a powerful way. But so few are willing to listen, and less are willing to respond to the wonderful message of the Gospel. They are not interested, do not see a relevance of the gospel to their lives. What can we do?

"Continue earnestly in prayer...that God would open to us a door for the word, to speak the mystery of Christ, for which I am also in chains, that I make it manifest as I ought to speak" (Col. 4:2-4). In Paul's prayer request we see how he worked. He would move into a new area, proclaim the gospel and reap a spiritual harvest. For this kind of evangelism he needed an open door for the word. In every place he would try to find those who are prepared for the message. In the synagogue he would find those who were prepared by God through the message of the Old Testament (Acts 16:13; 17:1-3). The Lord directed the apostle to other individuals who were ready to receive the word (Acts 16:30). Then Paul would teach the new believers, form a church and move on to other places. Of course the new believers should learn to continue the work, including evangelism. But how are they to reach out?

"Walk in wisdom toward those who are outside, redeeming the time. Let your speech always be in grace, seasoned with salt, that you might know how you need to answer each one" (Col. 4:5-6). Since all who were open had become believers, Paul does not ask them to follow his example by using the same method in evangelism as he did. He does not ask them to preach in the synagogue or market place. This had been effective with Paul, and a harvest had been brought in. Those who were prepared had given their life to the Lord. Now the process of evangelism needs to start again with sowing. The way they walk and talk to the people around them is important. This shall make them curious, start thinking and ask questions. The salt will make them thirsty and they will want to know more. Our life can be a help or a hindrance for others. Therefor we need wisdom in our daily walk and talk.

Evangelism should become a lifestyle for all believers. They should not see it as an event such as when an evangelist has a crusade, but as a way of life. A life full of love to the people around them to reach them for the Lord. The people God has placed around us are the ones He wants us to reach. This might be our family, neighbors, work mates or others whom we meet again and again. Like one man who was healed from demon possession we need to go back to them (Lk. 8:39). Since a prophet is not honored in his own town or family (Mt. 13:57), we need not behave like a prophet or gospel preacher, but like a member of the family, team or community. We can show that we love them by serving them in a patient and friendly way. This should be accompanied by wise talk, which does not get on the nerves of people, but respects their opinion even if it is wrong. Sometimes it is even better to be silent, when we want to win people who are very close to us (1 Pet. 3:1-2). It might take time until our friends and relatives are ready to hear more.

Therefore the Lord explains that evangelism is a process. He likens it to the work on a farm (Jn. 4:35-38). To make a harvest possible, the farmer has to prepare the field, sow the seed, water it, get rid of weeds, and wait. The process takes time. When the wheat is white, the farmer will harvest. After the harvest the process of sowing and reaping has to start again.

From this we can learn several lessons: The presentation of the gospel is just one of the last steps in evangelism. It is likened to the harvest. In order that there can be a spiritual harvest, there needs to be plowing, removal of weeds, sowing, and watering. And it will take time.

We can participate in this process. By observing and listening to the people around us, we can find out where they are spiritually. They might believe that there is no God, or that there is some higher force behind nature. Some think that God exists, and that they are responsible to Him. Others might know more—they feel guilty for what they have done. Later they will understand that they have sinned and are lost. Then they will see the need for salvation, understand the way of salvation and finally get saved. Evangelism would be to help them to move toward the Lord, to go one more step.

One good way to participate in the process of evangelism is to develop deeper relationships with others. The apostle Paul had very close friends among the religious leaders of Ephesus (Acts 19:31). His goal was to reach all kind of men with the gospel (1 Cor. 9:19). In order to do so, he came as close to them as possible, he became a Jew to the Jews (1 Cor. 9:20-23). He could be their friend, without being a friend of the world.

The Lord Jesus was a friend of sinners. He spent time with them, even to the extent that others complained. The Lord answered: *"Those who are well have no need of a physician, but those who are sick"* (Mt. 9:12). A doctor needs to go to the sick, even if they have a contagious disease. They need him, and it is his calling to go to them. But when he goes to the sick, he does everything to avoid getting the disease. He uses all kinds of hygienic measures. In a similar way we need to go to sinners (Mt. 28:19). They need the Lord Jesus. In going we need to do everything we can to avoid falling into sin.

We need to be so close to the unbelievers around us that they can see our life and hear our words. We need to be so removed from unbelievers around us that we will not lose our fellowship with the Lord. We lose our witness when we develop sinful habits.

Now some suggestions how we can deepen existing relationships and build up new ones. Make it a priority to spend time with the person. Do something together that you both enjoy. Talk about your convictions, values, and difficulties and learn to listen. Try to understand why he sees life like that. Pray for the Lord to give you ideas as to what to do and what to say.

When your friends are interested, you might want to invite them to read with you in the gospels and explore the life and teaching of the Lord Jesus. Or invite them to a suitable meeting where they can hear the gospel or get to know more about the Lord.

These are some ways you can prepare the people around you that they might also get to know the Lord Jesus.

APPENDIX C
LIFESTYLE DISCIPLESHIP
by Andreas Lindner

When the Lord Jesus called Peter, John and the other disciples, they left their work to follow Him (Mk. 1:20). The disciples spent much of their time with the Lord, saw Him at work and learned from Him. Their characters were formed and abilities were acquired. They participated in His work, going out to preach. Through all of this they were prepared for their future work.

Most of us do not leave our families and work in this way. But is our discipleship reduced to our free time on weekends or in the evening? No, we may also learn many valuable lesson in the daily experiences of life.

How can we learn from the Lord and be prepared for greater tasks?

One day the Lord Jesus used Peter's boat as a pulpit to address the multitude. Then He said to Peter: *"Launch out into the deep and let down your nets for a catch"* (Lk. 5:4). Peter did not expect to be successful: *"Master, we have toiled all night and caught nothing; nevertheless at Your word I will let down the net."* This was the first time Peter went about his daily work because the Lord had asked him to do so. When Peter did this, several things happened to him. And they will happen to us when we do our daily work as a service for the Lord.

1. Peter's crew caught a lot of fish. The Lord rewarded Peter. Everyone of us should turn his life over to the Lord, asking Him what He wants us to do and then do it for Him. Our service for the Lord will include such things as working for our living (2 Thess. 3:12), and managing our household (1 Tim 5:14). When a disciple is doing his daily work as a service for the Lord, the Lord will reward him. The reward will not always be success in business as it was for Peter that day. But there will be an eternal reward for everything we do as a service to Him (see Col. 3:24).

2. Peter fell down at the feet of the Lord, because he realized who the Lord is. Peter saw the power of the Creator as the Lord commanded all these fish into the net. Peter felt the holiness of God present and therefore said: *"Depart from me."* The Lord showed His love and care for Peter in providing food, and comforting him with the words: *"Do not be afraid."*

It was the apostle Paul's goal in life to know the Lord in a better and deeper way (Phil. 3:10), and it would be a good goal for us, too. Getting to know the Lord is not reduced to the time we spend in the Bible or in meetings. Like any other relationship, we get to know Him when we spend time with Him. *"In all your ways acknowledge Him, and He shall direct your paths"* (Prov. 3:6).

3. Peter learned about himself—that he was a sinful man. It is remarkable that he did not learn this while listening to the sermon, but when he was working at the Lord's command. The more we understand who we are, the more we will trust the Lord and not ourselves.

4. Finally Peter understood more about other tasks which the Lord wanted him to do. *"From now on you will catch men"* (Lk. 5:10). Peter was called to another sphere of service when he was doing his daily work for the Lord. And many things that Peter had learned as a fisherman he would be able to use as a fisher of men. For example, fisherman must go where the fish are, as evangelists must go where

the people are (Mt. 28:19); and both the fisherman and the evangelist need to have patience, work hard, stick to their goal, and use all kinds of methods to get the fish.

In the same way the Lord will use our daily work to train us for future tasks. The Lord prepares us for other tasks as long as we are here on earth, or other work which the Lord has for His faithful servants hereafter (Lk. 19:17). When David was tending the sheep he little realized that this was "training time for reigning time." As a king he was a true shepherd for the people of God. He learned many lessons for kingship while tending his father's sheep. *"If we endure we will also reign with Him"* (2 Tim. 2:12).

Fishing is hard and mundane work. Peter often went fishing for various reasons. This time he fished in obedience to the Lord, and as a result the Lord also sent him out to work for Him. Do your daily work for Him, at His command. This is the lifestyle of a disciple.

Peter was so impressed with this, that he devoted a large part of his letter to this topic. He lets the believers know that they all are priests, part of a royal priesthood (1 Pet. 2:9). What do the believers need to do to exercise their priesthood? Do they need to change their occupation? No, the Lord wanted them to stay where they were as servants or housewives, even when they had cruel masters or unbelieving husbands. They were given directions as to how they should behave as priests in these positions (1 Pet. 2:18-3, 6).

If we love the Lord and put Him first, our lives are not wasted. The Lord will use all things for our good (Rom. 8:28). We can learn to do our normal work—even everyday things like eating our food—to the glory of God (1 Cor. 10:31).

One important step in this is putting the Lord first: *"Seek first the kingdom of God and His righteousness, and all these things will be added to you"* (Mt. 6:33).

Some Christian might think: "My daily work is only to provide for my living. What really counts is the service I put in for the Lord after

I leave the office—distributing tracts, teaching a Bible study group etc." Unbelievers go to work to make money (Mt. 6:31-32); we should have a different attitude about our work. When we think like this we do not put the Lord first in our daily work. It is good to serve the Lord after office hours, but why not serve Him during office time by doing our daily work for His pleasure as well?

When we adopt the lifestyle of a disciple and do our daily work for Him, we will consciously seek His righteousness. The Lord is righteous. He wants to conform us to His image (Rom. 8:29). We can learn to be righteous in our daily work. With all the difficulties and temptations it can be the ideal training camp. This also applies to other character traits that the Lord wants to bring forth in us by the Holy Spirit (Gal. 5:22). At the workbench we learn patience. We might be challenged to be friendly with customers in difficult situations, or we learn to be obedient and meek in dealing with our foreman. We can learn to listen to advice, confess our sins, and regard others higher than ourselves.

Someone might think: In order to serve the Lord, I need to change my position; I feel like a slave. The Apostle Paul did write to slaves and said: *"Let each one remain in the same calling in which he was called. Were you called while a slave? Do not be concerned about it"* (1 Cor. 7:20-21). None of us is actually a slave, but we might be in situations which cannot be changed at present. Our present circumstances might seem a hindrance to our service for the Lord. A mother is tied to the sink, a husband is chained to his desk at the office, and a student is limited to his laboratory and his computer. Yet we may daily turn our lives over to the Lord, doing our work for Him, as Peter did when he said: *"At Your word I will let down the net."*

It might be that we get the opportunity to contribute more time to serving the Lord in a different way. Others need help, and they need the gospel. We can spread the Word of God by preaching it or by helping others who do so. The disciples left their work as fishermen and worked for the Lord in a different capacity when He called them to full-time work with Him. When we work as mothers and house-wives, in a shop or on a construction site, we can do it for the Lord. If we are freed from these obligations, we should use this liberty for the Lord and His kingdom.

The Lord Jesus was no less in the will of God when He was at the carpenter's bench than when He was going around preaching. He was spiritual and holy before His public ministry as He was in it. Let us remember this when we are doing our daily chores.

The wife of a missionary was getting frustrated because her hus-band traveled around preaching, while she seemed to have little opportunity to serve the Lord. She had to be home with the children, doing the dishes for all the guests who came through. One day it dawned on her that the Lord wanted her to do these things. She started to do her work for the Lord, not as a one-time thing—it became a lifestyle to her. And she pasted a sign in her kitchen: "The Lord's service here—three times a day."

APPENDIX D
I LIKE THE ASSEMBLIES

Pardon me, but I just happen to like the assemblies. It seems almost counter-cultural to say something like that. The "in thing" is to badmouth them, to highlight all their faults and failures. There are plenty of critics who pontificate on what is wrong with the assemblies. Maybe it's time for someone to step forward and say what is good about them. I'd like to be that person. Let me tell you why I like them.

I like the weekly remembrance of the Lord in the Breaking of Bread. For fifty years I have sought to remember the Lord every Sunday at the communion table, and it has never lost its charm for me. There is something special about a meeting where our beloved Lord is the sole attraction and the central object of worship. No wonder that when people leave an assembly for a different type of fellowship, they invariably say, "I do miss the worship meeting." It makes me sad that they ever left it.

The assembly has endeared itself to me because I have seen Ephesians 4:12 practiced as nowhere else. Gifts were given for building up the saints for the work of the ministry. I have seen unlettered men matured to the point where they preached the gospel with convicting power. I have seen homespun men ministering to the hearts of God's people and not just to their heads. I have seen devoted women finding fulfillment, not only in raising sons and daughters for God, but also in teaching other women and children, co-laboring with their husbands in support of their ministry, supporting the work of missionaries at home and abroad, visiting the sick and afflicted, and showing hospitality to saints and strangers alike. I have seen young men encouraged to exercise their gifts in a way that would never happen in the average church. Many prominent evangelical leaders give lip-service to Ephesians 4:12, and some even commend the assemblies for the way they practice it.

One of the glories of the assemblies is their steadfast refusal to divide an equal brotherhood into clergy and laity. To gather to the Person of Christ rather than to a charismatic preacher is divine both in principle and practice. The New Testament teaches a plurality of elders and never a one-man ministry. But assemblies who preach and practice this will always be speckled birds in the Christian community. There is a certain measure of reproach to being in an assembly of this type, and those who cast in their lot with the assemblies better be prepared to bear it.

I like the fact that each assembly is autonomous, responsible to the Lord alone. There is no headquarters on earth, no humanly ordained hierarchy, no organization coming between the Head and the body. This impedes the takeover of assemblies by liberalism, alien doctrines, or dictatorships.

The financial policies of the assemblies are commendable. It is extraordinary that in most fellowships, there is only one collection or offering a week. And yet that one offering, taken without fanfare or begging appeals, is sufficient to meet the local expenses and to help support Christian ministries at home and abroad. Traditionally, full-time workers have looked to the Lord alone for the supply of their needs without publicizing those needs. The world cannot say of the assemblies what it says of Christendom in general, "All the church wants is your money."

I appreciate the fact that the assemblies are willing to exercise godly discipline when it is called for, even if in doing so they may be limiting their chances of ever becoming megachurches. They are content to judge their fellowships, not by their size, but by the holiness of their members.

The literature ministry of the assemblies has been outstanding. Perhaps this has been their main contribution to the evangelical scene. The writings of Darby, Kelly, Mackintosh, Vine, and a host of others have exerted a profound and beneficial influence throughout the world. Some years ago the librarian of a Christian college attempted to compile a bibliography of "Brethren" writers. He later despaired of ever finishing the project.

And mention must be made of the missionary movement associated with the assemblies, a movement that is all out of proportion to the number of local fellowships supporting it.

Other people have other reasons for liking the assemblies, some quite unexpected. For instance, a sister who recently came into fellowship after years of church-hopping said she was delighted to be in one with male leadership. That was a strange note to sound in a day of women's lib.

Probably few groups engage in as much self-criticism as the assemblies. Frankly I feel it is grossly overdone, causing impressionable people to be unnecessarily disenchanted and turned away. Criticism comes best on the back of praise. It's time we balanced the two.

The foregoing does not mean that I am satisfied with the status quo. I recognize that there are areas in which we need to improve, such as evangelistic outreach and development of leadership in the assembly. While unalterably committed to biblical principles, I recognize the need for changing methods from time to time. I agree that some of our people, including the young people, have legitimate concerns, and need to be heard.

But instead of calling out the wrecking crew, we need to roll up our sleeves and tackle the problems. Give us men who will show us how to do a constructive job rather than armchair generals who blackball the assemblies or bail out altogether. And those who draw their support from the assemblies should demonstrate a measure of loyalty to avoid any appearance of "biting the hand that feeds them."

APPENDIX E
SHOULD WE HIRE A PASTOR?

While a salary is a suitable method of payment in most professions, there are peculiar dangers connected with it for those who minister the Word of God.

Doubtless it is for that reason that the idea of a salaried ministry is foreign to the New Testament. While the Lord Jesus taught quite definitely that *"the laborer is worthy of his wages"* (Lk. 10:7) and Paul confirmed that *"those who preach the gospel should live from the gospel"* (1 Cor. 9:14), there is no suggestion that these men should receive a stipulated amount each month.

One of the potential problems is that those who control the salary can often control the preaching. It does not always happen that those who pay the piper insist on calling the tune, but it has happened and can happen. Those who hold the purse-strings may be as carnal as goats, yet they can insist on suppressing any preaching that does not suit them.

It is also true that those who pay the salary can require certain standards of achievement. For example, they might require an increase in church membership, either through conversions or transfers from other churches. This might put a subtle pressure on the Lord's servant to lower standards in order to increase numbers. It is not in his power to produce true conversions; it is God who gives the increase. But he can produce shallow professions that look good in an annual report. Also he can speak softly on matters of discipline so as not to lose anyone.

Even apart from pressure from others, there is a temptation for the teacher to soft-pedal truths that might offend his congregation. If the people are wealthy, he might not think it expedient to speak on *"Do not lay up for yourselves treasures on earth"* (Mt. 6:19), or *"Command those that are rich in this present age not to be haughty, nor to trust in uncertain riches but in the living God, who gives us richly all things to enjoy"* (1 Tim. 6:17). The preacher must be the Lord's free man, free to declare the full counsels of God, free to be a mouthpiece of God, free to speak as the oracles of God. Anything that hinders this is a great tragedy in the work of the Lord.

In times of declension and apostasy, there is often a tendency for preachers to side with those who control his finances rather than to stand true to the great, fundamental doctrines of the faith. Concerning a denomination that is now riddled with liberalism and apostasy, David O. Beale writes, "There is a perennial 'joke' which pastors tell at each annual meeting: 'If the Convention splits, I'm going with the Annuity Board!' The Board does appear to be the 'cement' of the empire." Financial considerations have a powerful way of taking priority over faithfulness to the Word of God.

A fixed salary could very possibly weaken the life of faith. The servant of the Lord should be an example to others of one who walks by faith and not by sight. His life should be a perpetual crisis of dependence on the Lord. G. H. Lang gave his testimony:

> I have lived and worked in happy fellowship with workers in the gospel in many lands through fifty years and am satisfied that a guaranteed or regular income, because it dispenses with direct and constant faith in God as to temporal supplies, is certainly a spiritual loss, not by any means a gain.[92]

---

92   G. H. Lang, *Anthony Norris Groves*, London: Paternoster Press, 1949, p. 66.

In the ecclesiastical world, it is not uncommon for men to shop around for bigger salaries. They mistake material advancement for the guidance of God. It is all too easy to conclude that the offer of an attractive salary is an indication of God's call.

In the Old Testament economy, a bondservant was worth twice as much as a hired servant (Deut. 15:18). In other words, one who served because he belonged to his master was more valuable than one who worked for what he got out of it. Does this have a message for us today?

Of course, the question arises, "If not by a salary, how is a servant of the Lord to be supported?"

First of all, the believer must have absolute confidence that the Lord has called him to serve on a full time basis. This cannot be overemphasized. And he must not only be sure himself, but must have the confidence of his spiritual guides that he has received the divine tap on the shoulder. After all, no man is an adequate judge of his own gift.

Second, he must be thoroughly assured that, as Hudson Taylor said, the Lord pays for what He orders. He can then step forth without any visible means of support but with unwavering trust that the Lord will provide for his needs according to His riches in glory by Christ Jesus. That should certainly be sufficient.

But how will God do this? He will do it through His people. Someone has described the process as follows:

God can place an idea in a person's mind. He can cause someone to feel a strong "urge" or "conviction" to do something. So when we pray for a certain amount of money, God can cause one person to reach for his check book and send that amount, or he can cause a dozen people to send odd fractions of that amount, causing the total to be exact. You may not believe that He does this, but I am simply saying that when I talk about praying for money, this is what I mean.[93]

This is the thrilling part of the life of faith—to see income increase

---

93   Schaefer, Edith, *L'Abri*, Westchester IL.: Crossway Brooks, 1992, p. 126.

as needs increase, and conversely to see income decline when it is not needed. And it serves as a valuable system of checks and balances. As long as I am doing the work of God, I know that He will supply, quite apart from any publicizing of needs on my part. If I am serving according to my own wisdom, I cannot expect Him to pay for what He has not ordered.

Wrote Ray Williams in *Echoes* magazine,

> I believe this is the way. If not, how could we rely on His guidance? If I say to myself, "I want to do this" and say to my friends, "Can you provide the money to help me to do this job?" I might want to do it and my friends might want to help me, but I would not know if it was the Lord's will. If I only tell the Lord that I want to do this thing, and the finance to do it appears without anyone but the Lord knowing about it, then I know that this is the Lord's will for me.[94]

Hear the testimony of Silas Fox:

> In 1926, feeling that it would be better for me to look direct to the Lord for support, and be more free to take the calls that would come in for special meetings, I launched out, with a wife, and five children, and to the glory of God, after a quarter of a century, can give testimony that without a mission to support me, and without a deputation secretary to make known our needs at home, and without appeals, or on my part taking up collections...and without having my name on any "list," yet the Lord has graciously, wonderfully, faithfully met all the need for these twenty-five years, and we praise Him, and in this give testimony in this way.[95]

Finally, Dan Crawford adds his spiritual insight:

> A society missionary friend expostulated with me as a married man not

---

94   Ray Williams. *Why this Way?* Echoes of Service Magazine, February 1984, p. 75
95   Donald Fox, *The White Fox of Andhra*, Philadelphia: Dorrance and Co., 977, p. 153.

claiming a fixed salary—something sure was his idea. It was then that God spoke to me out of His Word. What settled the matter as to faith being the only definite thing was the following truth of God: *"The promise was by faith that it might be sure."* The only sure thing is faith![96]

---

96   Dan Crawford, *Your Salary*, Assembly Annals Magazine, June 1959.

APPENDIX F
THINKING AS GOD DOES

A Christian should learn to think God's thoughts after Him. This involves rejecting the world's standards and adopting those of the Kingdom. After all, the only test for anything is how it appears in the eyes of the Lord Jesus. The things that are valued by men of this world are opposite to those that are valued by the mind of Christ. Or to borrow the words of Jesus, *"What is highly esteemed among men is an abomination in the sight of God"* (Lk. 16:15).

The poor. Our Lord does not call many wise, mighty, or noble people. Instead, He loves to use the poor to accomplish His purposes. Solomon gave the world's opposing view that "money answers all things." If you just have enough money you can do anything. This idea has crept into the church. We are told that the greatest need today in the work of God is for money. But that is wrong. God is not a pauper. He pays for what He orders without the need for high-powered, tear-jerking appeals. When poor people do great exploits for Jesus, it is clear to all that the credit goes to the Lord. He gets the glory. Hudson Taylor was right when he said that what we greatly need to fear is not too little money but too much unconsecrated money.

The weak. God's strength is made perfect in weakness. What

could be weaker than a Man nailed hands and feet to a cross? Yet think of the millions who have been saved from eternal judgment through that weakness. The seeming contradiction is well described by Whitlock Gandy.

> *By weakness and defeat*
> *He won the glorious crown;*
> *Trod all His foes beneath His feet*
> *By being trodden down.*
>
> *He Satan's power laid low;*
> *Made sin, He sin o'er threw;*
> *Bowed to the grave, destroyed it so,*
> *And death by dying slew.*

The base. These are people who are low in place or position. They are on the bottom rungs of the social ladder. John Bunyan was a tinker. Yet God raised him up to write Pilgrim's Progress. For years it was second only to the Bible in sales. We read of unlettered Scottish coal miners who came up at the end of the workday, went home, washed up, ate supper, and studied their Bibles. They preached the Gospel with power and could see more on their knees than many scholastics could see on their tiptoes. They marvelously glorified God.

The despised. Here is a devoted Christian of a scorned minority carrying a sandwich board downtown with the warning "Prepare to meet your God." Passersby either sneer or feel sorry for Him. Or there is an itinerant evangelist preaching on a college campus. A few teeth are missing. Like Paul, he bears in his body "the marks of the Lord Jesus." Don't despise him. He is one of the Lord's choice servants, not seeking personal glory but only the glory of the Lord Jesus.

I have seen Christians meeting in living rooms, lodge halls, and rented storefronts. People poked fun at them. There were no pipe organs, stained glass windows, or cushioned pews. But the Lord was there and the Holy Spirit worked in power.

Things that are not. God takes a special delight in using things that are considered by the world as useless and people who are looked down on as nobodies, like the Spurgeons, Tozers, and the Ironsides. I speak of men who never had grandiose titles, who had no degrees to sport, and who never had to endure lavish introductions. They were men who prayed, like Charles Wesley:

> *Keep me little and unknown,*
> *Loved and prized by Christ alone.*

Foolishness. To men the gospel is arrant nonsense. The idea that a person can be saved by faith in Christ and entirely apart from good works of any kind is ridiculous.

The truth is that the Good News is the wisdom of God. It is the world's wisdom that is foolishness. The Gospel is the power of God by which sinful men are converted. What seems like God's foolishness really works in saving those who believe. What seems like foolishness is wiser than men and what seems like weakness is stronger than men.

Faith versus sight. Here is another way in which God thinks differently than the world. The world says, "Seeing is believing." God says, *"Believing is seeing."*

Jesus said to Martha, *"Did I not say unto you that if you would believe, you would see the glory of God"* (Jn. 11:40).

At the cross men cried out, *"Let the Christ, the King of Israel, descend now from the cross that we may see and believe"* (Mk. 15:32). But Jesus knew they wouldn't believe, even when He rose from the dead (Lk. 16:31).

Later the risen Lord said to Thomas, *"Because you have seen Me, you have believed. Blessed are those who have not seen and yet have believed"* (Jn. 20:29).

Our Lord is not pleased with the kind of faith that requires seeing.

Another shocking way in which God thinks differently than man is in the matter of leadership. Here is how the Lord explained the difference.

You know that the rulers of the Gentiles lord it over them, and those who are great exercise authority over them. Yet it shall not be so among you; but whoever desires to be great among you, let him be your servant, and whoever desires to be first among you, let him be your slave--just as the Son of Man did not come to be served, but to serve, and to give His life a ransom for many (Mt. 20:25-28).

There is a reproach to living the Christian life according to Christ's teaching. People will think you are strange. They will dislike you because you are unlike them. They will resent it that you do not engage in all their activities. They will mock you,

This is your great opportunity to *"go forth to Him, outside the camp, bearing His reproach"* (Heb. 13:13). Think as God does.

APPENDIX G
CHRISTIAN LITERATURE—THE POSSIBILITIES AND LIMITATIONS

It is admitted in secular circles today that the most explosive thing in the world is not nuclear weapons but printer's ink.

Why? Because a little of it, tossed into the alphabet, can detonate ideas that will move the minds of men with a force infinitely greater and more lasting than the whirlwind loosed by splitting an atom. Printer's ink serves good or evil, but the evidence on the positive side far outweighs the negative. For when a man with a vision of man's higher destiny touches ink to paper, its blackness holds the light of the world.[97]

Dr. Oswald Smith writes,

For more than 30 years I have prayerfully considered the problem, "How can we evangelize the world in the space of one generation?" Long ago, I was convinced that we could never send out enough missionaries. But there must be a way. After travel and study in 53 countries, I have come to the conclusion that the only way we are going to be able to carry out the Great Commission is by

---

97   From Dun's Review and Modern Industry

the systematic use of the printed page. Only in that way shall we be able to enter every home and reach every individual with the gospel message. The world is rapidly becoming literate. A million new readers every week offer us a golden opportunity for literature evangelism. Jehovah's Witnesses are wide awake, seeking to get their message across by means of literature. The Christian Church has not yet awakened. Soon it will be too late. Now is the hour.[98]

The advantages of harnessing the printed page for the gospel are astounding.

- The written word knows no fear—it flinches in the face of no man. It preaches the same message to the rich and the poor, the king and the commoner.
- It never loses its temper; never talks back in anger.
- It takes no note of scoffs, jeers, and insults.
- It never tires, but works 24 hours a day, even while we sleep and rest.
- It is never discouraged, but will tell its story over and over again.
- It will speak to one as willingly as to a multitude, and to a multitude as readily as to one.
- It always catches a person in just the right mood to be receptive, for it only speaks as he chooses to listen.
- It can be received, read, and studied in secret.
- It gets undivided attention in the quiet hours.
- It speaks without a foreign accent.
- The written word is more permanent than the human voice.
- It never compromises, never changes its message.
- It continues to speak and make its message plain after audible words have been forgotten and lost.
- It is greatly appreciated by the nationals of any country.
- It is immune to all disease.[99]

---

98   *The Harvester,* February 1963, p. 17.

99   From *The Revelator.*

The smallest tract may be the stone in David's sling. In the hands of Christ it may bring down a giant soul (Robert Murray M'Cheyne).

Books may preach when the author cannot, when the author may not, when the author dares not, yea, and which is more, when the author is not (Thomas Brooks).

No other agency can penetrate so deeply, witness so daringly, abide so persistently and influence so irresistibly as the printed page (Samuel Zwemer).

While we believe that literature has tremendous potential in the spread of the Truth, we must not assume that it is the only method or even the best method. While it is a wonderful help to the missionary in extending his outreach, it will never take the place of the missionary himself.

Let us be frank in admitting the limitations of literature:

1. It presupposes that people can read. There are still millions who can't. These must be reached in some other way.

2. Literature doesn't always answer questions that arise in a person's mind. This can be done in conversation more effectively.

3. The Lord sent out disciples who were to be living examples of the truth. There is no argument as effective as a holy life.

4. All evangelistic work should aim beyond salvation to grounding converts in the truth and to the formation of local assemblies. Literature can teach young believers about the local church, but the human factor (the missionary or preacher or teacher) will inevitably be necessary to lead them in the truth.

Dawson Trotman, former president of the Navigators, used to say:

The answer is the man, not materials. Maybe the greatest problem today is that we try to put into printed form that which should go from lip to ear and heart to heart. Materials are the tools. Tools by themselves are useless. If there were a young fellow beginning his study of medicine who had all the necessary instruments for a major operation, and an old doctor who just had a razor blade and a plain, ordinary crooked needle and some store string, I'd put myself in the hands of the old doctor for surgery rather than this boy over here with all his instruments, wouldn't you? It's not only the tools; it's the man who has the tools in his hands.